PF

W9-CNP-309

COLD FRIDAY

COLD FRIDAY

by

Whittaker Chambers

Edited and with an Introduction by
Duncan Norton-Taylor

Random House   New York

MANUFACTURED IN THE UNITED STATES OF AMERICA BY
The Haddon Craftsmen, Scranton, Pa

Typography by Tere LoPrete

Library of Congress catalog card number: 64-20025

A portion of *Cold Friday* first appeared in *The Saturday Evening Post*.

POWER *(to his companion, Force, and to their prisoner, Prometheus):* "We have come to the last path of the earth, in the Scythian country, in the untrodden solitude."

—Aeschylus, *Prometheus Bound*

This is to express my thanks to those friends of my husband who came to me with offers of help with this book, and those on whom I did call. I owe much to Mrs. Mildred Cole of Westminster, Maryland, for her patience and kindness to me as we transcribed the handwritten papers we found, and to Duncan Norton-Taylor —one of Whittaker's oldest friends at Time Inc., Managing Editor of *Fortune*—who has edited these writings with such understanding and given so unstintingly of his time and thought—my children and I extend our heartfelt gratitude.

ESTHER CHAMBERS

Pipe Creek Farm
Westminster, Maryland
April 1964

Contents

INTRODUCTION

In the early summer of 1961 Whittaker Chambers was
seized by his last heart attack. The labors of the mind ended,
and the basement study in his Westminster, Maryland, farmhouse became empty and silent.

After the years of exposure and vilification and final vindica-
tion he had retreated, with no sense of triumph, only a great
fatigue, to the farm in Carroll County, where he wrote his
book *Witness*. It was not a willing retreat: the one thing he
wanted to do was to return to journalism. But the opportunity
was denied him, at least in the active role he so much desired.
He had turned first to farming, working his three hundred
acres in hay, barley, wheat, and corn, tending a dairy herd
and raising sheep, until he was crippled by the first serious
onset of heart trouble. He wrote in despondency:

> I was still a man cursed with the temper of mind,
> which, with age, had passed into the habit of weighing
> reality as narrowly as possible; and that reality included
> my own. So I could see perfectly clearly the limiting
> personal facts. Fulfillment depends chiefly on a man's
> ability to command his environment, to win and justify
> his foothold in it. In a competitive society, where prac-
> tically everything, respect, self-respect, and the bank
> credit we live by, is measured by an earning power,
> the kind of job a man can get and hold, I had no credit.
> Due to my past, I was permanently unemployable, as I
> had more than once rather badly learned, in the one kind
> of work for which experience and ability fitted me . . .

Still a man is a man, and as such knows he can also find the inner resources to look to something else. And so I did. I looked specifically to farming. I have never been a successful farmer. But any averagely intelligent man who is willing to invest enough life and resolution can, with time and patience make a go of almost anything. I thought that I could, too. But I had scarcely begun when ill health in the form that ruled out physical activity ended such dreams. Henceforth I could do nothing ordinarily active, as I discovered from time to time. It would be hard to imagine a more complete stalemate, all gears locked. So for long periods of time my first thought on waking in the pre-dawn was: "Must I live through another day?" My life seemed utterly pointless. There was no point of issue from it, and I was completely incapable of making one.

He was quite wrong. The mind that had been so intensively, and tragically, preoccupied with the ordeal of revolution in the twentieth century, would not quit work. On his peaceful farm, where there could be no real peace, he continued to write. It is these writings that comprise this book and add both point and fulfillment to a prophetic career. In 1957 he did find employment again in journalism when he joined the staff of the *National Review*. But it was for only a brief time. The physical effort proved too much for him. Also, while he cherished the friendship of the magazine's editors and their loyalty to him, he never reconciled himself completely to their point of view. He never felt at home with any kind of orthodoxy, political or religious, after the betrayal of his spirit by the appalling orthodoxy of Communism. He was from beginning to end a revolutionary. In the summer of 1959 he and his wife Esther made a trip to Europe, and in the Austrian Alps he talked for days on end with Arthur Koestler, with whom he felt a true intellectual kinship. He had enrolled, meanwhile, for courses at Western

Maryland College, in Westminster. "I don't know why this should seem so whimsical to all, beginning with Esther," he wrote. "It isn't only the question of an earned degree and the completion of something left unfinished. I feel the crying need of formal, intensive training in history, philosophy and economics." He took the work with complete seriousness. He wrote to me one Thanksgiving: "Four days of recess. The luxury of being able to sleep until 7:30 A.M. I got through the mid term passably well: 97, 99, 99, 100 and 87. This last is a shocker. It is in Russian and represents a deliberate sacrifice of Russian to Economics in my study schedule. For I find Lord Keynes pretty difficult in a technical way. As somebody said: 'There is no subject, no matter how perfectly I understand it, that a graph cannot obscure to me.' Three mornings a week, I rise at 5 A.M. Three mornings I rise at 5:30. . . ." It was on a weekend's brief surcease from the drive back and forth between his farm and his classrooms that he died.

In time, Esther Chambers steeled herself to go down to the basement study. There were a half-dozen cartons and a briefcase filled with letters and fragments of writing—some of them typed, some of them still in his difficult hand-writing—which would take months of patient work to transcribe. A few of his friends had known what he had been about, of his determination to write a book which would be a supplement to *Witness*; it was to be a book he never would finish.

There were a number of reasons why he never finished, including the recurrent heart attacks. He was also trying to inquire into the meaning of history, but was continuously fascinated and distracted by its spasms during the years 1951-1961. He was not a codifier—he was too deeply implicated in humanity. "The true quality of my mind is poetic," he once wrote to a friend. There was no arrogance in the comment, only a recognition of the root of sorrow. He was a writer of sorrow and compassion—and sometimes of startling insight.

Like any other writer, he was plagued by the always formidable job of organization. He wrote in one letter, discussing his project:

> Tom Matthews suggested that the solution was something like a journal. Naturally I had thought of this before. I looked at it again, turned it over and rejected it again. I have always been an impatient reader of journals, random notes, *pensées*, what you will. Writing such a book: too much self-indulgence. Reading it: too much like a hot day's search, through a cluttered attic, for something which, when you find it, you find you don't really want it after all. A book should organize experience; that is what a book is for; author is artificer. The mind should impose order on experience without making you uncomfortably aware of the sweat. How else is meaning to appear? Besides, you would not sit down deliberately to bore a man to death in conversation. Why should writers think they are free to bore us to death with books?
>
> A book should start somewhere and go somewhere. It should take us somewhere, even if, at the end, there is no going-away present, nothing in your hands to guide you, Every Man, through all your days. Because there are no truths, valedictory or otherwise. There is only reality, through which you have been led. All the writer has to give at the end is the motion of his empty hand with which he points back (without too much comment) to the way you have come together . . .
>
> What has my book to say but, "As I came through the desert, thus it was as I came through the desert"? Comedy? "Laughing as I cried of thirst." What is still laughable after a thousand years? What joke does not stale with repeating except the one on ourselves, at

which we have no choice but to laugh unless we wish to be Calvin and burn? . .

Time is running out on me. I am rushing on to sixty. This is old age. Of importance, here, chiefly because, if I do not get my meaning down on paper, I shall die with *Witness* as my whole meaning. It is not my whole meaning. . . .

One day in 1955 he watched his son John drive off from the farm to register for the draft. He wrote in his notes:

It seemed to me as I watched him leave that the most important thing I could do for him was to report for him how his father had viewed certain aspects of our reality, what I believed the forces of reality to be, and how I saw their origins and development, which pulverized individual men, and caught peoples, like shovelfuls of corn in a hammermill. My book should be something like what past ages used to call an enchiridion —a little dagger to arm him against the swarming night, a little dagger that might help him to cut his way among the enemies and perplexities of his life. I meant no formidable treatise, for which I felt no competence. What I had in mind was a little book to which he could turn in doubt or trouble, when he could no longer come to me, and catch again his father's voice saying: "This is how it happened to me, these are the conclusions I drew from past experience. This is how experience seemed to teach me that a man should act, this is what a man is and should be against the scale of reality." My reward, never known by men, could be that he might one day say, "In the main, you spoke to me wisely."

I have put off the task too long. Few tasks have been so difficult as to begin this book. How many times I have sat down at my desk to begin it, and have then got up again with that slight feeling of nausea that I have sometimes known in testifying publicly or in writing much of *Witness*, which is, I suppose, the penalty that the body pays when the will overdrives the nerves. At the root of that feeling is the sense of hopelessness which besets most of those who have sought to carry on the struggle in our time. It can be put in a simple question: Since acts have done so little good, what possible good can more words do? Linked with this feeling is another that goes even deeper. It is the sense of a limit beyond which a man may not wish to drive himself. The effort of recollection forces me to turn back to horrors which no man can come through and live from day to day without putting out of his mind—not by a conscious effort but by that mercy of the mind which sinks what is too heavy to be borne into the grace of forgetfulness. To probe the scar risks each time reopening the wound. One of the best Latin tags says that perhaps at some future time it will be pleasant to remember these things. They can be remembered only in a turmoil of spirit that pushes the mind towards a longing for annihilation.

But the greatest difficulty in writing this book is something else. It lies at the point where the book itself is a parting much more final than my son's walking up a path. I write consciously in the belief that this is probably the last effort of the kind that I shall make, a kind of summary testament, a backward reading of what I have learned from experience to this point. I am haunted by the need for truth, the fear of error, at the point of life when truth has become the one consuming need, since nothing else has real worth. My son must read this as the effort at truth, knowing that I could wish for him only what is good and true.

I have a sense of leaving my son, that chapter by chapter puts us farther apart as if he were a figure compelled to watch from a shore another receding in a little boat.

From the cartons in the study came chapters, paragraphs, written and rewritten—fragments, excursions, luminous beginnings sometimes without endings, enigmas sometimes without answers. Would he have wanted any of it published posthumously? Possibly very little of it as it stood, for he was an exasperating reviser always reluctant to let his writing finally go. The responsibility must rest with Esther Chambers and her children Ellen and John, and to a degree with me, a friend. Actually there could be only one decision. Among the papers was one page labelled "Foreword":

> Spring has come to us again—a spring that I scarcely expected to see. Twice at night the wild geese have passed over. There may have been three such flights, since one night I dreamed that I saw hundreds flying overhead, so in the way we hear so much without ever quite waking to its meaning, I may have heard these wild geese honking without waking. The first flight, the venturesome, was small and the cries so faint that I was scarcely certain at first that I heard even them. The second flight was much bigger and so loud that I roused up, and I saw my wife already standing, listening, in the moonlight at the window. I said: "You hear the wild geese?" and fell asleep again. So my wife and I learned that, somewhat unaccountably, we had lived into another spring.
>
> I began this book deliberately with spring as the point of resurging life because this is a book, in general, about death—the death of an age and the death of a man and what relationship, if any, the experiences bear to each other.

It will suffice as the foreword to the book (or one of the books) that never was finished. All an editor could do was first select, and then impose an editor's artifice upon the hundreds of pieces patiently sorted out by Esther Chambers, so that the pages do "start somewhere and go somewhere." There is very little editing of copy; I sometimes thought, "But *he* wouldn't have let it go that way," but any argument between writer and editor was foreclosed. I began with some pages from a diary because they locate him in time and place after he finished writing *Witness*. (That book, an account of the role he played in the trial of Alger Hiss, the former State Department official convicted of perjury, was published in 1952.) From time to time, for what they add, I included some letters to other friends and to me, a few excerpts from pieces that appeared in *National Review*. Where the book takes us is into the experiences of modern history, lighted up by an extraordinary mind. Beyond that depends on where you want to go. You will at least discern in "the motion of his empty hand the way you have come together."

DUNCAN NORTON-TAYLOR

New York City
June, 1964

Invocation

Here I can stand;
See up, off, down.
This is the life-consuming air
This is the blood-drinking earth.
Silence is prayer
Holy and awful spirits of this place,
What you are is your own mystery,
What I reverence is mine.

Pipe Creek
Farm

From pages of a diary

June 10/52

Not to give way to hopelessness.

June 12/52

Yelping dogs woke me around 3 A.M. Pants, shoes, the shot-gun and out to the round-top. It was those hounds from the pecker woods behind us. One seemed to have gotten through the fence, was actually on the pasture. The other failed to get through—hence the commotion. Fortunately, all the sheep were in the orchard. I decided to go up and stand guard over them lest the raiders return.

As I climbed the lane, I made out John's figure in the shadows; leaning on his rifle. He had got on his shoes, but was wearing only his pajama bottom. The ear is so wonderfully selective in sleep. He had not heard my loud gropings in the house at all—they were a familiar noise. But the dogs' yelping had brought him awake. He ran out, to protect his sheep, supposing that he was alone. I sent him back to bed.

For about two hours, sentry go around two sides of the orchard. Pleasant watch. Up the lane between the apple trees and the wheat which is shoulder-high and musky. Then around the hayfield which John had finished baling after dark that night. The dogs, reunited, were tearing around in the wheat at the far side of the field. When the dogs were loudest, the sheep formed a huddle in the middle of the orchard. But they knew I was there and scattered again to browse or lie in groups with their lambs. "Old Yoe" the dowager ewe, with an eye wide-open and fierce as an eagle's, paced me along one side of the fence, sometimes pushing her muzzle to the mesh to let me scratch the short wool; no other sheep does this.

A big moon, dripping from the gun barrels whenever I turned a corner (from cells of memory untapped for years):

> . . . The three-quarter moon
> Rises deliberately,
> And gazes from her own height
> Of coldness and death—the satellite;
> And fills the lanes with shadow
> And the trees with light;
> And fulfills the night.

Toward dawn, fighting off sleep. To rouse myself, I climbed the ridge. The woods and the opposite ridge pearled with light, the hollows between filled with shadow. Behind, the grey band of concrete state road (no cars or even a truck at that hour). I thought: Quiet the land with sleeping. This is the oldest continuity, known to man—the peace of pre-morning in the fields, within which even I, for an hour, am one of the oldest of human figures—a man watching his flocks by night.

June 15/52

We have dug too diligently in the trash of the past and the penalty for deepening the archaeological horizon is that we know now not only that Rome fell. Civilization has repeatedly (the temptation is to say invariably) failed at the moment when it seemed to sum up most of the meaning that we put into the word, civilized. It is repetitious and alarming once we know that it was as true for Egypt, Knossos and the sixth city of Troy and Ur. They appall us with the intuition that their rubbish could have been disclosed only by the energies of a civilization which itself is at a toppling height.

Pipe Creek Farm,
August 10, 1952

Dear Dunc:

I have been awake since 3, up since 4. It is just turned 5, and in a few minutes I must go to the barn to begin my day's chores. Tomorrow, at 5, I am going down into your country—or the marches thereof—to a cow sale at Church Hill. For I am going back to being a dairyman. I have made up my mind. Made up suggests too much resolution. I went back to the cow barn, throwing Esther out, milk-stool and all. I found that what I was doing seemed to be what I should do. Back with my cattle and my chores, I am more content than I have been for several years. In fact, without this activity, I do not think that I could go on. It adds up to much more than a matter of personal contentment, though. I won't go into details. But it is all bound up with the writer in this century, the poisonous puddles of the intellectuals (so much less clear than barn gutters), and with the fact that, in our time, the West is swayed by a profound will to die. Since my desire is to live, I must live as far as possible outside the vapors of the perishing West even to the point of living as differently as possible from it. For, to survive at all, one must stand against it in its corruption (in this my instinct was never wrong and has never changed) even though one is not at war with it, is even committed to its defense. Actually, and with the profoundest vindictiveness of unhealth, it does not wish to be defended; it deeply resents anyone who would defend it and will seek to destroy him. And what subtle ways it finds in alliance with just those who seek its destruction! Because it cannot be defended without facing the truth about itself. Nor can anyone truly defend it without, ultimately, speaking the truth about it. That it cannot stand and so, first of all, it must long to destroy those who would save it. And so, I am taking refuge in my cow barn. Cattle, as Nietzsche pointed out in a well known essay (*The Advantage and Disadvantage of History for Life*), have no memory and hence no history. I, who am fairly history-conscious, find cows ahistorically tranquilizing. . . .

To the stable!

As ever,

Whittaker

Three months later, on Election Day, he was stricken by a heart attack and taken to St. Agnes Hospital in Baltimore.

St. Agnes

My heavy oak door stood always shut against even the corridor sounds of that citadel of pain in which I occupied one
of the pleasanter cells. I was permitted no visitors from the
outer world (though two security officers of the United States
Government managed to reach me surreptitiously my first
morning in the Hospital). Otherwise I could see only my
wife, and my two children, neither of whom was in a position to visit me often. A shock of sufficient force has the effect
of correcting our angle of reality, so that a certain type of
mind, at least, is first off struck not by a sense of its personal
disaster, but by the preposterousness of its individual plight
in the wider context of the human situation; thus it can view
its plight with a detached amusement. For me this amusement
began almost as soon as I could peer more connectedly between
the fog layers of drug and discomfort. Then, I could observe
my competent nurses executing in relay a kind of elaborate
minuet on tiptoe. What amused me was that I seemed to be
so much less the subject of a cure as the center of a presump-

tive wake, which I was privileged to assist at and make mental notes about.

This was followed, almost at once, by another strong impression—the impression that I was lying also at a center of almost absolute silence. It was due not only to the regulated sick-room hush. It was the more excessive quiet of the kind that seems to follow the sudden cessation of excessive noise. It was as if my life, which had long been lived in a din like that of a traffic tunnel where every sound is reverberated many times, had somehow burst into this silence because, at last, there had been simply nowhere else to go. Thus, I had the sense, too, that I was lying there not so much to decide whether or not I could manage to live as to consider, in that barely conquered peace, whether the minimum quiet necessary to life itself could be secured short of death. I was forbidden to move more than I could help; forbidden to talk more than necessary; forbidden even to laugh (a ban I quickly discarded). My mail was carefully censored by my wife, and I might not read a book or a magazine. Above all, I was forbidden to hear any news of the outer world or to read a newspaper. (This forced a special problem to my day nurse, an avid reader of the *Baltimore Sun*, the more so since my long-range vision is extremely good, so that she was compelled to do her morning reading crouched in the farthest corner with her paper at an angle that must have been almost as baffling to her as to me.)

Sometimes, in the first quiet days, my doctor would slip in, and, after instructing me not to try to talk with him, would stand by the bedside, or sit in a chair in the corner silently observing me. I knew what he was doing. He was trying to read from my face whether my will to survive was intact. If he had been able to ask me the straight question (in the nature of the case, he could not do so), I could have given him a straight answer. The decision to survive had been taken before I went to the Hospital. It had been made for me by my

son's frightened face, glimpsed for a moment as he watched
me thrash on the couch at home. But it was also abetted by
motives, which, for reasons which I shall not labor here, I
felt to be peculiarly a degradation of the spirit—the fact that
dying is a painful and ugly business, and the fact that by a
reflex stronger than reason the eye struggles not to close upon
the light in which the world exists.

But I should also have had to tell Dr. Alagia something else.
I should have had to tell him that I was not sure that the decision was the right one. For the question whether that
minimum of quiet could be secured without which it is worth-
less to live was not one which could be answered only in its
own terms, or in personal terms. It bore on, and the problem
derived its force from, the condition of the world in which
that life was cast, and the part which it was my lot to play
in it. No door however thick and no commanded silence could
keep that question out. It quickly made its entry, acutely,
and in the least looked for way.

There was one regular exception to the no-visitors rule.
Casually, at first, I became more aware, and I began to look
forward to the moment when, at the close of those long days,
the Hospital chaplain would open the shut door and take his
place in the easy chair in the corner. His name was Father
Alan. There was more to his name than that. But since that
is what I always called him, that is what I shall call him here.
Father Alan was a short man, small-boned and slight. As I
first studied his face, there was nothing particularly distinctive about it except a reassuring plain humanity and the play
of irrepressible merriment that rather undid the more severe
set of his chin and mouth. I knew that he came to me in the
course of his routine rounds of the sick and dying, and was
sometimes called away (as I became aware when I grew
more sensitive to the meaning of ambulance bells and a certain tenseness of the voice over the loudspeaker system) to
the raw horrors of the accident ward. I found myself thinking

about him sometimes, how almost no experience is so limiting as physical pain, both for those who suffer and those who minister to it. It would not have occurred to me that, in free moments, one of this man's chief interests was the theory and history of sea power and naval operations.

Something quite different first stirred my interest in Father Alan. He was a Passionist monk. I observed with some curiosity his black habit with its broad leather belt dangling the chain of heavy wooden beads and the Crucifix. I observed, too, the black metal insignia of his order, in the shape of a human heart on which were traced in white a Cross and the letters IHS which Father Alan wore over his own heart.

There was nothing distinctive about Father Alan's conversation either. He, too, was under the rule that nothing must be said that might disturb the patient. So he clung formidably to the weather with only prudent ventures about my fellow inmates—the milder, more hopeful, or more amusing cases; for like me, Father Alan must struggle all his days against his sense of the absurd or comic.

But in any wavering along the margin of life there is a need that amounts to a greed, for truth, since in the flux of existence, the crumbling or melting at the touch of all familiar reality, truth alone is felt to offer one austere, stripped handhold across a chasm. One night I decided to cut through the careful irrelevancies of our talk and try to discover what manner of man this monk might really be. I asked: "Father, what am I to answer those pepole who keep writing me that I was wrong to write in *Witness* that I had left the winning side for the losing side? They say that by calling the West the losing side, I have implied that evil can ultimately overcome good."

Father Alan studied his hands, which were lying in his lap. Then he glanced at me directly and asked: "Who says that the West deserves to be saved?"

If, in that softly lighted room, Father Alan had burst a

Verey flare, he could scarcely have lit up more effectively the ravaged landscape of that No Man's Land across which the West confronts its crisis, supposing that it is only an alien enemy it confronts, not knowing that the enemy it confronts is first of all itself.

For Father Alan's question cut past the terms in which men commonly view the crisis of our time. It cut past all ratios of opposed power, past the armaments race and the production race, past the atomic weapons, Bombs and the bombers, the guided missiles and the craftily guided policies, the marshalled divisions and the marshalled statistics. It did not ask: Has the West the physical power to survive? It asked: Is the West justified in surviving? Does that West retain within itself what alone in life and history ever justifies the survival of anything, and which is ultimately a play of creative force whose test and whose mandate is that it impels men to die for it, not because they wish to die, but because they feel its shaping power so completely that they would rather die than live without it? So long as men identify themselves with that force to the point where they will to die for it, it is living and provides that inner certitude, greater and more instant than any idea or reasoning, which holds nations upright as they pick up momentum in the terrifying slopes and turns of history. The moment men in masses begin to question that force, at that moment it has begun to die. However long the tremor of its decay may take, time will henceforth be no more than a delay. Every civilization embodies a certain truth to which it gives reality. When that truth, which is, in turn, embodied in a faith held religiously whether or not it is wholly religious—when that faith loses its power to inspire men, its downfall is at hand. When that faith and that truth no longer match and meet the reality of men's daily lives, there sets in a radical readjustment of reality whereby men seek to bring the faith by which they live into conformity with the reality they live in. Thus every social revolution begins with a spiritual and intellectual revolution. Men revolt first in thought, in order to be free to revolt in act. But revolt does not always imply violence. It may simply take the form of a question. When the gap grows too clear between the faith and forms of a civilization and the realities of daily life, masses of men are paralyzed by the discrepancy so that before the old faith they first grow numb, then apathetic, then questioning if not disdainful. They simply by-pass in one degree or other, what no longer corresponds to their reality. It has lost its power to inspire their lives. This happens even if they continue outwardly to conform to the old ways. This is the real crisis of the West and the point at which, across a No Man's Land of apathy, it confronts itself. Communism is only a secondary manifestation of this crisis, although Communism has reached a strength where it complicates and threatens to solve in its own terms the crisis of the divided West. For Communism is not an Asiatic or Russian growth, as some maintain. In its Soviet form, it has been shaped and colored by Russian peculiarities. But Communism is a way of thought and action, a way of reading history and its forces, which was developed in the culture capitals of the West. The growth of its power is inexplicable except as Communism appeals to the divided mind of the West, making each of its advances exactly along the line of the West's internal division, paralyzing each effort of the West to cope with it by touching some sympathetic nerve. The success of Communism, as I have written elsewhere, is never greater than the failure of all other faiths. Just as the threat of Communism is not the true crisis of the West, Communism is not the true revolution of our time. Communism is only one form and one sector of that revolution. The revolution of our time embraces the whole West, and, since, for the first time in history, our civilization, due to technology and science, embraces the whole world, the revolution affects the whole world. This revolution operates on many levels. It is a spiritual and intellectual revolution so that Henry Adams, sitting in his Manhattan club, watching the crowds marching up and down Fifth Avenue, had good ground for believing that they were marching chiefly to the end of a world—his world and ours. But the revolution is also a social revolution, a movement of masses of men, for a greater share of the goods which a technological civilization produces in hitherto unheard of abundance—and which is perhaps the sole justification for the existence of that system. Any attempt to see the revolution in either of those terms without seeing it in terms of the other —any attempt to see it only as a spiritual crisis or only as a social crisis—leads to a confusion of reality.

I opened recently a Fair Dealing magazine to find a two-page spread of American goods with a caption to the effect that this is our answer to Communism, this is what the free world has to offer the restive regions of mankind. It is well to offer this to whatever man needs it. Tactically— and he who receives knows even better than he who gives the degree to which tactics underlies the benefaction—these goods may forestall or defer a loss to Communism. Moreover, that deferment may be of incalculable importance.

But that will not solve the crisis either of the West or of the world. For the complacency which supposes that a crisis of the depth of ours can be solved by a dole fails to grasp that such a solution has thereby raised the other aspect of the crisis—the spiritual crisis—to the point of desperation. At that point, all stand under the judgment which humankind has always known at the moment when the ineradicable spirit bursts the shell that we try to raise between our lives and our inward knowledge that all life is tragic.

A civilization is justified in seeking to buy survival by sharing its material prosperity with a restive world—like any other form of endangered life trying to save itself. But a civilization which supposes that what it chiefly has to offer mankind is more abundant bread—that civilization is already half-dead. Sooner or later it will know it as it chokes on a satiety of that bread by which alone men cannot live. It will, in all probability, know it long before. For it seems to be a law of life and of history that societies in which the pursuit of abundance and comfort has displaced all other pursuits in importance soon cease to be societies. They become prey. They fall to whatever power can rally the starving spirit of man even though the rallying faith is demonstrably worse than the soft complacency that would suffocate the spirit in abundance. The fall is more certain because a failure of spirit leads invariably by some inward influence to a failure of intelligence.

Throughout the years between my break with Communism and the beginning of the Hiss Case, Father Alan's question had haunted me. It rose in its most terrible form when that case began. It was never absent from a day or night of that experience. Against nothing did I have to struggle so fiercely as against it. And nothing set me so apart from those who bore the burdens of that action in more important ways or sealed me off more completely in a circle of loneliness. For, unlike them, I truly supposed that that action was more than incidental, justified in the name of right and of necessity but powerless to affect the deeper crisis of our time which it subsumed in miniature. I never supposed that by my actions in that case, I could do more than give the children of men an infinitesimally better chance against the forces of dissension and darkness that were setting against them. Therefore, I sought to go a little in advance—to give them that infinitesimally better chance.

Every development of that case confirmed my view, and every development afterward added to it.

That is why, later on, when our nightly conversations had become something to which, it seemed to me, Father Alan looked forward almost as much as I, I spoke to his understanding with a freedom such as I would speak to few men.

Thus, one night, when our conversation had reached a certain turn, I said: "Two little imps sit at the foot of my bed, one on each post. They sit with their backs to me. But, now and again, one will turn around and grin and say: 'It was all for nothing?' Then the other turns and grins and asks: 'Why go on?'"

But it was not the absence of an answer to Father Alan's question ("Who says the West is worth saving?") that was most appalling. What appalled was the fact that, in its own mind, the West disdained the question, or, if it deigned to admit it to its consciousness at all, its complacent answer would be: yes. Father Alan's question spoke directly to my condition because it implied what we both knew—that at that point the West stood under the oldest and ultimate judgment, which could be lifted only in terms of more suffering than the mind can bear or measure.

> And unto the angel of the church of the Laodiceans write; These things saith the Amen, the faithful and true witness, the beginning of the creation of God;
> I know thy works, that thou art neither cold nor hot: I would thou wert cold or hot.
> So then because thou art lukewarm, and neither cold nor hot, I will spue thee out of my mouth.
> Because thou sayest, I am rich, and increased with goods, and have need of nothing; and knowest not that thou art wretched and miserable, and poor, and blind, and naked.*

---

* Revelations 3:14-17.

Pipe Creek Farm,
February 22, 1953

Dear Dunc:

Thank you for getting Tillich's *The Courage to Be.* I think I understand the tact and the point of the gift. Beyond realizing that it is a very good book, I am not yet far enough into it to have any world-shaking conclusions—at least not ontologically.

You were followed, a day or so later, by Father Alan and Father Morris together. Father Alan is your Passionist. Father Morris, no monk, is rector of the philosophical seminary in Baltimore. What a talk we had for two or three hours—everything from the evils of German philosophy and the pleasures of naval warfare in theory (Father Alan) to the pleasures of poultry raising and the evils of Descartes (Father Morris). You thought Father Alan was a minor miracle. You should meet Father Morris.

I thought I fielded very handily (for all our sakes) the one dangerous question you asked me: whether I was worrying about what I was next going to do. I worry about nothing so much. But I am fairly clear now about the main fact: The world is tight closed against me. No periodical editor is likely to publish me. None will give me a job. The two editors who might have been of some slight help are by chance gone from office. What will we do? We will milk cows and raise sheep once I get out of this bed. Which is better than going blind, like Wyndham Lewis, snarling and growling on Rotting Hill—as he calls it.

Best to all of you.

Whittaker

Pipe Creek Farm,
March 6, 1953

Dear Dunc:

I should have to read Tillich again and again before I would trust myself to get up at the State Fair and explain what he means.

Perhaps I can say a little better what he is doing. He is saying that man cannot describe God, no matter with how loud a voice: God *"ist ganz anders"*—wholly different (wholly other, to be literal). He is saying that man can know God only by overcoming that part of himself, of his very being which doubts God. He is also saying, at least to some extent, that the indispensable tool for scaling those cold peaks is the Hegelian dialectic (the one Marx converted)—the triad of positive, negation, and negation of the negation, which is the culminating synthesis of positive and negative, and brings us to a new phase of experience.

Tillich, in another sense, is saying, I think, what Dostoevsky said more memorably and briefly [in *The Possessed*]. The scene is that in Shatov's room when the cold, perverse Stavrogin stares at him with a faint smile and asks: "Is it true that now you even believe in God?" And Shatov grabs the edges of the table, is silent for a moment, and then shouts: "I *will* believe." Tillich, too, *will* believe, and he does not shout. He picks his way boldly and deftly along the frozen cliffs where Lutheranism has for some time been groping a faint path and foothold. It is a path that has great attraction, one might almost say temptation, for me. Who will say it is wrong because it leads to a glacier—to the Castle, in Kafka's image? You will recall that the Surveyor K. does at last manage to get the Castle on the telephone. Until then he has been kept away (although he had been ordered to come in the first place). He has been kept away on flimsy pretexts, has been humiliated and insulted. Then, at last, his call goes through and, for a moment, he hears an ethereal sound like children's voices singing. Then a gruff voice at the other end asks: "What do you want?" The Surveyor K. asks his tremendous question: "When can I come to The Castle?" The voice at the other end answers: "Never!" Between Man's purpose in time and God's purpose in eternity, Kierkegaard found an infinite chasm.

This, too, Tillich means. But, however cleverly he is saying it, he is always saying what Shatov said: "I *will* believe." All this, of course, is unfair to Tillich, who is much better reading than Chambers.

Father Alan and I once got on the subject of the Katyn Forest massacre. "There," I said, "were several thousand Polish officers marched out with their arms bound behind them, incapable of raising a hand to save themselves, and shot in the back of the neck. Some of them were arrogant, like Polish officers; some were stupid; but most were just simple men who loved their wives and children. The evil that conceived and executed the massacre was so monstrous that we have no word to encompass it. Tell me if God is a God of Good, why did He permit those simple men to be massacred by that monstrous evil?"

It is a monstrous question. And my respect for Father Alan really began because he could not answer it, and instead of trying, sat perfectly stunned and silent. I said, "There are at least four possible answers to the problem raised. The first is Dostoevsky's." I meant that moment when the lunatic, Marfa Timofeyevna, exhorts Shatov: "Water the earth with your tears, Shatushka, water it a foot deep with your tears."

The other answers do not now matter, because that is perhaps the best answer; or, at least, that is the one we all come to, even Tillich. . . .

Best to you all,

Whittaker

Pipe Creek Farm,
March 17, 1953

Dear Dunc:

I shall read him again soon. But I think that my final judgment, while a little more informed by then, will not be substantially different to what it would be now. In sum, it will be my reaction to all those fellows who try to catch the ever-lasting Why in terms of human reason. They perform a highly useful service. They are the framers of skeleton houses; they run up the studs, are the definers, the makers of distinction, the plotters of logic and logical consequences. They tell us why studs won't stand upright on a slant without supporting matter, etc., etc. People like you and me should follow them carefully, and know what their current blueprints

say, and what they have said as far in the past as the eye
can reach. Then, as wise teachers sometimes counsel their
students to do, we must "go out and forget everything we've
told you." Because living and architecture, while they have
much in common, are not the same . . .

I do not believe that you have met Father Bazinet, the
oldest of my Catholic friends in Baltimore. You remember
that we tried to see him at the Seminary. He is, altogether,
an impressive man. He was here the other day and I told him
I had been reading Tillich. He did not exactly grimace, but
a subcutaneous change of expression occurred. He glanced at
the book without touching it. He said: "I do not see what
those who have not really come to grips with evil, as you
have, can have to tell us about it."

But I think you are mistaken about Father Alan's silence
over Katyn—or perhaps I gave you a wrong impression.
First, my question was shocking. Then, his silence was momentary. Most important, and the point I was seeking to
make with you: a shallow man would have given me at length
the argument about inscrutable design. And Father Alan
did presently remember to mutter something about it. But
he knew that the question was too big for that and that, in any
case, such an answer would not work with me. Moreover,
what would you do if such a strange bird as I am had unexpectedly flown into your hospital?

I don't know whether I bothered you with the rest of our
plans, worked out in many talks of the kind we all loathe and
avoid. We have agreed to sell the herd, and eventually all
but the sheep. We have also agreed (this is an official secret)
to sell the farm we are living on. We will retreat in order
to the brick house on the back 200 acres. We also keep Medfield where I write. There are many good reasons for this
move. The details are too numerous to write about, but we
will discuss when next you are here. For various reasons, the
front farm has not yet been put on the market. But the

herd has. The commotion of selling is terrific—people in and out all the time. So that we live rather in the last act of the *Cherry Orchard*, but while we can hear them chopping down the cherries, nobody has bought the trees yet.

Best,

Whittaker

From pages of a diary

August 3/53

The capacity for probing and diagonal conversation, a rich and worthy faculty, has the opposite of charm for me. I am at the core a silent man. That generic silence is often taken for dullness or slowness. But I do not believe that it is. I believe that at root it is an asceticism of forces, which declines to be crowded or cluttered, and is highly selective in the sense that it feels itself rooted in a few unchanging truths, like its feeling about God, or soil, or the landscape in which it grew, and hence about courage, truth, and resolution. These are not ideas, but forces, to be changed or affected only by a basic revolution, such as joining the C.P.—not by the exchange or play of ideas, but by a total *Umschwung* or *Umwälzung*. The mind is not hostile to ideas. But such an *Umwälzung* is too total, too mortal, for a lifetime which is so brief. Exposure to it cannot be often risked, or lightly. Hence when the flow of ideas breaks over a mind like mine, it first listens, then resists, then grows silent. It is itself—fed by its own saps which pulse back and forth from the roots that basically sustain it and hold it upright. What it accepts from the atmosphere around it, it accepts only very slowly, imperceptibly, by processes which it would be laborious, and not even desirable, to probe. I am sure that I am saying this very badly, in part because I am trying to state in intellectual terms what is essentially not an intellectual process or position. In fact, it has always divided me from the intellectuals among whom I always return upon an inward silence which I think they find suspect because they suspect that it is hostile, whereas it is chiefly a difference in pulse rate. (Intellectuals in the sense that I use the term here—that is, people without any topographic horizons.)

Few men, I think, can love life with so intimate a particularity. But, progressively in the last two years, I have had to ask myself: Is there not something essentially base and ignoble in this mere fondness, like an appetite for bonbons in a grownup? One has seen it all. Another day's sun is just another sweet, rationed in minutes. Yet, when I look from the hills, it is the eye that betrays me always. So perhaps there are reaches of meaning beyond the bare command to pluck it out.

They write me continually that now I should be happy and tranquil, that I should be at peace. McCarthy asked me meaningfully if *Witness* was not a financial success. They envy me. It is as if the whole drama were played in a foreign language before an immense audience that catches only an intelligible word here and there, which, of course, it misinterprets, along with the gestures of despair and hopelessness —or just the silence they enjoin. As if peace, tranquillity, and happiness were not what I had irrevocably surrendered, knowing, too, what I was doing. As if anybody could envy me for any reason, now or ever. All these letters are by way of the most generous encouragement on the part of people who neither understand the enemy nor me. This is the heart of the great loneliness.

The kind of sad dignity that cannot be taken even from the captive apes in their cages. But then, one is not sure even of that since the main thrust of every force in the modern world is directed to destroying man's dignity. Above all, everything is set to make him connive at destroying it himself. The baits, as we know, are various in prospect; and, in the end, prove chiefly offal.

August 9/53

The alarm rang at 5:30, and as I came through my sleep, I was improvising a poem which seems to have been eight or ten lines long, out of which only the last line and part of the next to the last line came through sleep with me:

> Resigning all that went before,
> I shall live longer, not for more.

I often dream in rhyme. But I wonder how often I twang that theme, which was caught by the chance that this time the clock broke in on what the poor head thinks about in sleep.

August 14/53

We are having fall in summer—very autumnal. The gold-finches are loudly in evidence—always a wintry sign. And the swallows, all housekeeping done, are flocking on the telephone lines. Another sad sign. Twenty-three acres torn up for late-summer planting of alfalfa. More to come. Only a little less to plough for barley. And lespedeza harvest just ahead—the last hay crop. Two evenings ago, we cut the No. 1

Shropshire ram out of bachelor's quarters and gave him a
conducted tour the length of the farm to the ewes' pasture.
Ewes breed when the cool nights come. So, goodbye summer.
I was telling my wife about the ram's tour. "Poor fellow," I
said, "he did not know where he was going, and, when he
got to the top of the ridge, he gave such a sad blat." "He knows
now," said my son.

August 17/53

Searching for some papers, today, I came across Granville
Hicks' review of *Witness*, which I had not re-read since it appeared; and some jottings of mine made while I was still in
bed. It was only chance that the review and the jottings
were in the same heap. But perhaps it should not have been.

What struck me about his review, as at the first time I
read it, was that, after claiming me as a devotee of "consequent
logic," he adds that, to be truly consistent, I should return
to some point in time before the technological revolution in
order logically to begin my criticism of the secular, rationalist,
scientific mind *ab initio*. What seems to me characteristic is
his assumption that I do not know this, too, and have not
done it. There seems to be an idea that I have put everything
in *Witness*, which is certainly untrue, and, if true, would be
unmerciful. Is there to be no pity for readers? And as if it
were not our pleasure not to disclose all our thought but to
hold back a few windings to disclose at some time and place of
our good choosing. After which, it is at once necessary to say
that the striking feature of Hicks' review is an intellectual
and compassionate understanding quite beyond any other
liberal's who has dealt with the subject.

Now for the jottings, dated March 1, 1953, and intended
as part of some comment on a sermon of Father Bazinet's:

"More and more, I incline to a view, not at all original
with me, that the whole technological development of civiliza-

tion was a wrong turning; that we are harvesting its inevitable consequences; that we are at the end of a historical phase for which the only possible solutions are presently to be made by the Bombs. It is difficult at times to see it any other way. It is difficult to see how there can be anything less drastic than a new beginning; both because the illogic of the current situation has to reach debacle by the play of the forces that make it wrong; and because the sheer mass and complexity of historical error is now too great to be coped with by the mind in the form of good intentions. (This leaves out entirely the vast, complicating mass of bad intentions.) That is what I mean when I say that the only possible solutions will be made by the Bombs.

" 'Probable' would, no doubt, be a discreeter word than 'possible.' But the Bombs (A and H) do actually epitomize the ultimate refinement of the mind that dominates our time— the secular, scientific mind. They are its ultimate promise before which we stood sceptics—the promise that man could reach into the heart of invisible, more or less theoretical matter, and tear out its energy; then, by the devices of his further ingenuity, hurl it at inertia so that the literal heavens are threatened, and those who should know best seem unsure whether or not the charge will ignite the envelope of the world.

"This demonic genius has affected (or, if you choose, corrupted) the whole mind of the West. For, all those who think passionately, passionately submit, or in one degree or another, revolt from it. The only neutrals are the dolts, those who simply do not understand that there is a crisis. Put in the top grouping of them the college-trained technicians who understand only the sterile, dehumanized verities of card files, isotopes, controlled tests, or the purely functional mysteries of electronics.

"But the technicians are not the only lost minds. The whole population reflects a similar necrosis of the mind almost to the exact degree, I suspect, in which it has fallen under the technological spell. It is simply impermissible to question science and technology. And, in general, people no longer question much of anything beyond the range of very small children. It is as if the virtue of the mind has been lost completely; as if in one of Pavlov's horrible experiments with dogs, a part of almost everybody's mind had been cut away, leaving just a few faculties, more active for the excision of the rest—but faculties that react only to the bong of a bell, causing the subject to drool or show rage or fear. Say 'U.N.' to them, for example, and they drool. Criticize the U.N., and they foam. You could classify a whole series of well-known reactions.

"My point is, further, that it is particularly the intellect of the age that is affected in this way. The masses are powerless, if bumptious, due to the illusion of literacy. As a result, it has become almost impossible to communicate anything outside the stimulus and tone range of the bonging bell. Words, as agents of thought, have lost their force against the spell of the corrupted mind of the West (which, in One World, means also the East which reproduces the phenomena, only more sophomorically). The effort of individuals to understand retains, here and there, its integrity. But the hope of communicating understanding to others belongs among the illusions of childhood.

"This is a period in which only martyrdom is striking enough to teach anything, and then, perhaps, almost exclusively to the masses, and perhaps not to many of them. For one manifestation of the corruption of the modern mind is that science has succeeded in making even martyrdom suspect. In other words, the utmost effort that the soul can make for its fellows now seems, to a rather wide cross section of them, an evidence of personal instability. In short, modern men cannot be reached in general through their minds, and scarcely even through their souls. Therefore, I suspect, the argument must be completed by the Bombs. For no sound less tremendous can pierce that fatuous complacency beyond the tone range of the bonging bell.

"Nor do I believe that this conclusion must come under the head of pessimism. Surely, the prospect of a new beginning is more optimistic than a dead end. Diagnosis may be depressing. It does not follow, therefore, that a diagnostician is a pessimist. I venture that we should be extremely cautious in our guesses at Inscrutable Purpose, or our thoughts about what we deserve, or do not deserve to have happen to us. Here I am speaking less about individuals than about nations. 'Who says that the West deserves to be saved?' asked Father Alan. Does anyone think he would like to try to answer that question?"

August 21/53

The symptoms of a new heart attack are here—the dragging fatigue, that drained-out feeling, and that uncomfortable inflated feeling, which is not pain, but feels as if the heart were being steadily blown up—which, in a sense, perhaps it is; enlargement. There are also the never-failing pains in the left shoulder—sometimes quite difficult to bear. This will be the fourth attack, counting the one at *Time*, the one during the summer of 1952 here at Medfield, and the one that took me to St. Agnes. People manage to pull through a surprising number of such attacks nowadays. But four seems rather stretching things. The actual business of dying, the death struggle, the sense of breath being cut off and gasping through the mouth (which I remember from waking once during that night)—that is ugly. Most of our other thoughts and preferences about life and death seem to me silly. Like wanting to live to see grandchildren or not wanting to die in the cold time, in winter. There is really no best time to die. This is possibly true for the whole wider range of our relationships, and only the limitations of our understanding lead us to juggle with the theme: he should have died hereafter. The only thing about dying that seems to me really insupportable is that my wife should not go with me. Ultimately, it is perhaps simply incredible. I could face eternity—or nothing— without a qualm if her hand were in mine at the moment we slipped into it. It is curious. I took her hand as we walked through the yard to go mushrooming the other day; and I had the strange sensation then that we were walking toward death together, with great contentment, hand in hand. The image at the end of *Witness* is completely literal, like the whole passage, not, as I have reason to think that many people suppose, a matter of prose. Nor does this feeling rise from depression or is it selfish on my part. It rises from a simple sense of our inseparateness, a deep-going logic that makes it right that we should be always together. I cannot imagine eternity without her, just as she is the one soul without whom I should not have wished to live. The children belong to life. For the rest, I shall not regret anything but the sleepy summer heat on the fields and woods. W.C. *implora eterna quietà, eterna pace.*

This is the season when three little brown birds, scratching in the dry leaves, I noted this morning, make a sound like a platoon, crashing through the bushes. (Later) What I have written above does not mean, of course, that I shall not take measures to head off an attack. That is the point of duty— poor John particularly; Ellen has found a replacement for her parents. Those thoughts above belong to a soldier, tired to death of the war, who has picked up a grenade and pulled the pin and is counting six (or whatever they count). But he wonders whether, before he flings it, the thing will go off in his hand, knowing: if not this time, another—and only those who have not been to a war can indulge less literalness.

We do not really respect those who love life—none do who have once stood alone in No Man's Land at night and seen what fragments cling to the barbed wire. It heightens our appreciation of the sun, which becomes very dear. But each time, as we catch ourselves expanding in the light, we smile. And that smile cuts to the core of reality. We know. The rest are loungers on the beach, a little comical, perhaps a little gross.

August 29/53

The heart symptoms that I noted on Aug. 21, though less acutely now that I have been doing little but take medicine again. I can only account for the symptoms by supposing that a very small clot formed or was forming. How big is any clot? Discomfort, pain, and extreme weakness were most severe during the first three days; are now less, but all present every day at some time or other.

The swallows have gone; the clematis is in bloom. These two things always mark for me the end of the year. The rest is waiting for another spring.

I have now the truly paralyzing sense of waiting for something that is going to happen without any real power on my part to do much about it. And I lack the energy to come to grips with the last things that I should do. Bad morale.

August 30/53

Henry Regnery complains that his book of saints by a Protestant was ignored by Catholics while Protestants don't seem to like saints. I do not think he will have an easy path in religious publishing. He might publish certain books for his Catholic clientele and other books for the Protestants. I doubt that he can successfully breed the two. Both sides will regard the hybrid as a unicorn. Protestants are suspicious of saints, don't like saints, are perhaps by definition bound to outlaw saints. They reject tragedy, they must. The matter goes to the core of the Protestant position and the whole puritan compulsion. My Lutheran landlady in Berlin, in 1923, was living flagrantly with a *grüner Polizist*, who was always around the house by day, while her husband was a cellarer in the old Kaiserschloss. But in her kitchen hung a litle embroidered motto which read: *Immer rein und fein/ Muss mein Flettbrett sein* (Always clean and nice/ Must my kitchen board be). Bundling is perfectly possible among Protestants, but not sanctity. Not while *cleanliness* is next to godliness. Saints are so often unkempt, while some of them have a truly dismaying grasp of political reality. The Protestant worldview is simplicity; but science has added nothing to the Catholic grasp of the complexity of matter and life; it has only explored, pin-pointed, charted, and loosed it for destruction.

Protestants favor prophets. On the other hand, the Catholic mind distrusts prophets. A function of the Church is to keep them from getting out of hand—by faggots if necessary.

December 30/53

All a man can ever really do against fate is to assert the forces of his ridiculous and prayerful courage, which is neither more nor less ridiculous than what the first man asserted against sabre-tooth and the enormity of a primal universe. It is all men have ever had to assert; and the enormity has merely taken new forms.

January 3/54

Mr. Pennington arrived New Year's morning to say that an angus heifer had just been born, presaging a prosperous New Year. The same day, the first robin of the winter came back.

This evening, at sundown, I thought I heard a sound I could not believe possible—a wren. Poor thing, it's turning cold, and it is a long way from warmth and the warm lands, probably too long to make it back. It is unheard of, a wren at this season. Day before Christmas, the first lamb was dropped. Today, a spray of forsythia bloomed . . . Who has been meddling with what?

Cold Friday

Farthest Field to the North

Height! A little height in order simply to be a little and to see a little—to win a little headroom to breathe in, a little look-out to take some bearings from. If you could get behind any pair of eyes that rest on you, I suspect that you would find that something like this is what the mind within the skull really craves. It scarcely matters what form the craving takes, how it is dissembled, stifled, or denied; or whether it takes no set form at all, but remains unstated, as that formless, frustrated, resentful restlessness that is a ground mood of our time. We all know the mood. It is certainly not despair. Those who know true despair act quickly to end it. And true despair is much more uncommon than we suppose. A German doctor, released to the West from a Communist slave-labor camp has told us, with the realist's faint sniff of superiority, how his fellow slaves would spend their days endlessly discussing ways to end their hopeless lives. Yet not one of them ever simply walked into the forbidden zone around the barbed-wire fences where each would have been instantly cut down by the stitching machine-gun fire of the guards.

We may even hesitate to call what we feel futility. For against that stands the unparalleled material accomplishment of the West, consuming in a total activity each of our lives each of our days. But is it not true that moments come when that effort suggests a play of energy without purpose beyond its own expenditure, leaving a sense of deprivation, so that the immense accomplishment leads always back to something that does resemble futility.

There is a sense of toppling culmination. But the forces that are shaping it, like the force at Hiroshima, remain remotely abstract, impersonal, yet violent and all around us. Hence a confusion and a bafflement, that feeling that we are never going to do anything; things are simply going to happen to us. It is the same with political as with technological and scientific forces. We see and feel their effects. Their inward meaning and laws of motion elude us. Always, too, there is a sense of something left out, which brings an almost physical sensation that the air is being exhausted around us.

It is to get above that exhausted air that we crave a little height, though we must reach it by crawling on our hands and knees. Height, then, from which to try to measure, in a little beset detachment, those forces (crush of others, crush of things, crush of happenings) that impersonally shape each of our lives each of our days. Height on which to try to rally, in a little wrested silence and apartness, a strength equal to the impact of such forces. Height, above all, to try to locate ourselves, at least once before the end of the line, in the universe as it rides through the fall-out of space and the constellations—to locate ourselves, if only once for a moment, in what is (not what we might wish or even pray for, but what really is), to locate ourselves in our own reality. For only by knowing reality unsparingly can a man rescue the one

power that justifies his life between earth and sky—his chance
to rise above it.

For this, height need not be particularly high. Nor does
it matter if, in part, it is illusion. It is possible that illusion
is as necessary to us as any other force, so long as we know
it for illusion and allow for that in our factoring of reality.
My little height is called Cold Friday.

Cold Friday is the name of a field on this farm. On the old
survey map, and in the older deeds, a number of our fields bear
odd names, given them at forgotten moments in the past by
men whose own names nobody any longer remembers. Thus,
a field called Legonier lies on the south and east slopes of the
middle ridge. Hit-Or-Miss is the outermost strip along the
county road. High Germany sweeps up to the crest of our
highest ridge. Cold Friday is the farthest field of this farm
to the north. Cold Friday looks to the north in more ways
than one.

It is a flat-top, as we say hereabouts by way of contrast to
the commoner round-tops. One of them, Little Round Top,
on the Gettysburg battlefield a few miles to the west, lifted
itself, in three days during barley harvest, 1863, permanently
into the horizon of history. From that "high water mark"
(though it was traced in blood) certain energies of this
Republic receded, though they did not end. Certain other
energies were violently liberated, though they were not necessarily the energies that those who fought or died there supposed they were fighting for, or could even imagine. For in
those dusty grain fields, woods, and orchards, a way was
cleared for the United States to become something without
its like in history: a technological colossus; and that fact, for
good or ill, was to be decisive for all mankind. The sounds
of that decision in the making must have carried clearly to
Cold Friday. This was, of course, a battle of the first great

modern, mechanized war; and the vast triangle of its action extended from Chambersburg (in the Pennsylvania mountains to the west) to Wrightsville (on the Susquehanna) to Pikesville (on the outskirts of Baltimore). The defeated past and the looming future, in the shape of detachments of thirsty, battle-frantic men, swept down the Littlestown Road, not three miles from Cold Friday, skirmishing fiercely in every quiet village where roads crossed.

Family tradition says that my great-grandfather, a Dr. Chambers, was at this battle, though it is typical of my family, and an attitude of many Americans, that I never learned his given name. Yet, typically, too, I was given a detail: that during the battle, he soaked himself in whiskey to fog his mind to the horrors of three days of amputations without anesthetics, which he was there to perform.

I labor this footnote because I hold that a nation's life is about as long as its reverential memory. Let me try to underline my meaning with a recollection. Shortly before General Walter G. Krivitsky was murdered by the Communist secret police, a few blocks from the United States Capitol, I drove him and his wife and small son into Pennsylvania. I pointed out, as we crossed the Delaware River, that General Washington and the Continental Army had crossed at the same place on the cold Christmas Eve, 1776. Tonya Krivitsky peered around her as if to try to imagine the passage, improbable in that lush countryside, of the beaten band which had re-crossed the frozen river to reverse defeat and decide by force that a new era of history had opened— one which included the French Revolution, and also the Bolshevik Revolution of which the Krivitskys and I were human jetsam. Then she made a remark, which, it seems to me, few Americans would be likely to make, in a tone which few Americans would be likely to use. "Ah," she said with a trace of wonder doing duty for obeisance before the greatness with which men have sometimes acted, *"eine historische Land-*

schaft." I call that reverential memory at work. Cold Friday is part of an historical landscape.

Weathering has left a platform of earth—some ten or twelve unlevel acres—hoisted above and apart from the other fields. For Cold Friday is thrust from the rock-oak ridge behind it, like an outwork. Most fields invite the world; Cold Friday confronts it. Its slope to the south looks directly down on the roof of the Creek Farm house. Below its steeper face to the north, the Big Pipe Creek forces the shallow rapids that check its fall to the Monocacy, the Potomac, and the Ocean. Cold Friday, therefore, is the kind of height on which, in the past, men have sometimes built their ultimate defenses, calling them, variously, strongholds, citadels, acropolises, burgs, or kremlins, but meaning always the site of a last stand.

Here, in my turn, I meant to sink my ultimate defenses, when I reached Cold Friday, somewhat late in life, stumbling out of the revolution of the twentieth century. Here I determined to root the lives of my children—to live here and die here in this particular earth—which was for them, in the routine language of deeds, "and their heirs and assigns, to have and to hold in fee simple forever." I meant to root them in this way in their nation. For I hold that a nation is first of all the soil on which it lives, for which it is willing to die— a soil bonded to those who lived on it by that blood of which a man usually loses a few drops in working any field like Cold Friday. I was also fully conscious of another resolve: to end the wanderings of my house which for generations has been in flight westward—as Huguenot fugitives from France to Ireland, as soldiers from Holland to Britain, as revolutionists fleeing from Ireland and Scotland to America. On this earth, I was determined, our line would remain or end. Thus, for me, Cold Friday stands also for all the fields a man must cross to reach it.

I did not take such thoughts to Cold Friday when I first

went there. First, I put it in corn. After the corn came alfalfa. But when the alfalfa wore thin, and grass began to run it out, I left the field in rough pasture, to cattle for three seasons of the year, or to the furtive life that drifts over it—the deer and the hunter, the random trespasser. For Cold Friday is a defiant field. Two of its free sides are too steep for modern farm machines to climb. The third is denied by a springhead that wells from the base of the hill and has settled in a wet spot that gains a little every year on the firm ground, and which I am content enough to see gain. It is my little sacrifice to the energies of nature, to all that is chthonian in it before which anyone who lives directly against the earth and under the seasons hourly stands. Machines can reach Cold Friday only by way of a narrow, twisting trace through those rock-oak woods behind. It is not worth the effort, or half a hayload knocked from the wagon by overhanging branches, with the labor of stacking to be done again for nothing. So I surrendered Cold Friday to itself. For long periods, I never went there. There was no reason to go. Cold Friday lies too far from the barns where people work and the houses where they live.

Then, in 1952, it became impossible for me to go anywhere. My life became chiefly a necessity to outlive a series of crises of health or to convalesce between them. During the first long convalescence, I lay in the room of this house which is closest to the sheep barn. Waking before daybreak on snowy nights, I could sometimes hear the thin, wiry cry that means that a lamb has been born and has probably got itself in some corner where the ewe cannot find it. (Ewes seem perversely to choose the coldest nights to lamb, and few lambs are so helpless at birth that they cannot get away and freeze.) I was powerless to go find the lamb, to rub it dry or restore it to its senselessly blatting mother. I could only lie and listen. At such times, I was surprised at how often the image of Cold Friday came to my mind. I could see the field clearly, in my mind's eye, under its unbroken cap of snow and the down swoop of the west or north winds. This distinct image, recurring so often, puzzled me. One night, there came with it the opening line of "Prometheus Bound": POWER (*to his companion*, FORCE, *and to their prisoner*, PROMETHEUS): "We have come to the last path of the world, in the Scythian country, in the untrodden solitude." I was first amused—the Scythian country; that is Russia. But then it seemed to me that some deeper logic of meaning had long been at work and had taken form in the image of the field before the meaning had risen to consciousness. The last path of the world—that was Cold Friday.

When I could move about again alone, I did not go at once to Cold Friday, though the thought was often in mind. The mind resists going, even on a junket, to the last path of the world. It resists the more, the more it suspects that such a phrase mirrors a reality. Reality can be a temptation, and the mind resists the temptation of facing the full reality, the ordeal of particularizing what, in part, it foreknows. But when I could get back to Cold Friday, I went again and again, simply to sit alone in the jeep, or stand, to look off from the field.

I had with many misgivings (I shall come back to that later on) given life to two children. I meant, in the simplest terms, to take those children to the soil as one of the few sound realities left in life that they might grow into and grow out of, and which, whatever forays into the world they might later make, they would never finally leave. I meant to found a line rooted in a particular spot of the earth which they would make their own by that effort of their lives they put into it by working it, and which their children's children would inherit by right of that energy of their lives which they had sown, like seed, in it. In the twentieth century, no purpose could well have been more deliberately unrealistic. Every energy which my intelligence told me was shaping the future was against it. No man could have been more conscious of that unreality.

This was all there was to give—the ground beneath their feet. I meant to give it to them not only against the forces of open revolution but also against that suffocating materialism, which, more than want or hunger, recruits the forces of revolution in the West. For some must at last have eyes to see the plain fact that the revolutionary proletariat in the West (including Russia) is not, and never has been, a factory proletariat. The forces of revolution in the West are an intellectual proletariat, disinherited, not in this world's goods with which they are often incongruously replete, but disinherited in the spirit. The revolt of the intellectuals of the West almost without exception begins (no matter how it ends) as the frantic threshing of those drowning in the materialism of the West, a convulsive struggle against the death of the spirit. This is the answer to the fatuous, reiterated question why men like Arthur Koestler or Whittaker Chambers became Communists. For the differences in background, which the shallow world magnifies, are trifling compared to that convulsion of the drowning spirit which carried us, and men like us (each in his own individual way with his own individual rationalization) into Communism, and which makes a second death for those who, recognizing at last that Communism is itself evil, must burst from that second drowning back into a West which has learned nothing and forgotten nothing. Hateful home truths! For they invite the West to stop looking at Communism and look into itself. Hateful home truths! (I said them all in *Witness*.) "Communism is never stronger than the failure of all other faiths"; "Men are by nature conservative; they become revolutionists only by despair"; "Communism did not attract, it repelled me; I became a Communist to escape the dying West." The inner meaning was lost in the coating of words. I am a man old now in experience and getting ready to die. I have no time left to coat the harsh truth. I have no other business on earth than to speak the truth as plainly as it seems to me. In the end, God commands nothing less for any man, as we know and seldom know anything more surely, for we seldom feel closer to God than when we speak truth at whatever cost.

So I meant Cold Friday to be a base for my children not only against the forces of revolution in the world, but also against the climate of materialism which breeds revolutionists. Nothing could have been more clearly foredoomed. Intelligence and experience alike told me this beyond question, and if I had acted only on their sense, I should not have acted at all. But it is my conviction, based on a reading of man's upward climb from shambling apehood, that man's progress is always a progress of the spirit. And that spirit makes its irrational forward lurch precisely at the moment it acts in defiance of a prevailing reality. The mind may not reject the knowledge of reality; the more coldly it weighs it the better. But the spirit may defy reality in the name of something higher. Cold Friday was therefore for me an act of hope and faith. The point of importance was not the failure. The important point was to act—the clenching of the will set in defiance of failure, because what is good and right remains good and right though buried in disaster and by centuries. So Cold Friday also looks to the north. For the mind, the fact-finding and fact-weighing mind, will not be denied and the reality it posits may be defined only at the price of sacrifice. That is why sacrifice stands always at the heart of every faith that has had power to move me, even of those faiths which from the viewpoint of the others were in error. And the blood on the altar is always real blood.

And God? "And Providence," a friend asked me, "where does Providence fit into your forecast?" It was a day or two before the Geneva Conference of 1955, which each of us, in slightly different ways, believed to be a milestone of disaster for the West. I had gone on, in answer to a question, to sketch in rough outline the terms in which I thought the foreclosure of our age may occur. It was then that my friend asked: "And Providence?" For he could not understand why, since both of us agreed that Communism is evil, I could also suppose a world where life is not. Everything that matters in life remains at best an insight. That is why Dostoevsky makes Shatov, the ex-nihilist, describe it "as the will to go to the end though it expressly denies that end. It is that river of living water, the drying-up of which is threatened in the Apocalypse." It is the drying of that river of living water that we feel though we cannot fix it more literally. That river of living water has little or nothing to do with the inventive mind or the critical intelligence. Both are plainly proliferating like cancer cells. That river of living water is something different: it touches, not the inventive, but the creative spirit. That it is drying we know by the simplest reaction—because we are dying of thirst.

That is why I am constantly puzzled that so many simply take it for granted that God must be on the side of the West, that God will, *in extremis*, save the West. I feel no such certainty, while my mind notes little that the West has done toward saving itself. It is very easy to suppose that, because Communism is evil, Communism must inevitably be defeated. It presupposes comfortably that we are good.

That is why, though I hold Communism to be evil, I did not believe that it was simply stipulated that God was on the side of the West. Originally, the title of this book was to have been *The Losing Side*. A friend expressed displeasure at the change. I answered: "In history, the losing side of anything, however numerous, is never more than a minority. But today the whole world has reached Cold Friday." That is another way of saying what I had already said in *Witness*, though so few had understood and so many had misunderstood it: that the struggle itself is its own solution. For in that test will be disclosed what virtue is left in us, whether that river of living water has wholly dried up or merely dipped underground for a dry season.

In 1954, I deeded Cold Friday to my son. I never felt that I possessed for myself the earth I formally owned. I held it in custody for my children. My son was setting out on a journey. I deeded him Cold Friday because it, and all it stood for, was all I had to give him at such a time—the ground beneath his feet. Here, there is that healing quiet in which a man can simply sit and observe, letting the impression of the time and place pass through his mind.

The lore of this countryside says that in Indian days the valley of the Big Creek was neutral ground. Here all tribes could come in peace to dig something that they needed. The banks of the Pipe Creek are clay banks (the bricks, of which the Creek farm house is built, were home-shaped and home-fired from them). The clay of the Big Pipe Creek differs in quality from that of the Little Pipe Creek which joins it farther down toward the Monocacy. From our clay the Indians shaped their bigger pipes, and from the clay of the Little Pipe Creek their smaller ones. Hence the somewhat prosy name of these streams. It seems probable that more Indians than white men have loitered on this neutral ground. It is likely that those last remnants of Stone Age man climbed the lookout of Cold Friday which commands the clay banks.

> Bands of nude coppery men passed
> This way on soft feet
> And stood thus, to listen,
> When the moon was overcast.

Cold Friday is part of the landscape of a history, older than mechanized war. It is only a little distance over these ridges to the east that the last of the Susquehannas were massacred and exterminated, man, woman, and child—a reminder that this nation, like all others, lives above the graves of those whose soil they took by force and must hold, ultimately, by force. For if few men can live guiltlessly, no nation ever can.

The basic problem of writing is one of creating a kind of order. This runs counter to a popular notion that writing consists in working felicitously with words. That is part of the craft of writing, just as a carpenter, if he is to run up a hen coop, let alone a house, must be able to cut boards to a true angle and join them solidly. But the real problem is to impose upon the diversity, the chaos, of experience an order which will sum up, for himself and others, its essential meaning. It is this that makes writing more exhausting than field work—more like the labor of childbirth. If the labor succeeds, if a vision of truth evolves, it will have its own resonance—what the poetry of common speech calls "the ring of truth." That tone no art of words can add. It comes from within and instantly marks its distance from the eloquence of rhetoric which is an eloquence of the surface.

As a man ages, the more avid of truth he becomes until, as he nears the Hit-Or-Miss, the No Man's Land of a lifetime, the need becomes a craving. He comes to realize that every man's life, viewed from Cold Friday, is essentially an enactment of his vision of truth. The lapses, fumblings, failures, are themselves part of the truth. He knows then, too, that that vision of truth is all he can take with him. It is also all that he can really leave behind him.

I grasped that I had deeded my son nothing—a heap of dirt—unless I also made the effort to leave him the vision I glimpsed from that height. That was all I could really leave him.

In effect, my son will be climbing Cold Friday beside me. I am somewhat short of breath these days. I cannot be wholly sure, as we begin the climb, that we shall make it all the way. But I am reasonably certain that, if we do reach the top of Cold Friday, or not long afterwards, my son will find himself his own man, alone on his own Cold Friday. If I know my son, he will go often to that field, to look off, to consider by himself the windings of the Creek below, the facing woods and slopes, the traces of his father's course. I have only one counsel for him at that point: not to show by a change of his face or a motion of his hand what he feels.

Exercises

There is a dark upward trend to the night sky,
And in it, infinitely high, stars.
The fence, here toppling on to the road, is built
Of untrimmed rails. The three gate-bars,

Laid on their weathered posts, transect
Cart ruts that lead across the frozen fields.
The dark irregular growth of cedar,
Silent by the fence rails, shields

These lands from the memory of the moon,
That shone too brightly last night
And, being obscured by clouds,
Shines now with a lesser light—

In which are visible short winter-rotted
Kale and cabbage stumps,
And the long broken spring furrow-turnings
Ending in briar clumps,

And dark separate cedars that gather
Into them the loose strands of the mists.

So that, seeing them, one marvels
How the spirit of the fields persists,

And wonders how long it was gathering when
The last band of nude coppery men passed
By on soft feet, and stood thus
When the moon was overcast—

And what it has taken to itself of the pale
Men who followed these; or whether a new race
Will flow out of the blood of those sleeping
In the houses round about, and will displace

The traces of our ways. As I wonder,
If I live on here, what sons will stem
From my blood, and what they will be
To these men, and what will become of them.

Of course, all animals have souls, though of just what kind
I can say even less than about people's souls. But I recognize
them at the point where the beautiful light of this world
enters the creature's eye, and it longs to persist in that light.

Someone whom I stood with on this hill stooped suddenly
and collected from the tall grass a small skull and some verte-
brae. He was a young man, cut wholly to the modern fit. He
studied his find with detached, objective interest. He thought
the skull and bones were those of a groundhog which a fox had
killed. I thought of the ferocious pursuit and flight that makes
any seeming-peaceful field a scene of incessant death struggle
and murder as horrifying as a battlefield, endurable only
because most of it takes place out of sight and hearing, animals being so discreet, from fear, since the greatest killer of
all is man. I thought, too, of the multitudinous necessity of
death—the multitudes, in numbers defying the mind, who
have lived, died, been killed, without leaving any memory,

without trace or so much as a pathetic small skull and crumbling bones. Millions upon millions, vanished absolutely, as if they had never been at all—no smallest memento or memory; no apparent meaning. The thought of those meaningless numbers thunders like surf in the mind, and drowns our probities in the surge of energy without purpose. The point is not that God notes every sparrow that falls, but that he lets it fall—without trace. I love the light. The groundhog loved the light. The sparrow loved the light. Night falls. I often find myself thinking very concretely of people I have known who have long been dead. You wonder what their ruinous remains look like after so long a separation—whether they have passed the condition of plain corrupting horror and have reached a skeletal minimum that produces only a mild repugnance. Above all, you wonder that they are completely forgotten. I may think of them once in a year, in ten years. They are an unreality that once lived, though it is impossible to grasp why, to what purpose. Wind in the grass and the little pines. The buzzard sails and sails above the hill, letting the wind currents carry him without working his wings. In the intense light. Kindness, courage—sometimes, the courage to be kind. I knew as much when I was twelve years old. And, further, no one has ever known more. All efforts come to no more, coolly looked at: a small skull and some bones for whom the fox is coming. The fangs! The fangs! The fangs!

I. *First Light*
   The fox pounces,
   The leveret screams;
   The sun rises,
   And it beams.

   "Light! Light!"
   The bird sings,
   Releasing, as it flies,
   The umbel of a flower that swings
   Unimplicated, over stones

Where blood already dries,
In fluffs of fur
And clotted bones;
While expeditious emmets stir,
Triggered mystically to feed
Before flies breed
Maggots to compete.

The morning's heat
Ovening the air,
The fox bespeaks his lair,
Sleeping, like an angel, where
Earth and torpor soothe all sound;
And does not hear the closing hound.

II. *Spring Rain*
All things work together for good,
As every field
Of springing grain
Is dunged with filth and death,
And rots the falling rain;
Which double-duty Rosarian, utilitarian does,
Multiplying yield,
And simulating peace,
Which is always for the ear
That cannot hear;
The eye that is blind,
Or fixed behind;
Is always for the ending,
Never for the beginning, breath.

Is the web where hangs
The suavely packaged fly,
That for only meaning has
A little sizzling cry
Whereby
It confides to the capable arachnid
The monotony of the agony

Of its plea to die,
At once and, at the same time, not to die:
A dualism that it sums
In the vision that it hums:
"The fangs! The fangs! The fangs!"

Son,

I want to tell you how it was with your mother and me. Almost every book is a kind of letter. And, as with almost any letter, I think it helps to know quickly in what circumstances it was written.

The winter of 1954-55 was hard for us—the hardest since the black winter of 1948-49. If you asked me: "What did Mother and you do during the winter?" I think I should answer: "We sat across from each other in silence, beside the big fireplace in the kitchen, and listened to the wind in the chimney." As you know, this is an old Maryland farm fireplace, almost big enough to stand erect in. Of course, there was nothing new, either, about the wail of the wind in the chimney-waist. But we listened to it as if we were hearing it for the first time in the new way in which people often first hear old things because they have acquired new meaning for them. The wind spoke to us of illimitable space and distance where there are no warming hearths of any kind and reminded us that we might presently be notes in such a wind. There is nothing bad or sad about that. But it is thought-provoking.

This picture is not, as a fact-fond age is fond of saying, strictly factual or intended to be. But the total impression is true. It is practically impossible, as you know, for your mother to sit anywhere for long if she can possibly think of something to be doing, or unless she has worked herself into exhaustion, as happened too often that winter. I, on the other hand, have always been able to sit quietly almost anywhere, making little observations, letting impressions drift through my mind—thinking, as we often mistakenly call it. That was fine in days when the choice was up to us. Now health had brought me to the preposterous condition, for an otherwise active man, where I had to sit still because I lacked the physical energy to do anything else while I seemed to be able to keep warm, even in late spring, only close to a fire whose heat drove others across the room.

And the sense of encasing silence was real enough. In part, this was due simply to the fact that you were 400 miles away at college. Your sister was 700 miles away, living near a camp with her soldier husband and their son. For the elders in a family so close-knit as ours, that is itself a change like winter. So your mother and I found ourselves, for the first time in the big house, in another preposterous position—like two old birds, as we sometimes said, who have outstayed the season, and sit in silence over last year's nest because they cannot lose the habit though the nest has lost its purpose and must presently lose its shape in the weather.

That was some of it. But the household silence only prolonged another whose causes were quite different and went much deeper. As we felt it encase us, I noticed that we tended to retreat into it as if silence were its own citadel. Thus, we cherished days of heavy snow, which drift shut our lane and cut us off physically from a world whose most generous attentions stir in us apprehensions beyond our power to stop, though we discipline them in meeting with others. So, I suppose, a native who has once been mangled and slavered over by a python, but somehow survived, cannot see the slightest stir of grass in his direction without an inward panic which only the passage of healing years can allay, however much he learns to check it. I do not expect anyone who has not known this peculiar experience to understand such feeling. Besides, the causes of apprehension are by no means all due to irreparable shock of oversensitive nerves. I cannot quite imagine how the world imagines our life. A friend once said to me: "You know, to the world you are a mysterious man." I was astonished, naïvely, no doubt. In that sense, I seem to myself about as mysterious as a cabbage.

This was the household silence. It merely happened to coincide with and prolong a deeper silence, as the stuck bass pedal of an old piano prolongs an unwanted resonance without art or reason. I can best touch on the nature of that other silence (I do not mean to do more here) through someone else's experience.

Friends came to us, of course. Looking back, I am surprised at how many came—kind friends, usually breaking journeys from New York, New England, the West to Washington to make the unhandy side trip here; or, like Vice-President Richard M. Nixon and Mrs. Nixon, taking time from great activities out of some loving care for us. The least we could do, in return, was to dissemble our condition. It implies no ingratitude to the others if I say that there was one for whom it was not necessary to dissemble anything.

Bishop Cuthbert O'Gara visited us first in the autumn of 1954, on a day when a heavy rain was taking down the eaves. The first time he came for fifteen minutes (we had never met) and remained for four hours because, as he wrote me afterwards, "it was like meeting a fellow missionary who

speaks English after a long stretch alone among the natives."
He came again in the cold spring of 1955.

Bishop O'Gara was the bishop of a province in the far West
of China, where, it was said by those who are almost always
wrong about the Communists but always confidently vocal,
the Communists would never come because the province was
so wild and bandit-ridden that even Generalissimo Chiang
Kai-shek had never ventured there in force. One day, the
Bishop was handed a note from the Sister who ran the hospital. It contained three words: "They are here." They might
stand for a legend of the age. After a short period of official
correctness while they consolidated their power, the Communists imprisoned Bishop O'Gara and brainwashed him for
about two years. At last, they carried him half across China,
and passed him through the barrier at Hong Kong because
they believed the Bishop, a man in his sixties, was dying, as
indeed he was at that time; and it suited their purpose to have
him die in other hands.

Each time Bishop O'Gara came to us, we sat together with
him in his far-off cell and went, day by day it seemed, over the
procedures whereby Communism seeks to break and master
the mind and spirit of its captives—methods reflected less in
his words than by the unconscious anguish on the old man's
face as he quietly recollected them. As his health improved,
Bishop O'Gara began to try to tell public groups what Communism had done to him and his life, the urgent danger that
he felt it posed to the lives of his listeners, and what he feared
it might presently do to them. After one such talk, an intelligent, authoritative woman, whom Bishop O'Gara took to be
an educator, came up to him. "Bishop," she said, "that just
isn't true." The ailing Bishop told me: "I said to my companion: 'Get me out of here. Get me out of here, get me out
into the air.' I thought I was simply going to faint." Bishop
O'Gara set the heel of his palm on his chin and pressed his
hand hard across his face to his forehead, in a gesture that

has become an unconscious habit. "And then," he said with a wry smile, "they expect us to remain sane."

It was unnecessary to dissemble anything for Bishop O'Gara. It was, in fact, impossible. For, at that point, we had moved into that other cell whose walls are not stinking stones but that encasing silence which I had mentioned earlier. That silence results not from simple disbelief or scepticism. It is a rejection, by the enlightened mind of the West in the name of a superior intelligence and reason, of the truth which some have struggled back to warn them of while there still is time, usually, in one way or another, from the margin of life. That rejection is life- and soul-destroying. But it does not kill simply. It slowly suffocates those against whom it is directed as if they were buried alive. It is invisible and intangible. Nobody really does anything. All that is necessary to maintain that silence is a glance, a tone of voice, the lilt of an impermeable, dismissing complacency, or someone to say from time to time: "No one can believe a former Communist." That seals the silence more solidly than cement sets against any wayward impulse to break it. And much else feeds on it too—little things which we know are exaggerated in the context of that mood. The knowledge does not help at all because it is neither big nor little that matters. It is the sense of an enforced futility that kills the active mind.

One day your mother and I went to Cold Friday. We did not go there to see the blooming dogwood. We did not go a-Maying. We went to see whether a line of fence through the woods in back of Cold Friday was being properly run. Behind that simple practical reason lay a decision: I had decided to deed you Cold Friday outright—for you and your heirs and assigns, in the language of the deed, "to have and to hold forever." Forever is a long word common as ink in property law. But history does not know it. History is always the history of tragedy, whether nations are rising, always at the expense of other nations; whether a nation is falling and desperately improvising ways to break or mitigate its fall, or simply riding a final flood tide of prosperous complacency such as has floated most great states toward the collapse which always first begins inwardly.

It seemed to me that to you, now growing into history in one of its late ages, the utmost I could give was the ground beneath your feet. Neither you nor I can foresee what that history holds for you as an individual man. Nor, since one of wisdom's larger lessons is not to wish to know too much, could either of us wish to foresee it beyond the point where a limited foresight is necessary for an occasional practical decision. Whether or not you would ever be called to defend this land with your life, I wanted you to have the direct organic sense that part of the total land you would defend would be your own.

I had a further reason. The world beset me to the point where I was no longer sure that my strength would suffice me to outlast or overcome its entrapments. I wished to be free of the responsibility of that trusteeship which I held for you. It hampered me. I wished to be free to act alone, unencumbered by afterthoughts of you. Insofar as my life was a true witness, it demanded this absolute freedom of action against forces that absolutely outnumbered me. Nothing less would suffice, for the struggle required that I be undistracted by any other consideration. It required, too, that I have nothing of my own except a choice of how I must act, especially when the range of my resources for action was narrowed by failing strength. So I deeded you Cold Friday and all that that implies. Thereby, in a sense, I deliberately cut your life free of my life at the moment when you were setting out on yours. I made you your own man.

The fence I built for you was something else, and yet related. Experience has taught me belatedly that a farm begins with its fence. It keeps your own cattle out of your neighbor's fields and his out of yours. A fence is a definition and what it helps to define is that ownership of property which is the final guarantee of freedom. It cannot be breached without breaching freedom, and if it is ended, freedom is ended. Property is the ultimate guarantor of freedom. The benevolence of those who would deny this has nothing to do with the case. And earth is the ultimate property, of which every inch is, at need, a last ditch of freedom. In this sense, I worked for it and held it for you. In this sense, I give it to you and counsel you to hold it if you can.

This is what Mother and I were on Cold Friday for—a kind of pleasant and deliberate obsequies to which our reality had brought us. But on Cold Friday something also overtook us which I think I shall tell you for what it may be worth. For in a way, it marked the break up of the winter for us, including our personal winter.

As you know, a little source rises near the Creek Farm house and sends a shallow brook below the eastern slope of Cold Friday. It is a shallow ribbon of water, a few inches deep and a few inches wide—a "run" as we call them. In places this trickle has cut itself deep banks as it falls under rank shrubs and ferns to the Big Pipe Creek. In the past, it was one of your mother's supreme pleasures, and mine, to loiter together down banks of that run. For seven years we had not gone there. We did not mention it. The understanding was tacit. We did not go there because, as even the best of lives must sooner or later teach you, it is better not to revisit in distress those places where we have once been happy.

We did not say anything that day, either. But we found ourselves again wandering beside the run. We walked in silence. Once, when we came upon a young blackthorn that had grown during seven years to a shrub higher than our heads, your mother wept—suddenly and briefly. That was the only deeper comment either of us made. As a younger man, I might have thought: "The world shall pay for those tears." Now I know that the world has always been paying for them and always will. But we soon found where the bushes of the run were starred whitely by mats of bloodroot in flower. Elsewhere there were stretches of spring beauties. Along the Pipe Creek we found ourselves in beds of trout lilies in bloom. We had not known we had so many of them. As you know, trespassers sometimes vandalized our farther buildings and woods—smashing windows or shooting holes in metal roofs, or, as on one occasion, girdling forty young trees in a night so that they would die. We have no such worries with our wild flowers. No one else knows or cares that they are there. They have no value known to mischief or malice. Their beauty places them below the vision of one who cares little for beauty so they cadge their security from his blindness.

In a sense, we too cadged the pleasure of that unexpected day. Both of us knew that it was a counterfeit pleasure, without duration or nourishment in our larger reality. But we dawdled in the sun where the Creek swept over its rapids, as those aboriginal clay-gatherers must sometimes have dawdled a few generations before us. Then we went home, and fell asleep, worn out by our foray, like children. I was going to say, more accurately, like the old.

But the effect lingered, as we had by the Creek. The earth is so life-giving, that it has only to be touched to stir something in the roots of life, as a few warm days in midwinter set the sap mounting prematurely in the stems of shrubs. We dreaded this stirring as a delusion that served no purpose, but whose untimely enjoyment would simply make winter harder when the cold came back.

Yet I felt more than this had happened, that, as we descended that little valley, there had been renewed in us a desire, a sense of the necessity which had been almost lost, to keep on going to the end. It was as if we had stopped to shift more firmly on our shoulders a load that had almost worked loose and which we were resigned to let fall—not by will or the lack of will but because there seemed no point at all in continuing to wobble under anything so cumbrous and so irrelevant to anything we most deeply are.

That is how the winter went, son. Or, I think I had better say: That is where we came out of one of the hollows—there below Cold Friday.

The
Direct Glance

I speak with a certain urgency both because I believe that history is closing in on this people with a speed which, in general they do not realize or prefer not to realize, and because I have a sense that time is closing in on me so that, at this point, I do not know whether or not I shall be given time to complete what I seek to say. I feel, too, a sense of my own inadequacy in many ways. I cannot claim to speak with the authority of many whose learning is greater, whose competency is certified by years of devout effort in special acreages of the mind. I may not claim for the larger meanings of what I shall say: This is truth. I say only: This is my vision of truth; to be checked and rechecked (as I myself continually check and recheck it) against the data of experience. Every book, like every life, is issued ultimately, not to those among whom it appears and lives, but to the judgment of time, which is the sternest umpire. What serious man could wish for his life or his book a judgment less final?

I write as a man who made his way back from a special

experience of our time—the experience of Communism. I believe the experience to be the central one, for whichever side prevails the outcome will be shaped decisively by what Communism is and meant to be, and by the conditions that made it possible and made possible the great conflict. *Man's Fate* (or *La Condition Humaine*, to use its French title, which fixes its meaning more clearly) seems to me one of the few books* which have placed a surgical finger upon the problem of man in this century—the problem of the terms on which man can wrest some semblance of his human dignity (some would say: save his soul) in a mechanizing world, which is, by force of the same necessity, a revolutionary world. After he had read *Witness*, André Malraux, the author of *Man's Fate*, wrote me: "You are one of those who did not return from Hell with empty hands." I did not answer him. How is one man to say to another: "Great healing spirit"? For it is not sympathy that the mind craves, but understanding of its purposes. I do not know, it is not even for me to say, what value may be set on those scraps and tatters of experience that I brought back with me. They, too, are issued for time to judge. I do not know how they may serve, or whether they have any power to prevail against the many voices in the West today that say, "These are scraps and tatters," and deny them any further meaning.

In *Witness* I sought to make two points which seemed to me more important than the narrative of unhappy events which, time has compelled me to conclude, chiefly interested most readers. The first point had to do with the nature of Communism and the struggle against it. The crux of this matter is the question whether God exists. If God exists, a

---

* Some others: Arthur Koestler's *Darkness at Noon* and *The Invisible Writing;* Czeslaw Milosz's *The Captive Mind;* the Abbé Henri de Lubac's *Drama of Atheist Humanism;* Manes Sperber's *The Burned Bramble*, whose French title, *Et le Buisson Devient Cendre (And the Burning Bush Sank to Ash)*, again seems to me more meaningful than the English rendering.

man cannot be a Communist, which begins with the rejection of God. But if God does not exist, it follows that Communism, or some suitable variant of it, is right.

More follows. A man is obligated, if he seeks to give any effect to his brief life, to tear away all mystery that darkens or distorts, to snap all ties that bind him in the name of an untruth, to push back all limiting frontiers to the end that man's intelligence may be free to realize to the fullest of its untrammeled powers a better life in a better world. I did not spell this out in *Witness*. "Be sure that nothing can be told to any who divined it not before." It is pointless and, indeed, impossible to press anything upon those who are unprepared for it. I set up the proposition and left it to those who could to draw the inference. Precisely, the enlightened community of the West, as could be expected, drew them first. That proposition was, in my opinion, the chief cause of the lightnings that darted at *Witness* and still play about it. They darted not only from the political Left. In time, elements of the Right began to sense that a question had been posed to them. That proposition questioned the whole materialism of the West, and the West is heavily materialist. It is, in fact, this materialism that Communism constantly appeals to and manipulates, not in terms of any easily defined political lines of Left or Right but in terms of a common investment in a materialist view of life, which an important section of the West shares with Communism, and which Communism has simply carried to its utmost logical conclusion in thought and action. This common interest in a common materialism—which nevertheless differs in the West and in Communism in form, degree, qualifications, and reservations—is the grain of truth and sincerity in the West's resentment against Communist "witch hunts." For it feels an affinity and a respect for a materialism which it finds liberating to the mind, while it feels itself unfairly threatened or hurt because reprisals against Communism inevitably touch it as a sympathetic

form, though it does not share Communism's political aims.
This is a distinction which the non-Communist materialism
of the West does not trust the anti-Communists to grasp or
respect—the more so since, in action, the line is frequently
blurred, so that even when the materialism of the West is
assertively anti-Communist it often serves Communist ends.

From this proposition—that the heart problem of Communism is the problem of atheism—followed the second
proposition which I set up in *Witness*, also without developing
its conclusions. This proposition implied that the struggle
of the West with Communism included its own solution. That
is to say, in the course of its struggle with Communism, the
West would develop or recover those resources (in the main,
spiritual and moral) which it held to constitute its superiority
to Communism, or in the struggle it would go under. Going
under might, I suppose, take one of two forms. The West
might simply lose the war in political or physical terms. But
I also allowed for the fact that the West might win the war
in such terms and still lose it, if the taxing necessities
of the conflict brought the West to resemble what it was
struggling against, *i.e.*, Communism. A turn in this direction
has been perfectly visible in the West for several decades.

The margin of success in the struggle, it seemed to me, lay
less in an equality of technology and weapons (so long as
weapons paced themselves approximately) than in certain
factors within Communism which are little appreciated in the
West. These factors were also spiritual and moral even
though they expressed indirectly contrary terms, even though
Communism expressly denied man's spirit and morality as the
West uses the words. These resources I believed to be peculiarly inherent in the Russian Communist Party.

For scale, complexity, and depth, the struggle between
Communism and the West is a conflict without any precedent

of human record. Other conflicts have unsettled continents. The rise and sweep of the Mongol hordes comes at once to mind and is often cited as a parallel. This was a great surface fire, fed by the dry rot of all the lands it swept, having no plan and purpose beyond plunder and the raw play of ferocious energies, dying out as those purposeless energies died out, and leaving upon history little more than the literal ashes of its passage and a haunting memory of heaps of human bones. It is most like a catastrophe in nature, hurricane or flood; and has, in fact, no parallel at all. Communism first of all asserts a purpose and a plan. Both feed a will to victory that operates on as many multitudinous levels as life is capable of. There is no human creature living in any region so remote that he is not, in some way, affected by that force which each one, sooner or later, faces in what Sir Thomas Browne called "the areopagy and dark tribunal of our hearts." For the distinctive feature of Communism is not that it threatens all continents as no other force has ever done or even that it seeks a radical readjustment of all societies. Its distinctive feature is that it seeks a molecular rearrangement of the human mind. It promotes not only a new world. It promotes a new kind of man. The physical revolutions which it once incited and now imposes, and which largely distract our attention, are secondary to this internal revolution which challenges each man in his mind and spirit. Thus, the phenomenon of Communism is closest in the experience of the West to the rise of Christianity and its gradual transformation of the mind of the ancient world. Hence our puzzlement before the discrepancy between the ends of Communism and its visible personnel, which more or less reflects the bafflement of Pliny in his well-known letter to Trajan about the early Christians. Hence our large-handed contempt for Communists wherever they do not yet hold political power, which almost echoes Lucian's remarks about the Christians in the second century A.D.: "They waste their days, running from Romanism to ism, and imagine that they are achieving great things in treating their friends to children's fairy tales. In the squares, where they all shout the same thing in the same way, they are eaten up with envy. From their dirt, their lousiness, their mendacity, they argue with conviction that they are called to redeem the world."

For the war of Communism with the rest of mankind is first of all a war of ideas. In that war, Communism rejects few means of any kind, or none (its system of ideas justifies this practice). But its first assault is always upon the minds of men; and it is from the conversion of minds that it advances to the conquest of mass bodies and their living space. Each advance enables Communism to expedite conversion by political control since, for those whom it controls, Communism has become the one reality. The West (whatever value the captive may give that word) becomes at most a hope, but a hope that has been defeated (that is why the captives are captive); and it is a hope continuously deferred. Hope deferred not only maketh the heart sick; it stirreth profound suspicions that there is something radically wrong with it. In this case, it stirs a suspicion that exactly to the degree that Communism is felt to be evil and monstrous in its effects, there must be something organically wrong with the West that is unequal to prevailing against a power so conspicuously condign.

This failure to grasp that the basic struggle with Communism is a struggle of ideas has led, in the West, to the failure to grasp the signal fact of the conflict. That fact is that Communism, which in all material ways has been for decades weak to a degree almost unimaginable to the average American, has rallied strength and made its staggering advances precisely at the expense of that West which is in all material ways overwhelmingly superior. With this goes the boundless complacency of the West in supposing that the struggle will be decided in its favor by material means. I cannot remember a time when there was not a lively conviction in the West that the Communist state was about to fall by reason of its own

malevolence and inadequacy. This stems from the easily observable fact that Communism is a philosophy of thorough-
going materialism, brutal in its practical manifestations,
because it denies the sanctity of the individual in terms of the
self-interest of the community, which, in practice, is the arbi-
trary will of the shifting consortia that run the state. Communism is a philosophy of brute materialism. But if we ask:
"What is the philosophy of the West?" is there not a certain
embarrassment? What *is* the philosophy of the West? In a
war for men's minds, what is it that we are offering whose inherent force is so compulsive that it instantly seizes on the
imagination of men and incites them to choose it in preference
to Communism? In the name of what do we expect them to
rise and overthrow Communism which can be done only by an
effort of incalculable suffering—and not the suffering of faceless millions (as we so easily think of such things), but the
suffering of this father or that mother who love their children
whose lives, rather than their own, are the first sacrifice in so
one-sided a conflict? Is it Christianity? There are millions of
Christians in the Communist Empire whose Western populations are overwhelmingly Christian. Some 40 million must be
practicing Catholics. I remember no appeals to the Christians
in the name of their common faith with the West. Individual
freedom is often mentioned. It is well, perhaps, to remember
that freedom, in our understanding of the term, has been re-
stricted largely to the United States and the fringe of Western
Europe. In the rest of the world it has no accepted currency,
and over large areas of Europe the Second World War and
the revolutions that preceded it utterly destroyed the conditions of freedom and raised strong questions in many minds
whether or not freedom is practicable in the conditions of our
times. "*Der Fahneneid*," said General Groner to the Kaiser
in 1918, suggesting that his swift abdication would be well-
viewed, "*ist jetzt nur eine Idee*" (The oath on the colors is
now only an idea).

Moreover, these people are not children. They have the

acute realism of those who live daily under impending tank treads. The satellite populations can look westward and see that individual freedom is constantly being whittled down in the West in the interest of centralizing government, and they are perfectly competent to infer that this is the result of the play of the same basic forces and factors that have destroyed their own freedom.

We tend to forget—life has been, in general, so good to us, we are so appalled by life under Communism—that thousands of acute intelligences in the East are also peering back at us. We tend to forget what spectacle we present to those eyes which weigh us with the close harshness of men facing awful alternatives. It is not necessary to particularize that spectacle here. But if we think about it a moment, think about it as those others may see it, adding in their sense that our failure fixed their fate on them, is it strange if they do not find the spectacle that the West presents overly reassuring?

When, in History, there appear in swarms such commanding and ferocious types as the Communist, and his bastard brother, the Fascist, our habit of viewing them first of all with aversion, a habit of mind very widespread, especially in the United States, is no longer helpful. The moral judgment may be justified. But is largely pointless. It condemns us to see them continually in terms of effect instead of cause. We limit ourselves to seeing the effects that the Communist, for example, creates. We keep pretty carefully away from the causes that create the Communist. This resolute flight from causes, and resolute dwelling only in effects leads us into the plight of a man in a maze or a squirrel in a revolving cage. We go round and round; we never come out anywhere. It leads, in thought, to a defeating confusion. In practice, it leads to some pretty extravagant hypocrisy. The spectacle of the West encouraging cultural exchanges with a Communism, which in the next breath it condemns as a barbaric and criminal force, is, to say the least of it, puzzling. It is sometimes argued that with respect to Communism, the West is merely stupid. But stupidity isn't good enough.

Surely it is not too sweeping to say that there is nothing secret about Communism. For decades, its motives, purposes, and specific strategies have been explicitly stated by Communists themselves, and freely disseminated in the West. Even its guiltiest secrets are known in wearisome detail. Seldom in history can the actions of any cause have been subjected to so minute a picking-over in the very course of their occurence. It makes not the slightest practical difference. On one hand, the disclosures lead to a hue of moral outrage. On the other hand, the West continues to deal with the Communist center as if this were not true. Thus, the West itself engages with respect to Communism in a kind of double-think which it supposes to be one of Communism's distinctive faculties. This singular behavior is paced by another even more singular. This is the cherishing of a notion, constantly blighted, ever ready to flower anew, that Communism and Communists are about to undergo a change of mind (or "heart") so that henceforth they will no longer act like Communists; they will be like us.

Yet we have seen this manifestation occur on a mass scale more than once. When it does, we enter the realm of illusion. There is a clinical name for it, but it is not stupidity. Stupidity cannot explain; such stupidity has to be explained itself. This persistent flight into fantasy and resistance to reality, accompanied by an emotional play like the boiling of an overheated engine, suggest much more the energy, now dogged, now frantic, with which certain patients sometimes resist knowing the facts of their condition and its causes because they find the facts too painful to bear. A suspicion stirs that we resist knowing about Communism because we do not wish to know about ourselves; that, in fact, we need scarcely fear Communism if we did not secretly fear ourselves.

This suspicion is fortified by an arresting fact, one which

requires no special knowledge to see (it is inescapable), and one, incidentally, that is not often referred to. That fact is that the Communist Empire, born in chaos, backward and weak beyond the imagination of the average man of the West in all the resources that make a modern industrial state powerful—this desperately weak state has, nevertheless, in the course of four decades, rallied its strength, organized a modern industry almost from scratch, and possessed itself of a third of the earth's land surface and hundreds of millions of new population precisely at the expense of the West which, in all material ways, is enormously superior to it and whose survival it now challenges. Moreover, the fall-out of its influence affects millions beyond its official frontiers.

There is a further fact. Communism has achieved this fear at the expense of a West which is not only vastly superior in material, but a West which believes itself to be vastly superior in moral and spiritual resources. It is popular to dismiss Communism as a grubby materialist philosophy imposed by force on slaves whom we expect, sometimes indifferently, sometimes hopefully (we are in one of our hopeful phases) to revolt and overthrow it. But what is the philosophy of the West? In the name of what are we inviting the slaves of the East to revolt? We speak of freedom. Every day that the Communist Empire endures, the word becomes more meaningless for millions.

It is the business of the Communist theoretician, with his eye on the whole sweep of history, to try to assess the relationship of forces in the world at every given moment, to calculate their rate of drift and general direction as a guide to action—in order to take advantage of the constantly changing relationships of force to promote a revolution which the Communist holds to be beneficent and, in some degree, fated.

This process in history, and this view of it, Communists call dialectical materialism (or, in that Communist shorthand that we commonly call jargon, Diamat). It is dialectic because it deals with quantities of force in motion, sometimes violent, sometimes gradual. It is called materialism because the Communist mind, like the scientific mind, rejects any supernatural factor in his observation of experience. In short, God is rigorously excluded from the equations of changing force in which the Communist mind tirelessly seeks to grasp, to express, and to act on history at any and every moment.

To try to explain Communism and the Communist while ignoring dialectical materialism is like trying to explain a man's actions while leaving out the chief clue to his mind and his motives and general viewpoint. Dialectical materialism is the central fact of Communism. Every Communist is a dialectical materialist. Ultimately, he cannot be understood in any other terms. This does not mean that all Communists are consistent or successful dialecticians. There are millions of Communists in the world and they show the same gradations of intelligence and character as millions of anybody else. There are millions of Christians, too, of whom only a comparative handful are theologians (Communists say: theoreticians). The mass of Christians is held together by a faith in what suffices to explain to them the meaning of their lives and history, although even highly intelligent communicants may be quite vague about the doctrines of their faith, or even specific articles of it. This is made possible because the center of efficacy of their faith is the Cross, using that symbol in its most inclusive sense. The Cross makes them one in faith even though at thinner fringes of Christendom the efficacy of the Cross is questioned or tends to fade. In much the same way, dialectical materialism is the effective force of Communism, and even when understanding is weak or lacking, it operates as a faith which explains satisfactorily to millions of Communists the meaning of life and history—reality, as Communists say. By this they always mean reality in a state of flux, usually violent. Dialectical materialism is the crux of Communism, and not to understand this means never truly to understand the Communist. It is one reason why the West still does not understand the Communist despite the heaps of other highly accurate data about him. Such data remain extraneous, almost irrelevant, because they miss, or by-pass, the central fact which makes the Communist a Communist.

This is the fact which absolutely sunders the mind of the Communist from the traditional mind of the West—which makes him in the mass a new breed in history. For our breeds, in this sense, are defined by the view we hold, unconsciously or not, of the world and its meaning, and the meaning of our lives in it. Obviously, a breed of men who hold that everything is in violent flux and change, moving by laws and in a pattern inherent in matter, and having nothing to do with God—obviously, that breed of men is different in kind from the rest of mankind. It is closest, in our time, to the viewpoint of the scientist for whom a simple, solid chair represents a form of energy whose particles, seemingly solid and commonplace, are in fact in violent motion. This, incidentally, rather than the "progressive" elements in Communism which are usually brought forward in such cases, is the instant point of appeal which Communism so often has for the scientists of the West. They feel in Communism the force of a faith based on a material reality which more or less matches their own vision of reality. It is an abstruse view, and the scientists who hold it are lonely men, since the masses of the West cannot possibly understand or sympathize with what the scientists are talking about. The intelligent Communist knows exactly what they are talking about though he may know little or nothing about abstruse physics. Similarly, the scientist may know little or nothing about the niceties of dialectical materialism. Yet each senses that the other's basic view of reality is much the same. The affinity is strong.

In the years when Communism was advancing successfully against the West there were those who believed that its disruptive power was its power to manipulate a Fifth Column composed of non-Soviet Communists, sympathizers, fellow travellers, dupes, opportunist politicians, hitchhiking with Communism as they would in any other vehicle that seemed to be going part of their way—in short, the kind of debris and dust that almost anything with sufficient gravitational pull attracts and keeps whirling around it. I held that such elements, while dangerous, were not Communism's chief power in the West. I held that power to be something else—the power of Communism to manipulate responsive sections of the West to check, counteract, paralyze, or confuse the rest. Those responsive sections of the West were not Communist, and never had been. Most of the minds that composed them thought of themselves as sincerely anti-Communist. Communism manipulated them, not in terms of Communism, but in terms of the shared historical crisis—peace and social justice being two of the most workable terms. They were free to denounce Communism and Communists (and also anti-Communists) after whatever flourishes their intellectual innocence or arrogance might choose. Communism asked no more. It cared nothing, at this point, about motives. It cared about results.

Unlike Communism, the West held no unified solution for the crisis. In face of the crisis, part of the West reacted with inertia—inertia, in the simple terms of the physics primer, that is, the tendency of a body to remain at rest or in a straight line of motion. But the responsive section offered a solution for the crisis. This solution, whatever differences it assumed from place to place and time to time, whatever disguises political expediency or preference draped or phrased it in, was always the same solution. It was the socialist solution. Derived, as doctrine, from the same source—the historical insights of Karl Marx—the socialist solution differed from the Communist solution chiefly in political methods. One difference consisted in the slower rate of speed at which socialism proposed to apply its solution. Another difference concerned the kind and degree of coercion that socialism would apply to impose its solution. In practice, no socialist government had yet pushed its solution to the point where full coercion must come into play. Therefore, this difference had not yet stood the test of reality. Otherwise, between the end solution that socialism and Communism both hold in view for mankind—the matured planned economy of the future—the difference was so slight that it would be difficult to slip a razor blade between them.

It was no innate charm of socialism that made millions in the West espouse it, just as it was no innate charm of Communism that recruited its millions. It was the force of the historical crisis that made masses of men entertain the socialist solution, which, in fact, sundered the West. It divided the West as a whole against itself. And it divided against itself every nation that might still qualify, in a diminished world, to the rank of great power. In fact, it split almost every great nation into almost equal halves, as major sections more and more tended to show. Hence the intensity of feeling, the swollen pain as around any unhealing fracture.

The divisions in the West passed beyond matters of opinion. The arguments had all been made; the returns were in. The division of the West was organic; it turned upon different breeds of men. The sundering point was a choice between political liberty and economic security. One breed of man held freedom to be the greatest good to the point where regimentation seemed to him the touch of spiritual death, so that he would prefer to die rather than live under the socialist state. The other breed of man held social security, and hence regimentation, to be a simple necessity if he were to live at all in a modern world. The difference had nothing to do with logic of argument. The difference had to do with breeds of men. One or the other principle would determine the future of the West. One would be paramount—one or the other; both could not be. It was increasingly clear that those who held the latter view were in the majority. But when masses of men are so evenly and fiercely divided, the readjustment of reality can scarcely occur without an earthquake, even if the revolution takes a form no more violent than mass balloting. . . .

I received a letter from a close friend of many years standing who is, as I once wrote of him to Rebecca West, "a Conservative by cell-structure." Though he talks about the matter only among intimates, he is an intensely religious man. This religion, too, forms a family climate. He and his family lived actively within their church, decades before church-going became a renewed fashion among us. My friend, though highly literate, is simply devout. In my experience, this combination of high intelligence and devotion is—though the fact may be somewhat dismaying to face—rather unusual.

It was this man who wrote me as follows. "The rector of our church took a reading of the so-called rebirth of religion in the U.S., which he thought had started about 1950 . . . 'The Epiphany has fizzled,' was the way he phrased it. This is sad, but the 'rebirth' was a phoney to begin with." My friend then mentions, as a peculiar token of the failure, the name of a celebrated divine, the author of immensely popular books of a kind of fatuous Couéism, which he turns out in such quantity that he may almost be said to farrow rather than to write them.

I found this a lapidary line: "The Epiphany has fizzled." Yet, when the amusing novelty has worn off, it is seen to express chiefly a disconsolate exasperation. It is a kind of continental sadness, like the wail of a locomotive whistle, rushing off (where?) in the night—haunting, yet not true music, a very American sound, just as the locomotive whistle is (or was) perhaps the most American of sounds. But for any depth of meaning, "The Epiphany has fizzled" isn't good enough.

A decade or so ago the eminent French Catholic theologian, Father Henri de Lubac, published a book called *The Drama of Atheist Humanism,* a study of rare understanding of certain of the great questioners or lay-sages of our age—Kierkegaard, Feuerbach, Marx, Nietzsche, Dostoevsky.

Father de Lubac quotes a letter of Jacques Rivière to the poet Paul Claudel, written in 1907 (when incidentally my generation was about seven years old; and such dates are meaningful for those of us who have survived so long into this frightful age). "I see," Rivière wrote, "that Christianity is dying . . . We do not know why, above our towns, there still rise those spires which are no longer the prayer of any one of us. We do not know the meaning of those great buildings (*i.e.,* religious institutions—Tr.) which today are surrounded by railroad stations and hospitals, and from which the people themselves have chased the monks. And on the graves, we do not know what is made manifest by those stucco crosses, frosted over with an execrable art."

"And, no doubt," says Father de Lubac, "Claudel's reply to that cry of anguish was a good one: 'Truth is not concerned with how many it persuades.' "

Then Father de Lubac goes on to cite "an almost daily experience" which shows that "certain of the harshest reproaches made against us come both from our worst adversaries and from men of good will. The tone, the intention, the inspiration are profoundly different. But the judgments come to much the same thing. An astonishing and significant convergence." There is more. Father de Lubac goes on to another experience, one that bears directly on the so-called rebirth of religion among us and thrusts close to the heart of an instant problem. It is the plight of those seekers who, in deepest sincerity, approach the churches in a need and craving, often desperate, for truth and a haven. They approach, but then they hesitate and stand still. In the end they go no farther.

There follows an eloquent passage. "Among those who thus disappoint us," says Father de Lubac, "some of the clearest-sighted and most spiritual find themselves torn by conflicting feelings. We see them ravished [*seduits*] by the Gospel whose teachings seem to them still full of force and novelty; drawn to the Church in which they sense a more than human reality and the sole institution capable of bringing, together with a remedy for our ills, the solution to the problem of our destiny. But, on the threshold, see what stops them: the spectacle that we make, we, the Christians of today, the Church that we are, that spectacle repels them . . . It is not that they condemn us violently. It is, rather, that they cannot take us seriously."

This needs no commenting on by me. But I submit that it needs long and careful reflecting on, and that this is inescapable wherever the question of the rebirth of religion, which is raised in general statistically, must be weighed qualitatively. For here is raised a question which lies at the heart of our conflict with Communism. The question is: What is the West's answer to Communism? It is pretty clear, I think, that the more or less anonymous thousands who yearly flee Communism (about whom and whose later fate we rather prefer not to think unless we are compelled to) are fleeing a misery, rather than embracing an alternative idea. Though it works out of necessity in rather different ways, much the same is true of many former Communists whose defections or later testimony makes a week's news. It is the wretchedness of life for them under Communism which impels them; it is Communism's failure in their terms that drives them to the West. This is clearly not the same thing as an answer to Communism. The lack of such an answer defeats our propaganda at the core—and the word "propaganda" used in this sense, is itself suggestive. By an answer I mean a rallying idea, capable of being grasped by, and so overmastering, millions of men of the most diverse kinds because its single force persuades that it brings "together with a remedy for their ills, the solution to the problem of their destiny." In the West, taken as a whole, this idea does not exist. We know this whenever the problem arises, as it does daily, to the people of Asia and

Africa, for example—a sense-making notion of what the West stands for, so that they quickly grasp it, and it stirs them to a willingness to die for it, rather than live for any other. Does such an idea exist? Let us not deceive ourselves, but answer truthfully: "It does not exist." "But what about Freedom?" you say. You are saying it to millions who never have been free in your sense, and grasp chiefly that they are free to starve. They will reach quicker for an idea that promises them an end to hunger, even if they suspect that the promise is over-blown (for even the most primitive starvelings are, in general, not fools; they are merely not sophisticated in your terms; but they catch on quickly).

So long as such a central rallying idea does not exist, we in the West are likely to go on defending frontiers, even if we are no longer losing provinces. And that regardless of how elaborately the frontiers are manned and weaponed. Maginot Lines are butts to ideas.

On the eve of our time, Stefan Trofimovitch saw our problem clearly enough, even though, as sometimes happens, it took him a pointless lifetime to reach the insight and his last strength to frame it: "The one essential condition of human existence is that man should always be able to bow down before something infinitely great. If men are deprived of the infinitely great, they will not go on living and will die of despair." It is for that we crave reality, for the infinitely great may not be on any less terms. It remains otherwise lies and illusion. It is for that we crave a little height, to reach some notion of the meaning of our reality, and so as not to die of despair. So that we can rise above the paralyzing mood of our time, which we feel as a sense that none of us can really do anything; that things are merely going to happen to us.

If the voice says: "But that is what men have always craved," we will answer: "Yes, always craved." But the problem presents itself in different terms to different generations. Yet the root problem remains always the same. It is: On what terms consistent with their reality men can have God, or whether they must seem for a time even not to have Him. When, also on the eve of our time, another voice cried: "God is dead," the unthinkingly shallow heard in that cry the wildest blasphemy, and the unthinkingly intelligent heard it as a stupid promise of emancipation. But Nietzsche was only reading aloud the transcript of his time. That time comes whenever men remake God so much in their own image that He no longer corresponds to reality. For, of course, God never dies. The generations simply seek how they can have Him in terms of their reality. You cannot offer to the half-starved millions of Asia God as a sole solution to their plight, with the best of them turning away with pity for your stupidity if not with contempt for your dishonesty. But something else is also true: You cannot replace God with Point Four. If you fed the starving millions four square meals a day and studded their primitive lands with automated factories, men would still die of despair.

"I want to know why," one of the most native of our voices [Sherwood Anderson] asked in a line that rises out of all else he did and said because it sums up all the rest. I want to know why. It is for this we seek a little height, and because of this we do not feel it too high a price to pay if we cannot reach it crawling through a lifetime on our hands and knees, as a wounded man sometimes crawls from a battlefield, if only so as not to die as one more corpse among so many corpses. Happy is he who finds any height, however lowly.

That craving for the infinitely great starts with the simplest necessity. It is the necessity to know reality in order, by acting on it directly, to find the measure of men's meaning and stature in that single chance of some seven decades that is allotted them to find it out in. Since, by reason of the irrevocable briefness of that span, life is inherently tragic, the effort to

wrest meaning from reality is tragic, too, and means always
the necessity to rise above reality at any cost. But it is not
the commonplace of tragedy, it is anything that blocks their
freedom to enact it meaningfully that kills men with despair.
And if the old paths no longer lead to a reality that enables
men to act with meaning, if the paths no longer seem to lead
anywhere—have become a footworn, trackless maze, or, like
Russian roads, end after a few miles of ambitious pavement,
leading nowhere but into bottomless mud and swallowing
distance—men will break new paths, though they must break
their hearts to do it. They will burst out somewhere, even if
such bursting-out takes the form of aberration. For to act in
aberration is at least more like living than to die of futility,
or even to live in that complacency which is futility's idiot
twin. We all know those grand aberrations of our time. We
have plenty of names for them, political and invective. Communism is one of them. But all the aberrations have one
common cause, and point, in the end, in one direction.

   Suffering is at the heart of every living faith. That is why
man can scarcely call himself a Christian for whom the Crucifixion is not a daily suffering. For it is by the hope that surmounts suffering that true tragedy surmounts pain and has
always had the power to sweep men out of the common ugliness of ordeal to that exaltation in which the spirit rises superior to the agony which alone matures it by the act of
transcending it. This is what we loosely call greatness. And
it is the genius of Christianity to recognize that this capacity
for greatness inheres in every man in the nature of his immortal soul, though not every man is called upon to demon-
strate it. For it is by the soul that, at the price of suffering,
we can break, if we choose, the shackles that an impersonal
and rigid Fate otherwise locks upon us. It was the genius of
Christianity to whisper to the lowliest man that by the action

of his own soul he could burst the iron bonds of Fate with which merely being alive seemed to encase him. Only, it could never be done except at a price, which was suffering. It was because Christianity gave meaning to a suffering endured in all ages, and otherwise senseless, that it swept the minds of men. It still holds them, though the meaning has been blurred as Christianity, in common with the voices of a new age, seeks new escapes from the problem of suffering. But the problem remains and the new escapes circle back to the old one. For in suffering, man motivated by hope and faith affirms that dignity which is lit by charity and truth. This is the meaning of the eternal phrases: lest one grain perish, and unless a man die, he shall not live—phrases as hackneyed as history and as fresh as the moment in which they rose upon the astonishments of the saints.

Nothing is more characteristic of this age than its obsession with an avoidance of suffering. Nothing dooms it more certainly to that condition which is not childlike but an infantilism which is an incapacity for growth that implies an end. The mind which has rejected the soul, and marched alone, has brought the age to the brink of disaster. Let us say it flatly: What the age needs is less minds than martyrs— less knowledge (knowledge was never so cheap) but that wisdom which begins with the necessity to die, if necessary, for one's faith and thereby liberates that hope which is the virtue of the spirit.

But let us not suppose, like children, that suffering must not take its toll. Suffering implies growth and all growth is an hourly and daily dying. Age is its price as maturity is its crown. Both enjoin their blessings, among which is, supremely, a liberation from the interminable compromise in which all life is lived. Thus, at the end, or with the end in sight, truth alone becomes the compelling need and the quest for truth the only worthwhile occupation, while those engaged in it achieve that good humor of the spirit which most of those achieve who are engaged in any engrossing labor. For they know that constancy rather than energy is the cost of accomplishment in an art so difficult and so long to learn, while tolerance becomes a function of that infinity that opens up to them so near at hand. Truth too is a suffering and may not be had for less. The quest for it is a labor, life's only permanently valid one, and like any labor humbling because only the laborer knows how many mistakes have to be undone or unlearned to make anything, or supposes that he can ever really learn the mystery of his craft.

But I have reached an age, in one sense or another, and a condition where I have no other real interest. The first men who thought at all knew that the sadness of life is inseparable from its beauty—so that wisdom always implies the reaching of a point where a man can smile at both, while minimizing neither. But leave-taking is also the great liberator. The grown man who looks around for the last time has no room in his mind, and no time, for more than reality. And he wants it plain. He has no longer any reason to share it as men do to make it endurable in life, and no reason to care how others share it. This is the ultimate freedom; and what man can count that suffering a cost which has led him to the direct glance that measures what it leaves without fear and without regret?

Morningside

One view from Cold Friday was of a young man entering college in the year 1920.—D. N-T.

It was in the fall of 1920 that I made my way along 116th Street to my first class. Belatedly and reluctantly, I was doing what was expected of every bright youth of my age and class: at last I was going to college. It would have been much more realistic to say that I was stepping across what my geology instructor would soon teach me to call a line of fault—the line along which the seeming-solid surface of the earth was secretly cracked and under pressures and stresses beyond our sight or knowledge would one day, in a twinkling, tear apart, upheave or sink, engulfing cities whole in that readjustment of physical reality that we call an earthquake. Only this line of fault did not run invisibly under our feet. It flawed the whole structure of civilization. Two years before, the first four-year shock had ended after levelling Europe to a ruin that could not be measured merely by its physical wreckage. For the ruin took place in men's souls before it was made visible in the rubble of cities.

Columbia University, like the whole United States, stood far from the epicenter of that earthquake. But because it was by its nature and purpose a focus, a high concentration of the forces of that civilization that was in disaster, every vibration of the catastrophe reached and shook it, though the nature of the shock was not understood, though minds were rigidified in an effort not to understand it. Yet every one of those highly sensitive and informed minds to which I was soon to be exposed swung with each shock like the indicator of a seismograph, and often with no more understanding of what they reacted to.

They reacted, know it or not, to the crisis of history in the twentieth century, of which by their vocation of teaching they were inescapably a part. They reacted the more wildly sometimes the less they understood what they were reacting to. This was the zone of earthquake that I first stepped into on 116th Street. It was only chance that for me that zone was called Columbia College. It might just as well have been called Harvard (see John Reed) or Princeton (see Scott Fitzgerald) or any other top university in the country. Each, in its own way, with characteristic variations of time and tone, would register the same catastrophe, just as individual students would react to exposure to that shock according to differences of character and temperament and to differences in the stage and awareness of the earthquake when they first felt it sway them. The great mass would not, of course, react at all. This is always true. The sensitive react first.

In the crisis of the twentieth century neither Harvard nor Columbia could be other than what is was—a citadel of the mind swaying in the vertigo of a civilization changing (without admitting it) the basis of its faith from a two thousand-year-old Christian culture to the new secular and scientific culture. That is to say, changing the nature of its organism. This change Nietzsche heralded and in part prescribed. To it he gave a useful term: the transvaluation of all values—which is the pedagogue's way of saying that the change was a change in the moral, religious, and intellectual organism of Western civilization. In that revolution (of which Communism, socialism, and related forms are only logical political developments), Western civilization slowly and only half-consciously, and by a process reaching much farther back in time than it is common to suppose, rejected its two thousand-year-old Christian faith, which placed God at the center of man's hope, in favor of a new faith, secular, exclusively rational and scientific, which set Man at the center of man's hope. I cannot remember ever hearing the word Communism or the name of Marx mentioned in a classroom. Lenin as a writer of political theory was then locked up in Russian or unread in German. No member of the Columbia faculty was remotely suspect as a Communist. The words Communism and Communist were almost never heard.

There was nothing to tell me the day I walked across the Columbia University campus as a freshman that the path was to lead me into Communism. No member of the Columbia faculty ever consciously guided me toward Communism. The problem of Communism and the colleges was different then from now because the stage of history was different. Otherwise, it was the same problem because it was another expression of the same crisis of history. Columbia did not teach me Communism. It taught me despair. I loved Columbia and still love it in the physical way with which most men ever after love the campus on which they passed formative years of their youth. In the last decades I have sometimes gone up, to move alone—a foiled circuitous wanderer among the hordes of later alien undergraduates—among its remembered walls and walks (now greatly changed). But as a citadel of the mind, in the second decade of the twentieth century, I found its experience

a trap. I thought that I had found the perfect description of
it when one day in Hartley Hall I read T. S. Eliot's *Waste-
land*, just published in the old *Dial* magazine:

> And upside down in air were towers
> Tolling reminiscent bells, that kept the hours
> And voices singing out of empty cisterns and
>   exhausted wells.

I was fit, rather rugged, more athletic than I had ever been
in my life. I spent days playing endless games of handball in
the college gym, swimming, or running around Grant's Tomb,
and working out at 145 pounds with the wrestling squad. For
the first time in my life, I was consciously religious. I had
begun (in my nineteenth year) to read the Bible and to try
to grasp its meaning. I sought this meaning chiefly in the
Old Testament, and then chiefly in the Books of Job, Isaiah,
and the Psalms and Ecclesiastes. Quite unconsciously, I was
finding the route past this terrifying Book which is the modern
mind's favorite detour—I was reading "the Bible as literature."
The New Testament I merely brushed. Even in the Pauline
Epistles I simply read isolated passages ("There is one glory
of the sun, and another glory of the moon and a third glory
of the stars") as I might gaze from time to time at the night
sky. I read these passages, and only these, less for their
meaning than because they were to human utterance what the
constellations were to space: mystic.

The figure of Christ troubled me, indefinably but certainly,
as it had troubled me in the Sunday School books of my early
boyhood. I left that demanding Presence hidden between the
skipped pages of the Gospels. There was no one to help me
comprehend then the meaning of the Crucifixion. Insofar as
I was a Christian at all at that time, it was in the sense of
the famous celebration of charity in 13 Corinthians: "Though
I speak with the tongues of men and of angels and have not
charity, I am become as tinkling brass or a sounding cymbal."

All that the Bishop of Digne (in *Les Miserables*) had impressed upon a spirit naturally receptive to such imprint was here summed up in perfect utterance. Its benignity was boundless and effortless. This was what I had always believed. I would have believed it just as effortlessly if I were a Hindu or a Confucian or simply nothing at all. (I was forty years old, and the father of children, before I knew that charity without the Crucifixion is liberalism.)

This religious impulse in me was in large part instinctive, and I believe that the wise men agree, insofar as they agree about anything, that it is a commonplace of adolescence. But in part, too, it was the result of two personal relationships and other influences, and my exposure to the beliefs of two Protestants.

The first of those influences was a remarkable woman whom chance set down for a short time on the South Shore of Long Island. Her name was Dorothea Mund Ellen. She was a German, the daughter of a famous *Kapellmeister* of the Court of Hanover, and herself at one time the music and language tutor of Nicholas Roosevelt. She was an accomplished musician and she read the New Testament in Greek. She was a *Kulturmensch*—not in the sense in which my parents were "cultured people." She was not in the least interested in collecting culture, but in the sense that her mind had naturally absorbed and expressed simply and spontaneously in its least thoughts and references all that was greatest in human thought. Knowledge interested her little; she was not learned. Greatness interested her. She reacted to it instantly, as people react to sudden sunlight, and she found it in the least likely places, since there was greatness in her, and related it without effort and without pedantry. It was in her home (not in mine) that I first learned to know the meaning of Michelangelo. It was she who first played Beethoven for me. She first read with me the German masterpieces, and we spoke German together.

Insofar as my mind is civilized at all, she chiefly civilized it in the sense that she inured me to a tradition of life and of the mind in which nothing is so important as the human soul, its vicissitudes and its destiny. This influence I was never able to dispel even as a Communist. I was an editor of the *Daily Worker* when by chance I first opened Horace; and, as I read those purest lines

> *O fons Bandusiae,*
> *Splendidior vitro,*

it was her spirit that made me re-learn enough Latin to read the *Odes*. In this sense, she never ceased to draw me from the evil of Communism even during the years when it separated us completely. She herself knew this, and as she lay dying while we were estranged, among her last words was the question: "Where is he?" and the last triumph of her faith in me: "He will be all right." For to her I was always a soul. To me, she was my revered friend, and the greatest single human influence for good in my life until I met my wife.

She was intensely religious—a woman of immense spiritual probity and energy. For reasons which I found myself inadequate to follow, her religious energy took the form of Christian Science. She made every effort to bring me into that church. It was she who gave me my first Bible. It was for her sake that I read through carefully *Wissenschaft und Gesundheit mit Schlüssel zur Heiligen Schrift (Science and Health with Key to the Scriptures)*, for she gave me the German version. Under her influence I attended Christian Science services. I retained from this experience chiefly the sense that up to a point health is an aspect of the spirit and the sense that evil is an active force in life. The influence of Dorothea Ellen was powerful in that religious experience I was undergoing when I entered Columbia University.

It soon blended with another, very different influence of the same order. I made friends with the son of the Methodist minister in a village not far from my home in Lynbrook,

Long Island. In my second year at Columbia, I roomed with this boy. I was often at their house and sometimes attended services with them. In the sense of simple goodness, few men could have been better than that Methodist preacher. Nor was his goodness soft or weak; it had a hard human core. In the services and surroundings of his church, I found a bareness that touched some need in me and seemed congenial up to the point when I began to sense in it (rightly or wrongly) a spiritual thinness. Later, this need of mine for plainness would find its natural resting place when I met it as a function of Quaker mysticism.

Under the influence of this man and his son, I tried to pray. I felt it as an awkward, dutiful, and fruitless experience which I presently gave up. Yet like so many such experiences, the effort left its trace so that when, more than a decade later, in the turmoil of my break with Communism, I once more sought to pray, it seemed as if I were resuming an experience I had broken off rather than abandoned.

Emerson, too, had his influence on me at this time—an imperfect influence since I had not read him well or consistently. But the concept of the evidence of God in nature could not fail to take strong hold of me to whom nature meant so much. And in Emerson's law of compensations, I vaguely grasped the motion of a force that I sensed but which always remained just beyond the reach of the reasoning mind. I grasped its meaning crudely as this: that every act, however small, strikes the whole of life with incalculable consequences; that in the sum of things, the least may have the greatest consequences, and the worst effect the best result, a doctrine as elusive as the mystery it was intended to enmesh rather than to illumine, and which I found stated nowhere more elusively or conclusively than in Emerson's "Brahma":

> If the red slayer think he slays,
>   Or if the slain think he is slain,
> They know not well the subtle ways
>   I keep, and pass, and turn again. . . .

Politically, I was a conservative when I entered Columbia, and under the impact of postwar unrest, strikes, and the IWW outbreaks in the Northwest I was intensely preoccupied with politics. I was inclined to believe that Calvin Coolidge might be another Abraham Lincoln. I admired his prompt action in ending the Boston police strike, and I also admired Ole Hanson, the long-forgotten mayor of Seattle, who had performed a somewhat similar function in Washington. I knew almost by heart Coolidge's terse speeches, collected in *Have Faith in Massachusetts*. Constituting myself a one-man campaign committee, I had written to practically every Republican newspaper editor in the country, urging Coolidge's nomination for President of the United States. (Though I have lost this first careless rapture, I still rate Coolidge somewhat higher than the current quotation.) I had an extreme admiration for Theodore Roosevelt, as man and statesman, and an even greater admiration for his Secretary of State, John Hay. I believed that John Hay was one of the few Americans who had ever had a realistic grasp of international politics and that he had evolved a foreign policy so true to what would now be called the geopolitical position of the United States, that no one could depart far from it without jeopardizing the nation.

More importantly, I was reading widely and constantly in the lives of the Federalists—Washington, John Adams, Hamilton, John Jay, John Marshall and Gouverneur Morris. I was also studying the Federalist papers where in a paper of Madison's I would find in embryo a concept of the class structure of society that I would meet later fully developed in Karl Marx.

My political views were touched by the religious phase through which I was passing. I had a crude concept of conservatism which, if I had taken the trouble to phrase it, would have gone something like this: The family is the basic unit of history. The State exists for it, and the health or the failure of families is the history of the State. (The failure of my own family strengthened, rather than weakened, this belief.) The father is the ultimate authority in the family. But the source of all authority is God. From Him, the line of authority passes to the authority of the State, whose heads are simply the best men that election or tradition can provide. One line of authority descends from the State to the heads of its families. But another line of authority descends directly from God to the heads of families. A nation is a series of these lines of authority, descending from man to man, and deriving their ultimate force from God. Therefore, in respecting my superior, or in rendering obedience to him, I am merely respecting that authority within myself which also derives from God. When, at any point, this network of authority is broken, the nation is sick and in danger.

Sporadic and callow thoughts, but the fact is that I had them.

It was liberalism that I was now about to encounter, often without knowing the nature of the force that worked on me, and it was to perform on me its historic task in our times. It was liberalism (both in the honest meaning of that word and in its current sense as a cover-name for socialism) that, in the form of the higher intellectualism, was about to work on my immature and patchwork beliefs. In its bland, emollient, persuasive climate, all the more effective because I could not even identify it, the bond of my frail ideas was gently to leach and melt away until they crumbled in absurd ruins. My religious gropings first hesitated, then ceased, embarrassed by their own callowness in that warm light of reason, smiles, and tolerant irony. My instinctive sense of practical purpose in life and in politics was to yield to a glorification of the purposeless play of ideas for their own sake in the mind untrammelled by convictions. Any sense that some things are true and some things are false was to yield to the moral relativity summed up by Hamlet and quoted by one of my instructors: "There is nothing good or bad but thinking makes it so." At last, where there had been something, though uncouth, there was nothing. Into this vacuum, there sprang something which was waiting just around the corner—something which at first I had no way of identifying, but which I presently learned was Marxism. And as I watched the havoc of the liberal influence, first appraisingly, then bitterly, and condemned it at last as negative, aimless, and mischievous, I welcomed the positive and radical force the more eagerly.

I would have done well on my first undergraduate morning to have glanced less loftily at the landscape of Morningside Heights and more intently at the landscape of history. It would have swarmed up at me from all sides in dark contrast to the permanent illusion of sunlit campus. And it would have told me more about the past, present, and future of all men and of myself than anything I would ever learn in Contemporary Civilization (required for all freshmen).

Two years before, the socialist government of Hungary, feeling its power slipping, had taken the Communist leaders out of jail and turned over the nation to them. One year before I walked down 116th Street, the Hungarian Soviet Republic had fallen. I scarcely knew more than the fact that it had fallen. Yet its fall was to touch me closely in more than one way, and not long after. Five years later, I was to study the causes of that overthrow with an absorption that no college course ever moved me to. The fall of the Hungarian Soviet loosed upon the world a swarm of professional revolutionists of whom I was to glimpse one briefly (its commissar for war). Another I would meet under strange circumstances (as a secret agent whose name I never knew). A third was to play an important part in my life, as in the lives of many Americans. Under the assumed name J. Peters, he was to be the head of the underground section of the American Communist Party.

In that same year, the Bavarian Soviet Republic also fell. The organizer of its Workers and Soldiers Soviets, Eugen Leviné, would soon make to the court-martial that told him that he was under sentence of death the response that I would later echo to a grand jury in New York: "We Communists are always under sentence of death." And Leviné's picture, with the gaunt, ascetic face and the sensitive eyes and nose, would hang on my wall beside the pictures of Sou Chow Jen, the Communist leader of the Canton general strike, and Felix Djerjinsky, the Polish head of the Russian Red Terror.

A few months before I walked down 116th Street, the first calculated aggression of the Soviet Union against Europe had also been broken, just as the Red Army, under Marshal Tukhachevsky had headed for the suburbs of Warsaw. Even before that, history's beam had already picked out Tukhachevsky for a blurred instant, like a crouched fugitive whom a searchlight picks out in the barbed wire of a concentration camp. And there had been a second meaningful figure crouched beside him. For as an Imperial Russian officer in World War I, Tukhachevsky had been captured by the Germans. In a prison camp he found himself together with an obscure French officer, Captain Charles de Gaulle. The captive Russian and the captive Frenchman—the future head of the Red Army and the future head of the French armies—discovered that each, independently, had arrived at a revolutionary new concept of war (*blitzkrieg* it would be called when de Gaulle fled it). Its immediate purpose was to end the deadlock of those long lines of fault, the parallel lines of trenches in which for four years the manhood of Europe stood, maimed and murderous, from the North Sea to Switzerland, from the Baltic Sea to Bukovina. Tukhachevsky, too, would touch my life when his last march to a Communist execution cellar would help to dislodge me from the Communist Party at the moment when it killed him.

That Russian lunge at Warsaw, little noted and soon forgotten by most Americans, had been broken in part by the counsels of another little noted French officer, General Maxime Weygand. History was to pick out his figure, too, but in the full glare of its floodlight and in the crash of his own nation —its cities, armies, and its soul—before another totalitarian power, the Nazis. And when at the eleventh hour he was given supreme command of the shattered armies, he would utter the words that would toll for our generation, "Gentlemen, you have handed me a disaster."

Even more obscurely, in the year before I walked down 116th Street, another unnoted figure was flitting through sullen and defeated Central Europe. He was the late Edward Bonsals, an American from Maryland about whom most Americans probably know less than they remember of Weygand. Colonel Bonsals was the seeing-eye of an even more cryptic American, Colonel Edward House.

Of all the reports that Colonel Bonsals regularly fed to his secretive chief, few capsuled so much more meaning as history than one that was not secret at all.

One night, Colonel Bonsals had stepped from a cold and hungry Berlin into the Hotel Adlon (blockbusters would make rubble of it in World War II). In the Adlon elevator, he found himself in the company of a curious trio—an old woman, blind from cataracts on her eyes, and two younger women who were guiding her. All were Russians, of Europe's first wave of displaced persons, fugitives from the recent Bolshevik revolution. In the blind old woman, Colonel Bonsals suddenly recognized the Countess Kleinmichael whom he had known a few years before as the reigning beauty at the Tsar's court.

The young women were urging her to do something and she was peevishly resisting. They were urging her to have the cataracts removed from her eyes. "Then," said one of them with the triumphant logic of youth, "you will be able to see again." "But I don't *want* to see," cried the Countess Kleinmichael, "life has become so ugly, so ugly."

In that same year that I crossed the Columbia campus, Bernard Shaw would put it in another way. "Civilization," he would say (in the Preface to *Back To Methuselah*), has exploded in one of "those gigantic boils that must be lanced with a million bayonets." "One half of Europe," he would add, "having knocked the other half down, is trying to kick it to death. . . ." He warned that "it is extremely doubtful that our civilization can survive." A world whose attention Shaw had learned he could hold only by clowning would wonder uneasily what the point of the joke was.

A French writer who had survived the western front would put it another way. In *Le Feu* (*The Fire*), Henri Barbusse, soon, like me, to be a Communist and, like me, one of the editors of the *Labor Defender*, would re-live that agony in one of the first of the war novels. A few years later, I would be reading his appeal to the intellectuals of all countries to end the forces that made such agonies possible—a pamphlet surgically titled *Le Couteau Entre Les Dents* (*The Knife Between the Teeth*). For Barbusse had sensed what I would not know for some time after I walked down 116th Street: that the World Wars were themselves great revolutionary wars, smashing, effacing, dislocating, regrouping, and compressing decades of history and of change into brief terrible charges of blood and violence—convulsions whose meaning men could not read, but that led to a revolution that some men read as hope and some as outrage.

Three years before, a plain, bald, prosaic man had mounted the rostrum of the All-Russian Congress of Soviets. He was Lenin, and he opened the Congress with one of the plainest, baldest, and most prosaic statements with which any man has ever turned the iron page of history: "We will now proceed to organize the Socialist State." The British Ambassador, who was present, permitted himself a comment. "A rather unimpressive little man," he observed. The diplomatic gallery, perhaps, was not the best vantage point for foreseeing that within thirty years there would be no truly capitalist power

left on earth. All, to one degree or another, would be social-
ized, while Britain, the most self-consciously socialist of them
all, would lie on a brink of history under sitting-duck range
of the atom bombs of the unimpressive little man's political
heirs.

An American had foreseen matters less complacently. He
was Woodrow Wilson's seeing-eye, and shortly before or after
I reached Columbia, he summed up the Communist revolution
in Russia for his chief: "I have seen the future, and it works."*
The man was Lincoln Steffens, inveterate muckraker, also
a friend of Theodore Roosevelt, friend later on of innumerable
Communists.

But as I walked down 116th Street, these things reached
me, insofar as they reached me at all, only as a man knows of
a tumult beyond mountains. The mountains were my ignorance and my inexperience. I was acutely aware that the
First World War had been a disaster. My understanding of
the nature of the disaster was that of a child, and therefore
differed little from that of almost everybody else around me.
But I also sensed that the one positive result of the World
War was the Russian Revolution. My understanding of that
upheaval too, was like a child's. I saw it as an undifferentiated
savagery which reached my mind from the dark immensity
of steppes as through a curtain of permanently falling snow.

I detested and feared the Russian Revolution. I saw in it a
threat to civilization (Western civilization we would now say),
and I felt that threat precisely in its religious form. I was
soon to discover at Columbia many young men of my age who
understood the Russian Revolution much better than I did.
For they were just as politically minded. But none of them
was conservative and none of them was in any sense religious.

Almost from that day forth, blindly, gropingly, ignorantly,

---

* One of my gloomier anti-Communist friends was later to re-
arrange this to read: "I have seen the future, and I am afraid that it
works."

I was to seek an answer—which nobody seemed able to give me—to a question which I did not know how to phrase: What is the nature of the crisis of the twentieth century and what should a man do about it?

I was to seek the answer more and more insistently and desperately as I became better able to phrase the question. In the end, the question and its answer were to become the whole meaning of my college experience and, indeed, of my life. It would be a long time before I would learn that on the day I first walked down 116th Street I had been closer, in my ignorance, than I would again be for years, in my enlightenment, to that answer which I would finally learn in large part by enacting it.

Into my seeking I threw myself with the intensity of those forces. What I was seeking I was neither mature nor informed enough to know, and though I sometimes had strong intuitions of a unity of purpose that just eluded me, I was, presently, shy and even ashamed to suggest what that unity might be. In effect I was asking: Please tell me what our civilization means in terms of God and man, for I cannot make head or tail of it.

It was very much as if I had gone to a madhouse and said, cap in hand: Please explain to me the principles of sanity and sane living. Again, this is entirely without any special animadversions upon Columbia University. Exactly the same thing would have been true, in one degree or another, if I had gone to any other of the top secular universities in the country. Nor would the colleges have been at fault. Their failure merely mirrored a much greater disaster which was the failure of Western civilization itself.

That civilization lay maimed and broken, when it was not buried in those two immense facing graves—the trenches of the World War which was only two years over when I en-

tered college. On all sides of those dreadful ditches Europe
was a desolation over which the shell-shattered Cathedral of
Amiens and the guildhall at Ypres stood like symbol monu-
ments to the estimated eleven million casualties they had cost.
While the statesmen of Europe, having participated in making
that desert, were making something they were calling peace,
they were basing it in part on one of the most disintegrating
principles ever proclaimed by man—the political self-deter-
mination of minorities.

The human and material catastrophe was staggering. But
what of the catastrophe of religious, moral, and intellectual
forces that must have occurred before the visible catastrophe
was possible? It was that catastrophe which was basic and
which made it inevitable that peace was merely an interval
between disasters, like a pause between earthquake shocks.
For the whole structure of the West was in collapse and was
shaking down the East in its fall.

And it was against that backdrop of disaster that I sought
the meaning of God and man. It would be untrue to say that
I asked it. I did not know how to frame the question, for I
did not understand the nature of the forces involved and I did
not even yet grasp the depth of the disaster. The answers I
received, insofar as they were answers to anything, were
themselves disastrous. I am convinced that there were men
at Columbia University in my time who grasped clearly the
nature of the crisis of civilization and might perhaps have
been able to illumine part of the answer. It was my ill
fortune never to meet them. It is also possible that they could
not have helped me greatly if I had—possible, but not, I think,
very likely.

In soberest reckoning, I do not believe that I carried away
from those to whom I was exposed one fact or insight which
would help me to grasp or comprehend the essential nature
of that civilization of which we were presumed to be among
the most conscious units, or what was happening to it.

．　．　．

Contemporary Civilization was happily free from any pre-
sentiments. The course, if I understood it rightly, was intended to toss us into the ages as if from the end of a desk;
to shake up our minds and teach us to swim in waters which
some of us would soon guess were mid-ocean. That was, presumably, the Civilization part. The Contemporary part was,
at least in my classes, entirely missing, or so very cautiously
hinted at that it missed me almost completely. My first instructor had been a conscientious objector during the First
World War. He edited his thoughts so carefully that I was
aware merely of a kind of twittering. For I had not yet
learned the language of the birds—the arch indirections and
cunning allusions with which intellectuals can convey very
secret meanings.

My first, and one of my few abiding memories of Contemporary Civilization is of my instructor slumped, less from
collapse than organic ineffectualness, against a wall of the
room. In his hand he holds our red-bound textbook, written by
Irwin Edman. A somewhat pallid little man who lisped of
Santayana to small coteries of selected students, my instructor's eyes are half-closed behind his glasses and he recites,
with a weariness that would be funny if it were not pain-
fully authentic, from Swinburne's "The Garden of Proser-
pine," which Mr. Edman has included in his book:

> From too much love of living,
> From hope and fear set free,
> We thank with brief thanksgiving
> Whatever gods may be
> That no life lives for ever;
> That dead men rise up never;
> That even the weariest river
> Winds somewhere safe to sea.

I do not recall ever hearing in Contemporary Civilization
that the dimensions of the disaster of World War I could not
be measured by the physical ruins because the ruins had oc-

curred in men's souls before they were visible in the ruins of cities.

Nothing that I can remember was said about the Russian Revolution. No one in Contemporary Civilization parted the curtain of falling snow to show me Petrograd with a cold rain blowing in from the Gulf of Finland on a day in November, 1917. The tottering republican government of Russia had ordered the drawbridges over the Neva River to be raised. The great spans tilted slowly through the air. The Red Guards and the Communist Party resolutes had begun to execute that careful plan, the brainchild of Comrades Trotsky, Podvoisky, and Antonov-Avseënko which proved to be a master technique for the revolutionary seizure of a modern city. The Communists were occupying the public buildings, the ministries, the police stations, the post office, newspaper and telegraph offices, the telephone exchange, banks, powerhouses, railroad stations. To cut off the working-class Viborg quarter on the other bank of the Neva, and to prevent its masses from re-enforcing the insurgent Communists, the falling republican government had raised the bridges.

In from the Gulf of Finland steamed the armored cruisers of the Baltic fleet whose crews had already gone over to the Bolsheviks. The cruisers nosed into the Neva within point-blank range of the bridges. Their slender guns rose with mechanical deliberateness, and, as they rose, the spans of the bridges slowly dropped again. The masses streamed across into the central city. This was the crisis of the uprising, and one of the decisive moments of history.

The upraised guns of the cruisers—one hopefully renamed the *Dawn of Freedom*—did not lower. They swung, and lobbed their shells into the Winter Palace, which stood next to the Admiralty on the river bank. Inside, the rump of the government was in its final, dying session. Outside, fierce fighting was going on. Directing it, was one of history's most grotesque figures, Antonov-Avseënko, the Communist math-

ematician and tactician, the co-contriver of the *coup d'état*,
the man with the scarecrow face and shoulder-long hair under the shapeless felt. Antonov rushed toward the guns at
the head of the steps. His armed rabble followed him. They
stormed the doors. The Winter Palace fell. With it, in that
vast, snow-afflicted sixth of the earth's surface, fell the absolute control of the destinies of 160 million people.

A few hours later, the chairman of the Revolutionary Military Committee, Leon Trotsky, rose in the Petrograd Soviet
to announce the triumph of the revolution. As if silenced by
the force he was invoking, he stood for a moment, staring
through the permanent pall of tobacco fumes rising from the
booted, jacketed, somber, heaving sea of workers and soldiers.
Then he found the words equal to the event: "We, the Soviet
of Workers', Soldiers', and Peasants' delegations, are on the
point of making an experiment that has not its like in history."

"Only those who have lived through the revolution," said
Lenin's wife, "know its grand, solemn beauty."

Thus, with the slow raising of those guns was raised the
central fact of the first half of the twentieth century: the
Russian Revolution—and the century's central issue: Communism. Thirty years, the span of a generation, had scarcely
passed before that fact in the form of Soviet military power
and that issue in the form of Communist faith, would crowd
the Western world into its retreating borders. And men of
many nations, who were not born when those slender guns
were raised and on whose minds that tremendous imagery
of history had left no trace, would die from their delayed
fragmentation in Germany, in Hungary, in Finland, in Bul-
garia, in Rumania, in Greece, in China, in Indo-China, in
Korea.

For Antonov-Avseënko* and his ragged troops had stormed
more than the Winter Palace of the Tsars. They had stormed

---

* After a brief embassy to the Spanish Republican government,
Antonov-Avseënko was shot in the great Purge.

the Winter Palace of the human mind. More than the masses of the Viborg quarter had streamed across the Neva bridges. Mankind had crossed with them from one age to another— an age which, in Trotsky's words "has not its like in history." On one side was an augmenting power which utterly denied all the standards and values of two thousand years of Christian history. On the other was the shrinking frontier and failing faith of a pseudo-Christian world.

Yet the failing world had created within itself that new world unlike itself—a world which, though it paid public homage to the older standards, in fact denied or disregarded them. This was the new world of reason, science, and machines, which the dynamo, the automobile, the airplane, the radio, chloropicrin, trinitrotoluol, the machines that procreate machines and the factories that breed the masses had made manifest. It had stood up to declare its reality against the unreality of the failing world. It was in the name of this world that Antonov and his followers had stormed the Winter Palace of the mind. This process whereby a world begets its opposite, and in the mortal struggle between them a new world is evolved, Communists call the dialectic of history, the law of movement in history. The history of the rest of the twentieth century, the moment of history at which we now stand, is the last spasm of this dialectic process.

Other forces, too, were released at that fateful moment of history in Petrograd. The Russian Revolution began as a political revolution, an effort to replace the tsardom with a republic (the Kerensky government). But before the Communists had achieved the strength to overthrow that weak republic, a social revolution had set in, transforming or destroying the old political and social institutions. It was the momentum of this social revolution that carried the Communists to power. With the workers of Viborg, the masses rushed across the Neva bridges into history. Henceforth, all the political history of our time would be a struggle for the control of those masses. The revolution in which that struggle first took form would move in ever-spreading convulsions, and many changing forms, from its Russian epicenter, until every important area of the earth had known it or its intermediate forms. Everywhere it would be a movement of the masses, and everywhere it would be a struggle to capture and control the political power of the masses by granting their demands in full or in part.

In China, the revolution would take the form of Communism, and its triumph would tip the balance of power in the world in favor of Communism and against the West. In Italy, the revolution would first take the form of fascism; in Germany of Nazism, in Spain of falangism, in the United States of the New Deal, in Britain of socialism. Each might cry out against the others, and the followers of each might look with horror on the others. Each differed according to national conditions or traditions. One might engage in mortal war with another for supremacy (that is to say for control of the masses)—as the Russian Communists and the Nazis. But in effect, each was a form of the same revolution, in different terms, in different stages—the revolution of the masses in the intellectual and physical conditions of the twentieth century.

Not to know this was not to understand anything that has happened in our lifetime. Not to understand it meant to be unable to read the chart of history in this century. That was the failure of Franklin Roosevelt, who sensed what forces were at work but failed to understand how they worked or what they were working toward. The same failure of the mind lies at the bottom of the latent desperation of our time, which insists on regarding our history in terms of individual catastrophes because it cannot grasp the complete logic by which they relate to one another and develop out of one another.

For the Russian Revolution and its administrative form, the Soviet government, are not merely Russian manifestations.

If they were, they could be dealt with like any other form of aggressive nationalism. They are phases of a greater revolution, whose ideas and intellectual force and physical force are not Russian at all, but derive their force from the modern Western mind. It is that mind which it is everywhere substituting for the mind of the earlier Christian world.

The revolution of our time is an elemental wind that blows not from space, but from what, after space, is most terrifying: from the masses of mankind, from the human depths of the world. It dies down, but it merely gathers strength, and it returns again in successive blasts until everything that is old, worn, traditional, diseased, disordered, failing in that shaken world has tumbled or been transformed. This will happen certainly if the revolution succeeds. But it will also happen in part even if it fails. Nothing will be more changed by it than that which finds the power to withstand it. For in that fearful resistance, the world that resists will transform itself more and more into the likeness of its antagonist in order to be able to resist it on equal terms. This transformation too is dialectical—the action by which opposites become more like in order to be more equal in power.

These were the forces and meanings implicit in the seizure of power by the Bolsheviks in 1917. This was the issue and the problem that was raised with the turret guns of the *Dawn of Freedom* and the storm of the Winter Palace.

I remember only one or two things about Contemporary Civilization. Early in the course (we were just about to enter the Cro-Magnon caves), I recall learning with a start that the Java ape man is probably a fraud. It is quite impossible, my instructor said, for scientists to reconstruct a man from a single jawbone, or even to be sure that the jaw was that of a man. Most reconstructions of prehistoric creatures were pure guesswork.

The instructor sometimes hurrahed for the IWW—the only radically vocal instructor I ever met at Columbia (he did not last long). I once heard him turn savagely on a freshman who had made some slurring remark about those restless syndicalists, and treat him to a brief personal and intellectual assault that left the facts of political life in much the same questionable shape as the Java ape man and the reconstructed monsters.

One freshman talked back. "You are destroying all our beliefs," he said. "That is exactly what this course is for," said our instructor. "We want to destroy your beliefs, to shake up your minds and teach you to think for yourselves." I was reminded of my mother with the pie balanced on her fingers, telling me that I must keep an open mind, that the world was made, not by God, but by gases cooling in space.

That was the frontal attack. Since it was not clever, for it was recognizable, it was less effective than the bland treatment. It was not the high wind but the warm sun that made us abandon our intellectual coats.

Mark Van Doren (of whom I wrote briefly in *Witness*) was the master of the sunny influence. His influence on me was great, greater perhaps than he knew, both because he was my appointed faculty adviser, but more importantly, for his own charm and trenchancy of mind; like a burning glass, his influence focussed for me most of the disintegrating rays in that environment. With his mocking humor, he also refracted and broke most other qualifying influences. My first English themes were editorials for him. He advised the class to look for its models, not in the daily press but in *The Nation*, a New York liberal weekly in which "some of the best editorial writing in the country was being done" (and of which Van Doren was soon to become an editor). I doubt that I had ever heard of *The Nation* before. Certainly, I had never read it. I hastened to the nearest newsstand.

My editorials were terse and brief and received As. I remember one against the Russian Revolution which ended with a Biblical quotation: "Why do the heathen rage, and the people imagine a vain thing?" Another quoted Calvin Coolidge approvingly. Mark asked me into his office after class. He praised my editorial writing, but he wondered, with his infectious chuckle, whether the Russian Revolution was really as bad as I supposed, or whether Calvin Coolidge was as good. I perceived that in Mark Van Doren's world, which I was prepared to admire intensely because it was intellectually admirable, people thought that Coolidge was something much worse than bad. They thought he was funny. I presently learned that they thought Theodore Roosevelt was also funny, but with a difference: an element of venom entered in. I began to have that uneasy feeling, to which youth is especially susceptible, that my intellectual shirttails were showing.

One day I brought Mark a long hexameter dithyramb in which I celebrated my discovery of God in nature. No doubt Mark was appalled by the badness of the poem, though he was too kind to say so. But he was even more appalled by something else. "That's the pathetic fallacy," he said severely. I had never heard of the pathetic fallacy before, but I realized that it was an intellectual lapse so old and sorry that wiser minds had long ago tagged it. Had I been older, I could have gone a long way in agreement with Mark about the pathetic fallacy, and from a purely Christian viewpoint. As it was, I began to wonder from that tiny episode, and others, whether my religious gropings were not a little childish.

Good poetry, Mark taught me, was seldom didactic. The business of poetry was not to advance religious or moral ideas. The business of the poet was to discuss, and the business of poetry was to communicate the inherent beauty of simple and familiar things, and the closer this communication was to the patter of common speech, the better it was likely to be. He referred me to Robert Frost and quoted the last line of the "Hyla Brook": *We love the things we love for what they are*

—(a fairly didactic line, by the way). In all this, Mark Van Doren taught me nothing that was not good and helpful.

In a related way, he gave my mind a nudge that was to affect the course of my life. Less by anything he said than by his whole attitude of mind and literary excitement, he infected me with the idea that the literary life is the best in the world and that to be a poet is among the highest callings known to man. This is a viewpoint that I share wholeheartedly with him today. The difficulty for a man (and more especially for a boy) is to know when he is called, or to what degree, if he is called, he must compromise between his calling and the life of the world. To my unformed mind, the idea that I was to be a poet became the central thought and carried with it the strong implication that nothing else mattered—how I was to live, what obligations I might have to the community or to my family (even the simple obligation of finishing college or making full use of its facilities while I was in it) had no meaning beside the impulse to poetry. This was unfortunate, for I above all needed discipline and integration in a community. And in this Mark abetted me by assuming (or leading me to suppose that he did) that I was to be a poet, by laughing with me at the foibles or the stuffiness of my teachers, his colleagues, and at what I soon came to suppose was the whole folly of higher education and the whole way of life of which it is an expression.

I was a boy who, above all, needed firm and wise direction. Moreover, the natural habit of Mark's mind (like that of many academic liberals) was to treat ideas as having an existence apart from life; their delight was in their multiplex play; ideas never implied acts. The natural habit of my mind was the exact opposite. Ideas as intellectual game scarcely interested me at all. For me, an idea was the starting point of an act. The history of ideas and their play had value for me chiefly as the means whereby a man might test and select those ideas which had meaning for himself and the world at the moment of history in which both found themselves. A man did not play with ideas—he rejected or accepted ideas on the basis of their meaning for life. A man accepted an idea or a system of ideas because he found it better than other ideas. A man did not accept a system of ideas unless he meant to act on them. Their serviceability in life was the test. Thus Mark was always half in jest and I was always deadly serious. These attitudes are inborn and irreconcilable. I would say that for all my immaturity, my attitude made me inherently more adult than Mark. Mark would say, I think, that my attitude is a limitation of the mind and marks it as forever immature. I believe that Mark understood something of this difference; that it amused him; that he, by way of intellectual sport, wanted to see what would happen; that at worst my habit of mind was something to be corrected or outgrown. I did not understand at all the deep gulf between our basic attitudes or what might come of it.

Others did. There was in the English department, another young instructor who outwardly seemed the opposite of Mark Van Doren in all the grace of mind and manner. Moreover, he had a rasping and quavering voice. Mark and I sometimes joked about him. One evening as I was passing Hamilton Hall, I met this second instructor head on. He stopped me, grasped both lapels of my jacket in his two hands. There he held me, fixing me, like the Ancient Mariner, while in his quavering voice, he quoted James Thomson's "Proem":

> We stagger under the enormous weight
> Of all the weary ages piled on us.
> With all their grievous wrongs inveterate,
> And all their disenchantments dolorous,
> And all the monstrous tasks they have bequeathed;
> And we are stifled with the airs they breathed;
> And read in theirs our doom calamitous.

Then he said: "Be careful of Mark Van Doren. He is clever and he is kind. But his mind has no boundaries."

Mark Van Doren's classes were by no means the only ones in which dissolving influences played on me. In my German classes, for example, I learned little German. But I learned that talk about war guilt was nonsense. The war had been a mere struggle for power. In three years' time, Lenin would tell me the same things more convincingly, for he would give me plausible reasons for his opinion.

For some reason, I remember very clearly a large, rather informal discussion at which half a dozen faculty members presided—a class in General Honors, I suppose. The subject was Rabelais. We were discussing his ideal Abbey of Thélèma, whose motto was *fay ce que vouldras* (do what you like). The senior faculty member was a distinguished musician, a persistent if unapplauded poet who later in life had a remarkable success as a popular novelist. He was also the possessor of a voice of great depth and resonance of which he was well aware. In lecturing on "Paradise Lost," he would always refer to Milton's "gawjus owgan voice." "There have been just three of those gawjus owgan voices in English literature," he would observe in his own organ tones. "John Milton, (somebody else whom I have forgotten)." Then he would pause, self-consciously twirling his Phi Beta Kappa key. The third gorgeous organ voice went modestly unmentioned. The great dome of his head encased a formidable weight of learning. Blandly he explained that Rabelais' "do what you like" lay at the root of the conception of a gentleman. For it invokes that innate honor which distingiushes the gentleman and which always prevents the motto "do as you like" from passing into mere license. He paused, smiling tranquilly. The problem of the gentleman was explained from other sides. Even then I knew that there was something wrong, or at least something lacking in that suave comment, although I did not know what it was. Yet I felt it sharply enough so that over the years I never forgot the scene.

But I was forty years old before I grasped from very different sources what the collective intelligence in that room, honorable gentlemen all, had brushed across so bravely—namely, the distinct possibility that Rabelais with his *fay ce que vouldras* had shattered the moral structure of European civilization. I was even older before I sensed that the basic issue raised by Rabelais had been an irreconcilable conflict—a belief in original sin and a belief that man is by nature good. By then I knew that Rousseau had only echoed Rabelais in his "man is born free but is everywhere in chains," and that the issue between the two basic views of man's nature lay close to the heart of the central conflict of our time—Faith in God or Faith in Man.

The almost professional mood of doubt of all established values soon led me to doubt something that I was not intended to question. I began very seriously to question the value of higher education. The atmosphere of a liberal arts college in the modern world is by its nature subtly unsettling. Unlike professional schools, it is not definitely preparing most students for anything. I found myself asking: What am I doing here? What are any of these boys, whose parents have deprived themselves to send them to college, doing here? Why are most of these rather dull young men picking up a smattering of knowledge, which they can never assimilate, but which will unfit them to be the salesmen and clerks they were meant to be? The intense unreality of the whole college experience disturbed me. I would listen at night to the great city roaring around the campus, while mooning students caterwauled on the campus or from the dormitory windows dropped paper bags filled with water on passers-by on Amsterdam Avenue. (I dropped some myself but that did not change the equation.)

It seemed to me that that great intellectual factory was scarcely moored in the life around it. No ladders, no lines reached from this superstructure into the life of the real world. What good was a culture that had no roots in life and no connections with it?

How much was said that passed over my head or that I missed from personal immaturity or other inadequacy? A great deal, I would be inclined to say, invoking a rough law of averages. And yet I was intellectually curious and often sat in on courses which I was not taking. I remember one on the Renaissance. The class was huge so that the lectures were held in one of the science amphitheaters. The instructor, a man with a round face and somewhat startled china-blue eyes, used to sit at his desk in the pit. Sometimes he would rest his chin on his clasped hands, gaze out upon the ranks of football players (the course was considered a snap) and others, and utter a few exquisite names in a beautifully spaced and modulated voice: "Pi-co del-la Mi-ran-do-la, gentleman. Gui-do Gui-ni-cel-li."

One morning he opened his discussion by fixing the blankest looking of the football players and saying: "Mr. Blank, imagine that you are in Athens this morning. You are crossing the a-go-rrra. You meet So-cra-tiz. What is the one question you would inevitably ask him?" Poor Blank shuffled his feet. I thought: "This is the most expensive nonsense I have ever listened to," and ceased to drop in on the Renaissance.

The Columbia faculty was not, of course, composed wholly of young sceptics and esthetes. By any count of academic noses, they were a small minority. But they were closer to the younger students, and their appeal was great. Their minds gave off a stimulating sense of ferment. They seemed to be surging along paths to a newer life, while their staid colleagues seemed plodders, incommunicably learned, aloof, or simply dull. And the younger instructors did not repress a smile at their elders, which undergraduates were quick to catch and share.

In time, I came to think that Professor George Dinsmore Odell taught me more solid fact, and gave me more important insights (into Wordsworth, for example), than any other man at Columbia. He was the brother of a former governor of New York State. He was a big man in his sixties. He had snow-white hair crowning the aging face of a gentle, kindly child. His eyes were peculiarly blue and innocent.

He gave a course in the English Romantic Poets. It was considered hopelessly dull but a snap, and the class was also always crowded with the football team filling the backfield. His method was to take the Romantic poets in chronological order beginning, if I remember rightly, with Cowper and ending with Wordsworth. He would read a poem in his thin and rather soporific voice, and then make what seemed to me, and I am sure to everyone else, rambling and sometimes puzzled comments on it. I remember his reading Shelley's "Stanzas Written in Dejection near Naples." When he came to the line

Like light dissolved in star-showers thrown

he stopped and read it again.

"What does he mean, gentlemen?" he asked in his querulous old voice, 'Like light dissolved in star-showers thrown.' What does he mean? I do not know, gentlemen, I do not know." Then he paused and stared at us puckishly from under his thick eyebrows. "I only know," he said, "that it is beautiful."

In "Epipsychidion" he reached the lines

See when the son of heaven with wingèd feet
Runs down the slanted sunlight of the dawn.

He smiled puckishly again. "Shall I tell you, gentlemen," he asked, "how a modern poet would write that? 'Pipe Moicury comin' down the sunbeams.'" No doubt he had been making that crack for years and no doubt it always brought down the house. He would spend the rest of the period discoursing on his mystification at modern poets while the footballers caught up on their sleep in the back row—as he sometimes noted without impatience.

At last we reached Wordsworth. Wordsworth was a poet
I never read. I had tried once or twice and found him in-
tolerably dull, not even good prose since it jingled with rhyme.
I had heard how Alfred, Lord Tennyson, as a jest, had written
the perfect Wordsworthian line: "A Mr. Wilkinson, a clergy-
man," and I thought that summed Wordsworth up.

Now Professor Odell read Wordsworth's "Ode, Intimations
of Immortality." He came towards the end:

> Though inland far we be,
> Our souls have sight of that immortal sea
> Which brought us hither,
> Can in a moment travel thither,
> And see the Children sport upon the shore,
> And hear the mighty waters rollings evermore.

This time he made no comment, arch or querulous. He simply paused. He paused so long that I grasped for an instant
that he was simply listening within himself to something that
he could hear and we could not: The mighty waters roll for-
evermore.

While I was still rocked by the surf-beat of the great lines,
he passed to "The River Duddon." He read

> For, backward, Duddon! as I cast my eyes,
> I see what was, and is, and will abide;
> Still glides the Stream, and shall for ever glide;
> The Form remains, the Function never dies. . . .

"What *does* that mean, gentlemen?" he asked in mock
exasperation and went on

> We Men, who in our morn of youth defied
> The elements, must vanish;—be it so!
> Enough, if something from our hands have power
> To live, and act, and serve the future hour;
> And if, as toward the silent tomb we go,
> Through love, through hope, and faith's transcendent
>   dower,
> We feel that we are greater than we know.

Again he paused without comment.

Then he turned to the "Lucy Poems." Of all the Wordsworth I had glanced at, the "Lucy Poems" seemed to me the silliest tinkle-tankle. Now Professor Odell read

> A violet by a mossy stone
> Half-hidden from the eye!
> —Fair as a star, when only one
> Is shining in the sky.

" 'Fair as a star,' " he repeated, " 'when only one,' only one, gentlemen, 'is shining in the sky.' " That worked the wonder that gave me the meaning of Wordsworth for the rest of my life. There flashed upon my mind the evenings of my boyhood, especially autumn evenings, when I stood in the garden, beside the last roses, tossing in the crisp wind, waiting for the frost that would burn them. Then, as I glanced upward, from the dim blue sky a single star would palely detach itself. That was what Wordsworth meant.

A year or so later, after I had published an atheist play, Professor Odell became my implacable enemy and argued with Dean Hawkes for hours, I was told, to have me expelled from college. I do not blame him.

His was a benign influence. All that I know about English Romantic poetry, he taught me in his rumbling way, not by serving me with facts but by exposing me to something of which all that he himself would say was: "I only know that it is beautiful."

By the end of my sophomore year at Columbia, I had ceased to be a conservative. I was nothing. God, when He was not an intellectual embarrassment, was an admission or a convention that one conceded for the sake of tradition, civility, or an argument. Truth was wholly relative. Nothing was absolutely true and hence, by inference if not by direct evaluation, nothing was absolutely false. In other words, nothing was absolutely good or bad, though those other words were held to be a little naïve or uncouth, just as the word "truth" was avoided in favor of the word "fact." My mind, which from the hodgepodge of my boyhood reading and other influences had begun in adolescence to sort out a crude conservative order, was once more a hodgepodge. Now it was the higher hodgepodge, a spiral nebula which caught up the whirling dust and fragments of literary and philosophical ideas from Homer to Gertrude Stein and the pre-Socratic philosophers to T. E. Hulme.* Insofar as my mind was not a hodgepodge, it was a vacuum. Its law was scepticism.

My mind is by nature positive; it shrinks instinctively from negation. As between life and death, it is for life. I came to acknowledge scepticism as an invaluable tool of the mind. But a tool presupposes a purpose. The sceptics and the scepticisms around me served no purpose discernible to me. At most they were defining a pattern of irresolution. Most of them I sensed were organically unhappy. For believing in nothing included an inability to believe in themselves. Mockery was a habit of their minds and it acted most savagely upon the least truant faith in themselves. To me they came to epitomize the modern mind for which I found the perfect image in Ibsen's *Peer Gynt*—the onion, which we peel, skin by skin by skin and find at the heart a hollow. Only slowly, and less by any action of my mind than by an organic revolt of my whole being, I began to grow sceptical of the sceptics. I saw that they had destroyed for me all traditional beliefs (in part justifiably, for a certain amount of demolition among old and fixed ideas must take place before the mind is free to use its energies). But they had absolutely nothing to put in their place. In a quieter world that might have made little difference. But the world in the twentieth century was in turmoil.

My revolt occurred at the moment when I began to sense

---

* In my years at *Time* magazine I had a rare opportunity to observe a good many minds recently emerged from many universities. It seemed to me that the higher hodgepodge was still in force, but now it had become economic and sociological.

the dimension and to seek the nature of the human crisis; to which they had no answer but aversion or doubt, and of which I suspected they were themselves a symptom. It was at that point that I began consciously to seek a new positive answer to problems which I suddenly saw petrified in the ruins of Europe and rigidified in its millionfold grave markers. I did not return to the rubble of those traditional values that had been pulverized for me. That job had been too well done. Moreover, it was clear that the crisis was, in part, a crisis of those values. I sought for a new answer to the new problems —the search that was to bring me to Communism.

During my freshman year, I had commuted to Columbia. I brought a package of lunch from home, filed it away in my gymnasium locker, and at noon ate it in the locker room.

I was not alone. Several dozen undergraduates, day students like me, also ate in the gymnasium, sitting on the narrow benches between the lockers. They lived an intense, intellectual life, almost wholly apart from the life of the campus. They were a cohesive group, bound together by a common origin, a common flight from a common fear, and a common poverty.

To me they were an entirely new race of men. They came from the Bronx, the East Side and from a region I had never heard of—Brownsville—somewhere far out in what they themselves used to call the "steppes of Brooklyn." They spoke a dialect which was almost wholly unintelligible to me, and which, oddly enough, was one language I was never able to manage. It was Yiddish. They were Jewish, of course, but my inexperience in such matters may be judged from the fact that for a long time, I supposed that Schapiro was an Italian name.

All of them were intensely serious. Not that they did not laugh. They laughed a great deal. Their humor was at times

highly intellectual (there were among them one or two authentic wits—rarities in any group). At other times, their
humor was extremely earthy. Some of it was completely unintelligible to me, for its point derived from allusions to a kind
of life and to people I had absolutely no knowledge of.

Their seriousness was organic. It was something utterly
new in my experience. It sprang from a struggle in which to
gain an inch was the achievement of a lifetime. "*Ist er ein
ernster Mensch?*" I used to ask later on like most Communists,
as my first question about any new person we were dealing with: "Is he a serious man?" My strange luncheon
companions were *ernste Menschen*—and with good reason,
for most of them were sitting there as the result of a struggle
with a warping poverty impossible for those who have not
glimpsed it to imagine. They sat there, that consciously separate proletariat, loudly munching their sandwiches, because
they came of a stock that, after God, worshipped education
and the things of the mind. They were there, in most cases,
by acts of superhuman sacrifice and contrivance on the part
of their families. To me that seriousness was deeply impressive. It was unlike the attitude of any group I had ever known.
It spoke directly to a seriousness within myself, that sprang
from no such struggle as theirs, but partook of a similar organic attitude toward life. It was years before I would understand that the root of that seriousness was religious. That
fact was not to be changed by the fact that most of these
young men were intellectually irreligious; even while they
were working to destroy my faith, I nevertheless sensed that
I had come to Gerar, and that the voices I heard preaching
the new faith of socialism and revolution had been heard also
at Tekoa.

My first relations with those strangers were not particularly
friendly. They talked a great deal about writers, books, and
plays, but they were writers, books, and plays that I had
scarcely heard of: Sudermann, Hauptmann, Tolstoy, Dos-

toevsky, Turgenev, Chekhov, Gorky, Ibsen, Strindberg—the modern literature of central and eastern Europe. They talked about it not as something they had read but as something which was a part of their lives. Most of these writers they had not read in English, but in German or Yiddish. It was, in the main, the literature of social protest that they were absorbed by, and they were absorbed by it because they found their lives reflected in it. These were the wretched of the earth, speaking with twentieth-century voices and climbing twentieth-century barricades. When I once wetly mentioned Victor Hugo, there was a pause of smiling embarrassment at my simplicity.

They talked about matters less familiar to me than Strindberg and Hauptmann. They talked about socialism, atheism, the Russian Revolution, socialist Sunday schools (Sunday meetings for young atheist socialists—a new term to me), experiences in speaking from soapboxes (another new term to me), Eugene V. Debs, Upton Sinclair, V. I. Lenin, Leon Trotsky, Marx and Engels, Hegel, Feuerbach, Kropotkin, Bakunin. Without knowing it, I was in the presence of a new way of life, a new culture, which I felt to be deeply antagonistic to my own and which I lunged out against. I brashly asserted my own religious, conservative, and anti-socialist views. To Eugene V. Debs I opposed Calvin Coolidge, but without marked success.

There was great intellectual stimulation in those arguments. The gates of a new experience swung open to me, even while I fought against it. Some of the best minds in the undergraduate body were in that dingy proletariat. I was learning more in that intellectual rough and tumble than I learned in my academic courses. Some of my locker room opponents knew more in certain fields than their instructors, who stood a little in awe of them. To equip myself for the daily battles, I began to read the literature of protest to protect myself. The revolution came to me first in literary form.

Hauptmann's *Weavers* suddenly presented me with the social conflict from the viewpoint of the starving Silesian textile workers. Ibsen's *An Enemy of the People* suddenly laid bare to me the corruption that takes the form of gentility and respectability. His *Peer Gynt* gave me the permanent image of the twentieth-century man without convictions or faith in anything but success. Chekhov's plays showed me the middle class which had lost the will to survive, charming, futile, and foredoomed. Gorky's *Lower Depths* whispered to me that misery is an international fellowship. Tolstoy's *Fruits of Culture* taught me the hollowness of mere civilized forms without human content, a lesson that was continued in his *Resurrection*. For it was not the Christian parable that impressed me in that novel, but the human suffering in the prisons and the superb court scene in which the mechanics of justice contrast inhumanly with the human foibles of those who are administering it.

In those books, the soul of man uttered its cry against the suffering of the twentieth century, and that cry echoed in my soul. Here was no unfocused liberal scepticism. Here was a scepticism fiercely focused on human institutions. If the cry took this form, if the authors were revolutionists and atheists, the cry issued from their lips because those who might better have uttered it were mute. Long before I had spelled out that fact, I sensed it. Long before I would admit a change, my viewpoint had shifted.

The shift, I think, can be accurately fixed in one small basic concession. It was my growing susceptibility to my opponents' insistence that political democracy is not enough. In a political democracy, they often told me, freedom, in the last instance, is only freedom to starve. Of what use is such freedom to a hungry man? I remember vividly the day when one of my friends laughingly quoted me a line from Anatole France: "The law, in its impartial majesty, forbids the rich, as well as the poor, to beg for bread and to sleep under bridges." I remember it because that smiling irony marked a tiny turning point in my thinking.

In time my strange luncheon companions no longer seemed strange to me. I felt for some of them a strong affection. And through them I had met others on the campus, friends of their childhood with whom they had grown up. Most of these others came from comfortable homes, but shared the same general view of life as my locker room friends. They were also *ernste Menschen.*

Thus began my friendship with Meyer Schapiro, one of the most brilliant minds in many fields I ever met, and one of the most loyal and generous friends I was ever to know. There was also Charles A. Wagner, an authentic lyric poet, now a New York newspaperman who is also my loyal and generous friend. There was Louis Zukofsky, also a poet who was for years my close friend until his poetry achieved a complexity (and perhaps a depth) beyond my comprehension and his friendship passed to Ezra Pound. There was John Waldhorn Gassner, whose personal kindness to me in my student days was very great. For years he had been a literary adviser to the Theatre Guild and was, for a long time, co-editor (with the late Burns Mantle) of the best plays of the current year. There was Irving Kaplan who in those days was engaged in daily philosophical dogfights with Mortimer Adler (whom I came to know better later on). There was Herbert Solow, now one of the editors of *Fortune* magazine, who was later to help me at the time I broke with Communism. There was Clifton Fadiman whom I came to know late in my Columbia experience. He was a friend who did me innumerable kindnesses, who, as an editor for Simon and Schuster, started me on my translating career, and one of those who, during the period of my break with Communism, lent me money. There was also Lionel Trilling, now a professor in the English department at Columbia, who later wrote a novel, *The Middle of the Journey*, in which I figured as one of the characters.

When a Hiss investigator asked him to testify against me in days when powers and personalities were mobilized against me, it was Trilling who answered: "Whittaker Chambers is a man of honor." There were many others.

As our friendships grew, they began to take me into their homes. There was a geographic difference in these houses, but in all was the same unvarying, unbounded hospitality. Although some of my friends lived in the comparative comfort of outlying Brooklyn or the Bronx, others had not risen from the slums and never were to rise. These students also took me into their humble homes, diffidently, with what misgivings and secret shames I understand now better than I did then.

With them I first entered the deep slums. I entered them with a shudder that I could not repress but which I was careful to conceal. I was brought up on the land, and ingrained in me there is a countryman's, even a peasant's, distrust of cities, even those like Baltimore and Washington which I have come to love. New York City I loathe with an unabatable loathing.

Slums fill me with a revulsion so deep that I cannot now pass through them without feeling as if black waters were closing over me.

But a slum is not merely loathesome, or in Marx's phrase "a passively rotting mass." A slum is a mass of wretched people not all of whom by any means consider themselves wretched. A slum is a different nation, with other customs, other ways and values of life. Leave the garbage-cluttered, narrow streets, pass through the grimy, stinking halls of tenements, and there are merely men and women living as best they can their hard and useful lives. So I found the families of my slum-dwelling fellow students.

They were men and women of a palpable goodness that showed in their manner, which, uncouth by standards of etiquette, was refined by natural grace and generosity; and showed in their faces, in which a beauty of the spirit flooding through the eyes, transfigured features in themselves ugly. They were people of intense humility which had the quality of religious purity. Their lives were measured in years of hard, unremunerative labor in conditions often vile and always hard. Their families were circles of affection which often included three generations among which, with no jar or rupture, the oldest were devoutly religious and the youngest were revolutionary materialists. They lived in the night of the slums which does not lift even in the day, and in this night they had guarded the treasure of their goodness and sweetness untouched for ages. So that from them I first learned, not as a line from the Bible, but as a fact of experience, one meaning of the phrase: "The Light shines in darkness." These were indeed the wretched of the earth. But they made the earth seem better to me for their being on it.

The activity of their minds was equal to the labor of their bodies. Ideas were as necessary to them as food. Before I ever read it in Engels, I learned from them that "it is necessary to change the world." They wished to change it not only for themselves, and not chiefly for themselves. This vision included one human race insofar as it suffered and labored. Before I found it in Communism, I assimilated from them that vision of man who has repudiated God, by his own intelligence creating a new world of order, peace, and plenty. For in them, the vision lay close to the spirit of an older vision whose roots were in religion, and retained its spiritual force.

In those circles of light that forced back the darkness of the slums, I found an authentic culture of the spirit that was ages old, a culture of the mind that was cognizant of most of what had been said and thought over the centuries, and modern purpose that was revolutionary. Within its climate, I seemed like a half-formed barbarian blundering among forms and traditions as settled and as fixed as those of the Sung dynasty.

Here the revolutionary tradition was almost as formal and refined as the older cultural tradition of which it was merely an intimation. Here the same man who instructed me in Spinoza and Dostoevsky also described to me in detail how terrorists carried out their acts or revolutionists made jail breaks. There I first heard how Vera Zasulich, outraged because General Trepov had flogged the student Bogolepov, walked up to the General and shot him at point-blank range with a revolver. There I first heard how Prince Peter Kropotkin, distinguished mathematician and geographer, chief of the Tsar's cartological survey of the Amur country, anarchist and revolutionist, made his escape from the Peter and Paul Fortress in St. Petersburg—by calculating mathematically his own movements and those of his guard—while across the street a conspirator gave the signal by playing the violin.

There I first heard of the revolutionary poet, Edelstadt, and learned that most haunting of revolutionary songs:

> *Mein lieber Freund,*
> *Wann ich soll sterben,*
> *Trag an mein' Grab*
> *Ein' reute Fahn'—*
> *Mit den reuten Farben,*
> *Bespritzt mit Blut*
> *Ein Arbeitsmann.**

This was not ideas. This had nothing to do with soapboxes. This was not contrived. This was the voice of the wretched of the earth speaking, simply and tenderly, from the depths of life and death. With it went that song whose melody seemed to constrict the heart in which the imprisoned

---

* My dear friend,
If I should die
Bring to my grave
A red flag—
With red color
Splattered with the blood
Of workingmen.

revolutionist feels in his cell the stir of hope at the sight of the crows returning north with the spring. An immense sense of the realization of struggle gripped me without my even knowing it.

This living tradition of revolution, this tremendous imagery of history settled to the depths of my mind so gently that I felt no displacement of the waters of my mind. There it remained without my ever taking thought of it until the not-distant day when the impact of history made me a revolutionist in turn. Then it rose, like an island thrust in an instant from the sea by the force of a submarine earthquake, so that I was not like a man jumping from one ice cake of revolutionary theory to another—Marx's dogma and Lenin's slogan. I was like a man walking upon the firm earth of a tradition as old as human misery, as fierce as the instinct of struggle against it while the wretched of the earth asked me only to be at one with them in faith, in vision and in humility, so that of us revolutionists it might be said at last that the night of mankind would be a little shorter for our having lived.

One day, in the summer of 1923 (between my sophomore and junior years) I sat reading on a balcony in Brussels on a pleasant little back street that curved down a hill somewhere behind the Belgian Ministry of Agriculture. I was reading Aeschylus' "Prometheus Bound." I suppose I must have read it before in English. If so, it had made no impression on me. But as I began reading it in Leconte de Lisle's French translation, I was stopped by the opening lines almost as if the balcony had dropped off the building: "*Nous sommes arrivés au dernier sentier de la terre, dans le pays Scythique, dans la solitude non foulée*" (We have come to the last path of the world, the Scythian country, to the untrodden wilderness).

My classmate Meyer Schapiro and I had just come out of Germany, where I had seen something for which, as a young American even uncommonly conscious that World War I was an epochal crisis, nothing had prepared me. I had seen not only a country but also a people in ruins. It had begun in mid-Ocean. I was a third-class passenger on the S.S. *Seydlitz*. One day there was a great scamper to the starboard deck. I lined up at the rail with a crowd of homing Germans to watch the *Leviathan* (the former *Vaterland*), bound westward for New York. "That is our ship," a voice beside me snarled. "You took it away from us after the war." Then suddenly the men and women around me burst into song:

Es braust ein Ruf wie Donnerschall
Wie Schwertgeklirr und Wogenprall
Zum Rhein, zum Rhein, zum deutschen Rhein. . . .*

It could have been seen as extremely funny. Most of my fellow passengers were lower-middle classlings—*Kleinbürger*, *petit bourgeois* in most of the least attractive senses of that term. They were of various shapes and sizes, but prevailingly dumpy—the same people who clucked and gurgled over the thick German meals, assuring me that pickled herring was the sovereign preventive of seasickness, sometimes just before making an incontinent dash through the dining-room doors for the deck rail. Moreover, they were on holiday, which meant that they were set up in incongruous tourist caps, golf knickers, and other oddments. But I did not find their singing funny. I knew, in fact, that I was witnessing something fairly momentous, though I did not know just what it was. I did not know that what I was seeing was the certainty that there would be a second World War.

My education quickly picked up in Germany. From Bremen I took the night express to cross to Berlin. I had a

---

* A cry goes up like the roll of thunder,
The clash of swords and the crash of waves
To the Rhine, to the Rhine, to the German Rhine.

ticket for a seat in a third-class compartment. But men and
women were already standing between the facing seats in
the compartments. Through the night, half across Germany,
we stood in the corridor, sometimes sleeping, for we were
wedged in so tight that there was no possibility of falling.
Beside me stood a man who had introduced himself on ship-
board as an Austrian count (Austrian and German counts are
as numerous in those lands as the descendants of Irish kings
in Ireland). He wore knickers and a modified Tyrol hat, and
carried all his possessions in a rucksack. He told me that his
family had lost everything in the war and he had gone to
America to earn a living without much success. I asked him
where the crowds came from. "The French have occupied
the Rhineland," he said. "These are the refugees."

I saw crowds of these Rhinelanders in Berlin, among
whom I remember in particular a man and wife, professional
acrobats. I remember them for their habit of walking on their
hands at unexpected moments and because, unlike most Germans, they seemed always carefree, although so far as I could
see they had absolutely nothing to live on. For the inflation
was on. This was something the like of which Americans
were to know nothing until some seven years later in the
Great Depression. As an American I had traveller's cheques
so that the inflation struck me at first only in the preposterous
exchange of a check for a massive roll of hundreds of
thousands of marks, and in the necessity of eating meals
early because in the matter of an hour the value of the mark
had fallen again, and a meal eaten at one o'clock might cost
a thousand marks more than a meal eaten at noon.

I was in a great city, one of the most orderly and organized
in the world. Here, modern civilization had taken form in big
solid buildings, street lights, streetcars, a flawless subway,
automobiles—all the externals of modern life. Behind those
impressive appearances life had gone mad. I was reminded
of my Grandmother Whittaker's description of an earth-

quake—when the underpinnings of a world give way, the walls fall out and pipes writhe up from the surface of streets like snakes. That had happened in Berlin and all over Germany. But the solid form of things stood firm. The earthquake was invisible or visible only in its effects on the victims.

Well-dressed people walked back and forth on the Kurfürstendamm, like any Fifth Avenue crowd. Suddenly, the tears would stream down a woman's face simply as she walked along—the face of desperation, which asked and expected neither pity nor help, for there was no pity or help because there was no hope. The commonest of sights was to see someone snatch a purse and disappear in the crowd which rushed together for a moment, attracted by the victim's cries, and then walked on again with a shrug.

Some years later I saw a photograph of the Kurfürstendamm. Some of the sidewalk restaurants remained. There were even some people sitting at the tables. Around them were great gaps where bombed and blasted buildings stood, and neat piles of blocks where the retrievable rubble had been tidied up. The line of history that I suddenly felt under my hands in the summer of 1923 ran unfailingly from those weeping women in the street to those gutted buildings.

Sometimes I saw another aspect of the crisis that was even more baffling. There would be little knots of furtive figures selling newspapers at some of the street corners. At the appearance of a green-clad policeman, they would break and run. I was told that they were Communists. The Communist Party was outlawed. They were selling *Die Rote Fahne (The Red Flag)*. I did not know, of course, that the party was even then stockpiling rifles and machine guns for a revolution that was scheduled to break out in the autumn.

Once, I was awakened about three or four o'clock in the morning by a sound of feet softly shuffling and voices singing in a low grunting cadence. I went to the window. I could make out a group of figures marching off the Janowitz

Bridge. I suppose they were Communists returning from some late meeting, or making a surreptitious demonstration at an hour when they thought that the police would be in bed. I could scarcely make out the words of the song, but I never forgot the tune. I was to know both words and tune very well not so long afterwards. They were singing:

> *Schmier die Guillotine, schmier die Guillotine, schmier*
> *die Guillotine*
>
> *Mit Tyrannenfett.*
> *Blut muss fliessen, Blut muss fliessen, Blut, Blut, Blut.* *

I went back to sleep and all but forgot the incident. For, after all, I was in Berlin to see the magnificent Raphaels and all the rest, not to review the insurgence from its netherworld. Yet everywhere I looked there was destruction—the awful desperation that speaks silently from the stricken faces of people.

Meyer Schapiro had worked his way over on a boat and had joined me in Germany. We decided to leave Berlin and go to Belgium. I remember Meyer had to get his papers straightened out and we went to the American Embassy where we found the waiting room filled with quietly desperate men and women seeking to escape Europe's foreclosing future. One woman was almost out of her mind. She was waiting for some kind of official permit to get her into the United States. A suave and dapper young Embassy official emerged from the cool interior of the Embassy. He went up to her and said in a cool Harvard voice: "There is against you, madame, a presumption of expatriation." At the railroad station there occurred another of those perfectly pointless trifles. I asked the ticket seller for tickets to Brussels. "I can't sell you tickets to Brussels," he said. He was angry and incoherent. I insisted. He said: "To the West, I can

---

* Grease the guillotine, grease the guillotine, grease the guillotine
With the fat of tyrants.
Blood must flow, blood must flow, blood, blood, blood.

sell you tickets only as far as Hamm in Westphalia. The
West is blocked—*der Westen ist versperrt*." It was like an
oracle that was to ring in my inner ear for the rest of my
life: the West is blocked. I had never heard of Hamm, an
industrial and division point that the air raids of World
War II left in shambles. "Why can't you sell me tickets
beyond Hamm?" I asked. "*Besetztes Gebiet*," he answered—
"occupied teritory." In this tremendous, civilized Europe, it
was no longer possible to move for armies.

I bought the tickets for Hamm where we arrived in the
dawn. At Hamm, I bought two tickets. They would only
sell them as far as Cologne. "I do not think you can get
through," the ticket seller said. "People are not travelling to
the West."

The train crawled out of Hamm. At the first river bridge,
British troops came on board and made a half-hearted search
of the luggage and examined our passports. The train crawled
on. Belgian troops boarded it. In Cologne were more British
troops. But there I could buy tickets to Aachen on the Belgian
line. All afternoon the train ran under little bridges where
the French Senegalese troops sat with their machine guns
sighting the train. Every station was an encampment of
French soldiers. At one point, just at sundown, the train was
stopped in the open country. The coaches were stopped. A
detail of soldiers and an impressive French officer in a magnificent sky-blue uniform searched the coaches. On some
whim, he ordered Schapiro and me off and stood us under
guard in a field. The train started to move. But the Frenchman was dealing with Americans. "Jump," Meyer said, as
the Liège express gathered speed. We ran after it, wrenched
open a compartment door and swung in—leaving the
astonished officer and his soldiers staring.

All this was in my mind, whirling formless but vivid, as
I read "Prometheus Bound" on the balcony in Brussels. And
there was more. For I had lately gone down to Paris. But

nothing I had seen in that beautiful city had left in me so deep an impression as something I had seen on the way to it. As the train crossed northern France and the old battlefields of 1914-18, I saw in the distance a jagged wedge of wall and the fragments of a bell tower standing above foundations of what had been a town. Someone told me that that was what was left of St. Quentin.

That is why I read and re-read with a sense of new meaning the words: "We have come to the last path of the earth." It was peculiarly right that Aeschylus should have put those words into the mouth of his embodiment of Force.

I carried away from Columbia a mood in which scepticism was only one ingredient—a mood that was by no means peculiar to Columbia. It was shared in one degree or another by practically every intelligence and focus of intelligence in the world, and had been for more than half a century. It was a feeling of despair, not always explicit and seldom definite, but running like a wistful theme through any view of life that was not merely practically ambitious. It was the sense of historical sundown, the sense that man had reached one of the great jumping-off places—or what was worse, a place where it was impossible to jump because it was the end.

I felt, and most of the men I knew and most respected felt, that the world was too old, that it was late in its night, that that night was very dark, man was very far from home, he lacked inner strength to make the effort, and besides the right way was lost. No one quite knew how or why. Something was radically wrong. No one quite knew what. It was useless to seek an answer from any traditional voice (that was part of the despair), for all the oracles were dumb or lied because in the general darkness they could see no better than anybody else what threatened them, but feared it even more. Most people knew that something catastrophic was happening, but no one quite knew what, for one of the symptoms of the catastrophe was the discovery that there was no one left who could see realistically. The power to distinguish between reality and unreality was lost. The more frantically men tried to check the disaster, the more their efforts contributed to it, and the more hopeless they became because they saw how hopeless the task of redemption was.

At the same time, a great number of people—stupid, perversely confident, or personally untouched by the premonitory spasms—continued to assure the world that it was in perfect health if only people would stop worrying, if only they would do the day's work, if they would be more thrifty, if they would think less about pleasure and more about service, if they would practice the good old virtues. The pathos was that there was profound truth in all these exhortations. Those were exactly the things that people should do, and which in their hearts they yearned to do. Only, it does almost no good to tell a man who is trying to keep his balance on a reeling floor in an earthquake that the thing for him to do is to stop sashaying and go back to the good old habit of standing squarely on his own two feet. This is particularly maddening if he does not know what force makes it impossible for him to keep his balance, or what the nature of an earthquake is.

It was not the world of twentieth-century politics but the much more basic, pervasive world of the mind and spirit that I discerned was in extremity. The profound sense of the incurable sickness of the world made all men sick. In this mood, the undergraduate (I) wrote:

> And we on whom its shadow falls—
> A sober and containing air—
> Feel it as tired and late despair
> Between enfolding iron walls.

A generation of writers, the clinicians of every age, fixed the mood and the dimensions of the crisis—in four brack-

ish lines of Edgar Lee Masters' epitaph for the Unknown
Soldiers:

STRANGER: Tell the people of Spoon River two things:
First that we lie here, obeying their words;
And next that had we known what was back of their words,
We should not be lying here!

The mood was not a discovery of our generation. The first
rumblings of catastrophe had been uttered by a generation of
giants by contrast with whom we would clearly trace the
decline of the human condition and the deepening of the
crisis. Ibsen, Tolstoy, Nietzsche, Strindberg, Hauptmann,
Shaw, Hardy, Matthew Arnold, Tennyson had foretold
us.

It was a mood whose temper Oswald Spengler caught
exactly, not so much in his philosophy, which comparatively
few men read, still fewer understood, and many recoiled
from, but in the tremendous poetry in which he asserted his
vision of the crisis of twentieth-century man. It is in almost
every line he wrote . . . The mood was implicit in the title
of his chief work, *The Decline of the West* (written just before World War I), and even more expressive in the German
version, *Der Untergang des Abendlandes*—The Down-Going
of the Evening Land.

By nature, I was much less literary and much more political
than my fellows. That did not mean that my grasp of world
political forces was wide or acute. It meant merely that I was
not satisfied to seek the human condition only in literature,
but sought it also in political manifestations. It was not a
conscious attitude or effort of the mind; it was spontaneous, a
reflex. Instinctively I asked not merely: What is Nietzsche's
place in philosophy from the pre-Socratics to his day? I asked:
What were the conditions in Europe in the nineteenth century
that made possible these perceptions and ideas which found
their expression in Nietzsche? That was a basically different

approach from that of my fellows and was almost certain to lead me into action instead of reflection.

I did not need Marx or Lenin to tell me that the world was in catastrophe, or, what is more important, that the military form of the catastrophe, World War I, despite its massive human and material hemorrhage, had settled nothing at all. It had been sapped to a degree that I was as yet wholly incapable of grasping. But even I could see that with the destruction of the great dynastic empires—Germany, Austria, Russia, Turkey—was destroyed the stability of the West. I could also see that France and Britain had been organically weakened.

In this disaster, in which the whole fabric of civilization was heaving, I reacted violently at last from that climate around me which enjoined doubt rather than faith, and robbed all action of its energy in the name of uncertainty. I did not believe that life is hopeless. With my deepest instinct, I did not want to be told that there are no ways out of catastrophe and that that does not matter in any case, for it is alike indifferent to the sceptical mind how we live and die since good or ill alike are relative. I wanted to know what the nature of the crisis was. I wanted to know the way out. Everything that was alive and strong in me wanted to know those things and I believed in a solution exactly in the degree to which I was alive and strong. To the same degree I became restless. I wanted to know: "Doesn't anybody know why we are in this mess? Is there nobody alive with the intelligence to figure a way out? For God's sake, somebody give me a straight answer." At the same time, the suspicion kept gnawing at the mind that there was an answer, that my so-intelligent instructors knew the answer, knew both what was wrong and what to do about it, but that it was not expedient to give the answer, and that the melancholy of their mood was the despair of men whom expediency forbids to tell the truth.

At that point, the revolutionary mood takes rise with the feeling: Well if there is no answer, if nobody can say what is wrong, or what to do, let us do something anyway. Let us at least smash something, for our condition is a great stagnant pond where life rots in stinking water, and if we do no more than break the banks and let the water out, we will perform a service to life. That is the mood where the anarchist stops. It is the mood in which Bakunin celebrated destruction as a creative act. But only a child's mind or an arrested mind can stop there. A mind, rounding into maturity, whatever its jolts, lags, and lapses, and however much it may recognize destruction as the first phase of any building operation, must seek a constructive purpose. The answer to death is not more violent death. The answer to death must be more complete life.

Columbia College proposed to make me into the image of the educated man of my time. It was perfectly apparent to me, and to a great many of my schoolfellows, that the educated man of my age who might know all about clocks and the time-space concept, did not know how to tell what time it was. And the suspicion grew with familiarity that the educated man was an integral part of the crisis of our age about whose basic nature he knew less than the man who gave one wrench to each nut on an assembly belt. At last the mind cried: "I don't care what Plato thought about the philosophic being. Don't tell me what Aristotle said about the political animal. Tell me why, in the twentieth century, civilization is everywhere in collapse and man is everywhere in despair. For this is not man's age-old despair at dissolution. This is the nightmare despair of men who know the bombers are coming, know that they will be trapped in the rubble of shattered cities, know that their children will be crushed with them, but do not know why or what to do about it."

It made little difference that the vast mass of mankind, in many nations, went about its simple, ordinary, hard-working, good, devoted life. The mass of mankind is in all ages as patient as it is brave. It made little difference that most men asked: "What despair?" or "What has it got to do with us?" or that they asked it with the complacent superiority of the hard-working and the thrifty whom their lot spares tragic insights. They still ask it, especially in the United States. But history has already begun to give their complacent questions the terrible answers of the death of their sons, far away, in lands they have scarcely known of, in the dawning realization that it is no longer possible to plan a life which war and dislocations will not wipe out at any moment; in the knowledge, still scarcely conceded, that the crisis, which other men foresaw or suffered, has now reached them, inescapably, since they cannot flee it because there is nowhere to go.

Lenin said to me:

The old world is dying. The world wars, the economic crisis are its death spasms. In its terrible convulsions it will destroy everything it has created in its history, and everyone within it, especially everyone who seeks to save it.

It has become an empty house, with its walls torn out as in the moment of dissolution it tries to remodel itself along the dreams of its youth. It is a haunted house in which the upper class is like an insane grandmother who walks around with a knife, wearing a sealskin coat which is the symbol of her better days now gone beyond repair. She is persecuted by the memories of her own greatness. The mother and father are divided and the household has been split for years. The father is incapable of love. The mother seeks to dominate through sacrificial love. One son will kill himself in clear perception of the truth, but first he will die of despair. The other son? If he remains in that house, he will die with it. He can only live by fighting it and everything it stands for to his dying breath.*

---

* Chambers is using a very personal symbolism; the household he is describing is the one in which he grew up (See *Witness*).

Lenin said to me:

Look. To every man born into this age, there are two choices—only two. He may stand with the world that is dying. He may take his place in the world that is being born. Which would you choose—the living or the dying? What do you choose for yourself—life or death?

Lenin said to me:

Look, if you choose life, I will demand of you discipline, obedience, hardship, poverty, intelligence and courage.

But in the end, my choice was based, not on the teachings of Marx and Lenin, their historical or economic analyses, or even the faith of Communism and the vision of man's salvation on earth. In the end, I made my choice, because I became convinced that the intelligence and power of the West were no longer able to solve the continuing crisis.

This is an oversimpilfication. But in some similar way this is the form in which the turn toward Communism takes place in the mind of every man or woman who becomes a Communist. It is the crisis that keeps them Communists, sometimes long after dissilusionment or discontent with the realities of Communism have set in. Nor does the ex-Communist, returning to the world that he abandoned as hopeless, have any illusions, if he is intelligent and sincere, about the crisis. He does not return to the world because he believes that it is morally healthy or capable of solving the crisis which in fact is deeper than when he left it. He returns because he believes that Communism is evil. The crisis remains and the world remains unable to solve it.

The
Third Rome

Reality

The first bomb wounded several Cossacks of the Imperial Guard. Tsar Alexander II got out of his carriage to see in person to the care of the wounded men. He even spoke, "not ungently" we are told, to the terrorist who had thrown the bomb, and thanked God that the damage was no greater. "It is too early to thank God yet," said Grinevitsky, and tossed a second bomb between the Tsar's feet. The explosion tore him apart, and killed Grinevitsky. "Home to the Palace, to die there," muttered the dying Tsar.

The incident occurred some twenty years before my generation, that of 1900, was born into a world largely innocent of airplanes, automobiles, wireless, and almost wholly innocent of the fact that we, and our children, were heirs to a general crisis of history of which an episode in St. Petersburg was merely one curious disclosure. But one of an instructive kind, as if a violent hand had lifted a corner of a shade from a window of the Winter Palace, or from any other stately palace anywhere on earth, to reveal not just a quietly lighted room, but that the interior was a raging furnace in which the inmates were beginning to roast alive in various degrees of circling frenzy or resignation, and, in either case, rather futilely, because most of the exits had been locked from outside.

Perhaps it is because so many of us, at least in the Western Hemisphere, have managed not to peek into that interior, to retain, while living through a succession of catastrophes without any precedent of record (the two World Wars for example), so much of that 1900 innocence, that the meeting of Grinevitsky and Alexander II has haunted my mind.

In life there are no hard and fast positions. In life and in nature, reality is in constant flux. In an age like this one, it is in violent flux. We do not have to be revolutionists to know that there are energies within the inner earth that can in a twinkling (as our eyes measure such events) turn solid rock into a molten flowing syrup. During my lifetime, the site of the Mexican volcano Parícutin was a ploughed field—a *campo de labor*, a field of labor, as Spanish puts it. Within a week, those energies under the earth had turned it into a belching mountain and a desolation. The same forces, as we know, though we do not often turn our minds that way, exist outside the earth. Siberia, the ice-bed of Asia, was once a tropical landscape. We know this because Siberian explorers have come upon a deposit of the bodies of mammoths perfectly preserved in the refrigerated soil. We know that their fate overtook them in what we should measure as an instant, because pieces of the palm fronds on which the mammoths had been feeding, twenty thousand years or more ago, were still intact between their teeth. Their flesh was so fresh that it was possible to cut it up, twenty thousand years later, to feed to the sledge dogs. And God? a man cries out instinctively at this moment. Beware of having God too cheaply, of reducing Him to a comfort or a balm, and thereby reducing Him to nothing by willfully depriving His image of those energies that broke Parícutin from the ploughed field and, in a flash or a thud, locked the bodies of the mammoths in the earth for twenty thousand years. In this the ancient Jew hewed closer to the truth than we and puts us to shame. He knew at least that the thought of God is inseparable from the thunder and lightning and of the terror that walks by noonday.

In our time that terror has taken form in the forces of history—our shorthand word to sum up the effects of the play of those forces of reality whose energies are violently shaping our lives. Other ages have known a terror equal to, or a little more than equal to, their powers to endure it. Nine hundred years ago, a line had been added to the liturgy of Catholic churches in many parts of Europe. Men, women and children prayed: "From the Viking terror, Lord, deliver us." In our own time, James Joyce said: "History is a nightmare to which I hope never to wake up." Other ages have known a frightfulness equal to their imagination in inflicting or enduring it. Ours is the first age in which the havoc that men wreak on men has outrun the imagination, which can no longer cope with the plain reality and turns away, helpless, exhausted, and incredulous. Thus, the frightfulness of our reality gives the age its peculiar quality of unreality. Belief breaks in two. The mind cannot bear the reality of our condition. It wishes not to believe it. It turns away from the too-staggering evidence. Some eleven million people perished in the First World War. Do you remember those photographs of the mass death pits of Poland, with men, women, and children heaped higgledy-piggledly, arms, legs, heads obscurely intermixed, as we pile trash before it is hidden by the disembarrassing earth? No, you do not remember them. Their circulation was limited; there was no market for them. You do not remember them. Some Poles remember them. In the West, a few others. We are told that the mercenaries who revolted against the brutality and meanness of Carthage after its first defeat by Rome once came on an astonishing sight. They came upon a road bordered on both sides, as far as the eye could see, by two lines of crosses. On each cross was crucified a lion. A shudder passed through the horde of rebels and they asked one another: "What manner of men are these that crucify even the beasts that prey on their herds?" How childlike, how *literary*, such a spectacle seems by contrast with our own.

Ours is the first age in history in which duly constituted governments, duly recognized by others calling themselves civilized, practise the extermination of their own people by millions, as a matter of calculated policy. Within the lifetime of young men and women who have scarcely reached the age of twenty-one, the Soviet government had exterminated so many of its people that it did not dare publish the census figures; the population, despite all official pressures and inducements to breed, had fallen too steeply below the level of a few decades before. The same government decreed, because its peasants were hiding their grain, that they should be starved to death. So they were, from three to six million of them. The statistics cannot be confirmed. But what can millions more or millions less mean to a mind when a million is a measurement of individuals, each of whom is a unit of agony? I remember a traveller's description of how, at some way station, the children stood below his train window, simply stretching out their arms above their swollen bellies—silently because they had lost the strength or will to say: *"Dyadya, Khleb!"* (Uncle, bread!)—the ageless cry of famine. They did not all die of hunger, for mercy also comes in savage forms. An officer of the Red Army said to me: "Those God-damn peesants" (he could not produce the short a in English). "We had to put the machine guns on the hills and shoot them down." In personal relations, he was among the kindest and most generous men I have known. Here we reach something else—that the terror of our time is often, perhaps generally, inflicted by those who feel horror at what they do. So Czeslaw Milosz tells us that among the secret police in the satellite countries are practicing Catholics; and that by a deliberate effort they put their Catholicism out of their minds when they must commit acts that security police exist to commit. What else can they do? Be killed themselves for refusing to perform an act that someone else will perform anyway? Be killed to no point since no one would know what they had done or what had been done to them? This is the age which, among other achievements, has learned how to disarm that most dangerous of demonstrators—the martyr, the man who, in extremity, finds strength to make use of his last human right, his life, and throws it into the scales of good against evil.

We have been talking about Russians, Poles, Ukranians, the peoples of Europe's eastern reaches, which, when we think of them at all, we think of chiefly as vast pig farms where the people are scarcely distinguished from the pigs unless we make a rather prudish check and force ourselves to think: "Yes, these are people, too, backward, of course." I thought the unconscious viewpoint was well expressed by Allen Dulles, the head of our Central Intelligence Agency, when he said that there seems no reason to suppose that the Russian mind is inferior to ours. The Russian mind that, in one unparalleled continuous spiritual outburst produced Pushkin, Dostoevsky, Tolstoy, Moussorgsky, Mendelev—to keep the list short.

But what of the Germans who were not backward, who, until 1933, were by common consent among the world's three or four most civilized nations? I remember an American, dead now, who went into Poland with the Red Army in World War II to inspect the concentration camp at Maidensk. This was one of those death camps with the tall stacks from which eddied the clouds of soft, sooty smoke, since they were the exhausts of the gas-ovens where the German authorities weekly vaporized its contingent of Jews and others. But it was not the obvious ovens that my reporter stressed. It was the heap of shoes, piled high above his head—of men's shoes and boots, and women's slippers, no bodies (they had been tidily burned), just the shoes that had shod the bodies, and, most horrifying, among the others, the children's shoes. My informant stopped speaking.

And do you suppose that there were not, among the Germans who exterminated these children, men, like the Red Army officer who machine-gunned the "God-damned peesants" —men in personal life kind and generous? It would be a shallow and a simple thought, black and white, absolute good *v.* absolute evil. The tragedy of our time is not simple, and if you think so, it seems possible that you do not know what time you are living in, that in a sense, you are not living in it because you suppose that that tragedy cannot touch you. I think you are mistaken. I think you do not know what realities these horrors are evidence of. For if the mind clenches itself and peers for a moment beyond the human desolation, it must say that this is, above all, evidence. It is such evidence as a great flood brings in nature—ruins of people, cattle, dwellings. It is the energies that lift that flood that we must seek to know if we wish to understand its laws of motion, its causes, inertia, and duration. It is those energies that I call: reality.

The revolutionist understands what that reality is. Whatever mistakes he makes from that point on, he was not mistaken about that. The revolutionist did not make the flood. He sought to guide and channel its forces. By the force of his will to act and his will to understand, he sought to add to mere catastrophe: purpose. If you charged: "You have complicated and increased catastrophe," he will answer: "Which will you have, the purposeless catastrophe of world wars or the purposeful catastrophe of revolution?" We will add: "That is the margin of choice." You might do well to look hard at the history of your own lifetime before you contradict him flatly. "Facts," as Lenin taught us, "are stubborn things."

It was to give purpose to a catastrophe otherwise meaningless that the revolutionist had to overcome the temptation to live. For this he had to overcome the temptation to give life. But terrible is the temptation to live. This, it will be seen, is an echo of Bertolt Brecht's line: "Terrible is the temptation to pity." At root, perhaps, they are the same temptation. Either is fatal to the revolutionist who would grasp the nature of the realities shaping our history, and try to direct them. The revolutionist who cannot overcome those temptations becomes a counterrevolutionist. These positions are the cathode and the anode poles of thought and action in our time. That is why Liberalism, as the term is used among Americans, is simply revolution pursued by other means. While Conservativism, when it means anything at all, is counterrevolution pursued by other means. "Other means" signifies means short of violence. For the central reality of this age is revolution unfolding at every level of life. Let us try to grasp something about that reality.

Slon

In what now seems to me my late childhood (I was perhaps twenty-four years old), I found myself in touch with a little splatter of men and women, which included a Communist, an Anarchist, and a couple of others who were a little of both, which made them nothing at all that can be conveniently tagged by scholars. This was in New York City, and these people were poor with a poverty such as most Americans know does not exist. But if it does exist, we know that it is evidence of a lack of character (*i.e.*, ambition) which amounts to a sin. These acquaintances of mine lived in the depth of the slums.

When I stayed, once or twice, with one of them, we ate our thin borscht and kasha (a porridge made of buckwheat groats sodden with warm milk, which always had for me an aftertaste like the smell of liquid shoe-blacking). The little room I slept in was, I think, windowless. It was certainly airless. And it was difficult to fall asleep there for another reason, too. All night, the high voices of Chinese, of whom there seemed to be a great number crowded into a room in an adjoining tenement, came through the wall and sounded somewhat like the continuous mewing of abandoned kittens.

These Chinese were probably poorer than any poverty that even my poor acquaintances could imagine. Like their hunger, their conversation was interminable; and I supposed that it was a political conversation, that they were arguing the politics of the Chinese Revolution. We sometimes forget that it broke out in 1911, and has been going on, now in one form, now in another, while most of us have been growing old. We forget it, because until the Korean War most Americans did not know that "the mess in China" bore directly on their lives—on the lives of boys and girls growing up in quiet villages which run off into fields where baseball or football are played and the shouts of the players come pleasantly on an air that is heavy in autumn with the smell of burning leaves: the autumn smell of America. The high voices of the disputing Chinese in the slum night made you feel, while you tried to drowse in spite of them, as if you were in a Chinese quarter of Moscow.

So, in a sense, you were. For all of the older people I have mentioned were Russian, though they came, not from Moscow, but from Minsk or Pinsk or Verkhne-Udinsk. And they still lived in those places. They only existed on the banks of the East River.

One of them, the Communist, then seemed to me a man of great age (he was probably in his fifties). I remember him as a big-boned man. More likely, he was simply physically solid and temperamentally stolid. I do not think he was fleshy. Few of these people ever ate what Americans would call "a square meal." Instead, they chiefly drank—oceans of coffee (vile) and tea (strong)of which they kept the makings in a small, metal pot of "*sens*" (essence, I suppose).

The Communist is dead now, and I have forgotten his name.

So I will call him Slon, because that is the Russian word for elephant, though it is not pronounced "Sloan" but more like "slawn." Slon was Jewish. He was, in fact, the gross caricature of a Jew that frightens anti-Semites in their dreams, and of which on waking (and perhaps to exorcise it) they sometimes draw pictures. Slon had extremely thick lips, spoke an uncouth English full of phlegmy gutturals; and his face was set in an expression of permanent anger. To a young American, there was something goatish about him.

But there was something else that anti-Semites always miss. Slon would sit still for long whiles, almost completely still, staring, not into space, but into his thoughts. Eventually, he would glance up at you with a shy smile—a child's smile, you thought. But then you realized that it was not the smile of a child. It was a smile that was saying grace upon whatever Slon's thoughts had been. It said that the world was really an enchanting place, if only there were not people in it, if only men would let it be enchanting. It said more. It was a smile of the Semitic East. It summed up who knows what circling surveys of the Asian and North African past, and solitudes of waste sands. It looked past the ugly clots of slum, and New York's human and motor traffic, and, if it saw them at all, absolved them. It said without words: "Hear, O Israel, the Lord our God, the Lord is One."

This man was an atheist. A nineteenth-century atheist, to boot, whom Darwin had, one day, struck with a blinding revelation in which the image of the First Great Ape, our shambling ancestor, had once for all displaced Adam, just as the interminable trial-and-error coagulation of *Urschleim* (the primitive first jelly out of which evolved life) had displaced the great command: Let there be Light! For this man's mind was a caricature, too. I suppose that he had never had more than five or six years (if so much) of anything approaching formal schooling—probably in some unheated Russian ghetto school(he was grown when he reached the United States) with a little clump of pupils, chanting in chorus after their rabbi-teacher: "*Aleph, beth*" (A, B). But the fact that Slon was an aggressive atheist while his smile said, "The Lord our God, the Lord is One," will seem a paradox only to those literal minds which do not know that people often are—that life perhaps proceeds by—paradoxes.

Most of all, this man was a follower of Auguste Comte. Of course, a Communist cannot be a Comtist. But that is another paradox. Slon managed to be both. Despite his penury, Slon had amassed a considerable library of books by Comte or about him. How many days without eating anything at all the purchase of those books must have represented—books immaculately kept, dry almost to the point of unreadability, but for this man having the power of the speck of radium invisible in the ugly lump of pitchblende.

Comte's name is not often heard nowadays, for reasons which I do not understand. Yet I think it is not too sweeping to say that Comte has a throne in the modern mind. To most eyes, it appears to be vacant, so that we are startled, now and again, to catch an initiate making a furtive genuflection toward it. I should suppose that most American liberals, and almost all social scientists are, at least in part, Comte's progeny. But theirs is a derived, adapted, a filtered, and perhaps largely unconscious Comtism. Comte was not only an aggressive rationalist who began by ruling out of man's observation of experience all religious and metaphysical notions. Comte professed the "religion of humanity." He attempted to found a rationalist church, organized painstakingly, pedantically, on the Catholic model, but with faith in sociology supplanting religious faith, and the saints literally displaced from their niches by such secular benefactors of the race as Sir Isaac Newton. Slon, this devoutly irreligious man, professed the "religion" of Comtism in that arid form and with the abstracted fervor of an Indian holy man. Man, who every day of Slon's life, disenchanted Slon's world for

him, was transfigured in Slon's thoughts. There, man became
God.

Comte had worked this miracle for Slon, this most pathetic
of all the paradoxes whose sum was Slon. All miracles would,
I suppose, be essentially simple if only we could grasp the
point where their complexities unify to one focus of pure,
effective force. This miracle was simple, too. The clue to its
mystery lay at the point where Slon did not wish to disbelieve
in men; where he wished to have faith in men, despite a lifetime of experience of them. At that point Comte whispered
to Slon: "Have faith in me, and I will give you back your
faith in man." For man is only of necessity vile. We have
only to use our heads to become as souls again. But first we
must chip away all the nonsense with which man's mind has
defaced his use of the word "soul." That done, the streets of
New York City, or Minsk or Pinsk or Verkhne-Udinsk, will
be seen to swarm with potential angels, who only appear to be
bill collectors, insurance salesmen, policemen or pushcart
peddlers, needle trades bosses and workers, or housewives
desperate with the arithmetic of daily living which balances
the price of an onion against the price of a subway fare needed
to take a child to a shabby park, or to the end of the line where,
at the extreme limit of the crushing city, there is an illusion of
air and space—an illusion that (once bought instead of the
onion) is always sourly known to be just that: illusion, making the reality, by contrast, that much harder to bear. "Believe on me," said Comte to Slon, "and all these weary, dreary
multitudes will no longer simply be trampling one another
under, as they pursue, like rush-hour crowds at Grand Central Station, their dismal destinies toward a horizon which
is, above all, pointless, is not even a sundown, is simply:
Nothing." "Hope," Comte whispered to Slon, "can be real
only if it is rational; then hope and faith become one."
At that point, Slon fell forever on his knees before Comte,
muttering his guttural gratitude, never for a moment sus-

pecting that this, too, was a posture of prayer, that his abject thanks, whose sense seemed so much the contrary, said the same thing as his smile: "Hear, O Israel, the Lord our God, the Lord is One."

Slon also read Spinoza, Averroës, and Maimonides as others read breviaries. He read them by the hour, hunched over on a tall, supremely uncomfortable stool, directly under the best light there was—the ruinous light of a low-watt electric bulb. He read them with the fierce concentration of the self-taught, for whom the sense of every sentence, every word, must be won as a battle is won, by an effort whose intensity causes even the lips to move.

When a boy, I was stopped as by a miracle the first time I actually saw how a mushroom, so soft that a baby could mash it by closing his fingers on it, will, in its effort to reach light and fulfill the meaning of its life, force up a slab of concrete. From Slon I learned again how the mind, trapped in poverty, ugliness, night, will, for much the same reason, do much the same thing; though like the mushroom it may become a little lopsided from the effort. I never think of Slon, reading on his bookkeeper's stool, without also thinking of a campus on Commencement Day—the procession of black-gowned, mortar-boarded graduates, and the billowing robes of scholars with the various colors of their hoods brightly professing the degrees of their attainment—all moving solemnly through sweeps of lawn, past stately trees and halls, with the chapel bell tolling. In my fancy, it seems to me that that procession can be moving only toward one logical end—the moment when, by common impulse, they drop to their knees before Slon, grotesque on his stool, as Slon fell to his knees before Comte. But then, Slon would be too buried in his books or his thoughts to notice them.

For Slon was the thing itself: the raw thrust of the mind, groping, like roots, through dirt, through rubble, to light.

Slon had a small son to whom he was devoted with a

hovering, meddling, ferocious intensity that few American fathers would dream of or permit themselves. He was instructing this unhappy child in strict rationalist principles, teaching him not merely that scepticism is a useful probing tool of the mind, the beginning of wisdom, but also that all the wisdom there is is scepticism. The child was, I think, altogether the most ill-tempered, odious brat that I have known. Even in those days, he was already, I believe, enrolled in the Pioneers, the children's formation of the Communist Party; and while, as I have said, a Communist cannot be a Comtist, at least Comte had got him off on the right foot.

The strict sceptical discipline once paid off in a rather unexpected way. There was an eclipse, or partial eclipse, of the sun; and Slon took his son to the tenement roof to observe this grand celestial demonstration of physical laws at work, immutably free of metaphysical clutter. The moon, or whatever it was, duly passed between the sun and the earth. The world grew still and chill. The little monster looked. But, suddenly, he threw down his smoked glass, stamped his feet, and screamed, "It's a fake!" Slon liked, occasionally, to tell this story on himself, again with the shy smile, but also, it seemed to me, with a certain wonder as of a man who has been plunged unexpectedly into an atmosphere where there has been revealed to him, not only the orderly procession of the planets, but that there is a scepticism of scepticism.

Slon and the Anarchist once kept a little shop. It was located on a street of roaring traffic, a slowly crawling mass of drays, vans, cars, and constantly honking horns because the traffic was constantly clotted or blocked. The shop window was so cluttered that almost no light got through. Not many shoppers had the hardihood or the curiosity to penetrate that dim interior. Those who got in quickly left, and the shop presently went bankrupt. This unhelpful attitude of the shoppers was chiefly their own loss. For that dark, uninviting shop was only a front—not, I hasten to add, a front for anything subversive. (Slon's Communism was of the most hypothetical and passive kind, scarcely more than a habit, like his tea-drinking —routinely convivial or warming, and an aid to diuresis.) The shop was a pretense (necessary since one must pretend to live somehow) of earning a living.

But to eyes that could penetrate its dimness, it was something else. It was the mouth of that pit, which, when the unexpected slab has been lifted (in *The Arabian Nights*), leads the solitary explorer down a flight of cobwebby steps, through winding tunnels, until, in an amazed moment, he comes upon the room where, together with the baskets of precious stones, have been buried for ages the Singing Bird and the Fountain of Living Water. These treasures existed, of course, only for those who could distinguish them from old tin pots, heaps of work clothes, and the drip of a leaky faucet. They existed, for those who could read them there, only in the minds of Slon and the Anarchist.

Coming out of one of his long silences, Slon glanced at me one day with one of his shy smiles. Where had his thoughts been? One can only guess that they had been back in his own boyhood, far from the ugly New York street outside the window, though in streets just as ugly in their own style, but which memory had touched with the beauty and the pathos of what has once been known but never will be seen again.

Slon began to tell me how a peasant of the Moscow countryside prepares to go to the town to sell something—some wretched keepsake that will yield him, in his need, a few kopecks, or a few roots, or a necessary animal. If he sleeps at all before the great adventure, he wakes in his hut in the dark night. He walks till dawn. Then, in the breaking day, perhaps from the Sparrow Hills, he sees the first light strike the city's towers, the domes and turrets of the Kremlin, with their two-armed crosses (the slanted cross, the symbol of Christ's broken bones)—and the neighboring domes of St. Basil's. Those are the domes that Henry Adams called: "The turnip with its root in the air," when he visited Moscow in the summer of 1901. What he saw did not please Henry, who noted that "the turnip with its root in the air" is no improvement on "the turnip with its root in the ground."

Slon's peasant felt differently. At the sight of those golden domes, shimmering in the morning air, he always took off his dirty cap, bowed his verminous head, and said:

> *Moskvá, Moskvá,*
> *Zolotaya golová!**

Thus, I learned that Slon the irreverent, knew what reverence is.

From this man I also first learned something else that I was not to hear again for many years, and not to understand, of course, when I heard it then. One day, Slon told me, in connection with his peasant and glancing at me a little askance, that there are some who hold that Moscow is the Third Rome —"*Tretii Reem.*" This is a Slavophile concept, and the counting goes like this. The First Rome was the Empire, whose heirs were the Middle Ages and the Roman Catholic Church. The Second Rome was Byzantium, whose heir is orthodox slavdom and those upside-down turnips flaring in the morning sun. The Third Rome is to be the Muscovite universal state, which will once again unite all men in a common realm and a new faith. The Third Rome will be greater than the other Romes for it will include all mankind.*

---

* *Moscow, Moscow,/Golden head!*

† Nicholas Berdyaev in his *The Origin of Russian Communism* (London: Geoffrey Bles, 1937) wrote:

After the fall of the Byzantine Empire, the Second Rome, the greatest Orthodox state in the world, there awoke in the Russian people the consciousness that the Russian Muscovite state was left as the only Orthodox state in the world and that the Russian people was the only nation who professed the Orthodox Faith. It was the Monk Filofei who expounded the doctrine of Moscow as

This is an *idea* only to the minds of Pan Slav propagandists. But as a feeling it lodges deep in the Russian Communist spirit. No doubt, it lodges in the deeper folds of many Russian Communist minds no more incongruously than did Slon's nationalist principles that coexisted peacefully with, "the Lord our God . . . is One." Incongruously, because at its roots, the concept of the Third Rome is religious. It touches profoundly a conviction that the Russian is inherently good, as compared with the West, which has become wicked; is sound, in a primal moving sense, as compared to the West, which is old and exhausted.

Years after Slon had passed completely out of my life, I was to come upon the Third Rome (though the term is not expressly used) in Fyodor Dostoevsky's novel, *The Possessed.* This is among the most Russian of books, and more can be learned from it about Communism and that greater manifestation, the Russian Revolution (to cite the least of its meanings) than from libraries of works about Marxism.

"Do you know," cries Shatov, the defected revolutionist, (in that section of the book called "Night"), "do you know who are the only 'God-bearing' people on earth, destined to regenerate and save mankind in the name of a new God, and to whom are given the keys of life and of the new world?" And Stavrogin answers, faintly contemptuous (like Slon he is a rationalist): "From your manner I am forced to conclude, and I think I may as well do so at once, that it is the Russian people."

"Not a single nation," Shatov goes on, "not a single nation

---

the Third Rome. He wrote to the Tsar Ivan III: "Of the Third new Rome . . . Of all kingdoms in the world, it is in thy royal domain that the holy Apostolic Church shines more brightly than the sun. And let thy Majesty take note, O religious and gracious Tsar, that all kingdoms of the Orthodox Christian Faith are merged into thy kingdom. Thou alone, in all that is under heaven, art a Christian Tsar. And take note, O religious and gracious Tsar, that all Christian kingdoms are merged into thine alone, that two Romes have fallen, but the third stands, and there will be no fourth. Thy Christian Kingdom shall not fall to the lot of another."

has ever been founded on principles of science or reason. There has never been an example of it, except for a brief moment, through folly. Socialism is from its very nature bound to be atheism, seeing that it has from the very first proclaimed that it is an atheistic organization of society, and that it intends to establish itself exclusively on the elements of science and reason. Science and reason have, from the beginning of time, played a secondary and subordinate part in the life of nations; so it will be till the end of time. Nations are built up and moved by another force which sways and dominates them, the origin of which is unknown and inexplicable: that force is the force of an insatiable desire to go on to the end, though at the same time it denies that there is an end. It is the force of the persistent assertion of one's own existence, and a denial of death. . . ."

The Russian mind which feels these things was long in conflict with that part of the Russian mind that had felt the influences of the West; and so it is still. Before the Russian Revolution, that Westernized Russian mind believed that Russia was a collapsing, rotted strawrick. Even so, it shared a common Russian conviction that Europe was more deeply doomed. We hear both voices (also in *The Possessed*) in the words of Karamazinov, Dostoevsky's caricature of the Westernized Russian novelist, Ivan Turgenev. He is speaking to a nihilist leader about Europe: "If the Babylon out there [Europe] really does fall, and great will be the fall thereof (about which I quite agree with you, yet I think it will last my time), there's nothing to fall here in Russia, comparatively speaking. There won't be stones to fall, everything will crumble into dirt. Holy Russia has less power of resistance than anything in the world. The Russian peasantry is held together somehow by the Russian God, but, according to the latest accounts, the Russian God is not to be relied on, and scarcely survived the Emancipation [of the serfs]; it certainly gave Him a severe shock. And now what with railroads . . .

Holy Russia is a country of wood, of poverty—and of danger;
the country of ambitious beggars in its upper classes, while
the immense majority live in poky little huts . . . Everything
here is doomed and awaiting its end. Russia as she is has no
future."

This was written between 1870 and 1872. Now it has the
ring of prophecy, especially if we add Karamazinov's words
a few lines later on: "To look facts straight in the face is
only possible to Russians of this generation. No, in Europe
they are not yet so bold; it is a realm of stone and there is
still something to lean on."

But Europe did not remain what it was. The future came
on in forms that Karamazinov and Dostoevsky imagined all
too well. But at the same time, the Third Rome took forms
that both would have found unimaginable.

Still, the deep sense of redemptive mission implicit in
Shatov's words is the bloodstream of the Third Rome. I have
seldom known a Russian who did not, in one degree or another, share that sense however it was dissembled, however
he dissembled it from himself. But at the shadowy depth
of the Russian mind where the springhead of the Third Rome
wells out, shaded by slanting birch, firs, and springing mushrooms, the Third Rome is not a vision of Russia conquering
the world. That is only a form which, as we know, reality
sometimes regrettably takes. The promise of the Third Rome
is the dream of the Russian people redeeming mankind.

I knew Slon only for a brief time. He came into my life
as abruptly and passed out of it as completely as if he had
simply sunk. Presently somebody told me that he was dead.
There is a Russian legend about the Lake City of Kitezh.
Beseiged by the Tartars, the people of Kitezh prayed to God
to save them from the Mongol fury. And so it happened, in
a rather unexpected way. One morning, the Mongols found

that the City of Kitezh was gone. It had been transported to
the bottom of the lake on which it had stood. But even yet,
so the legend goes, in certain lights, the Orthodox people
can make out, dimly, the towers and houses of Kitezh at the
bottom of the lake, and, in certain sets of the wind, can hear
its bells, tolling faintly below the water. So Slon sank below
the surface of my mind and lay there all but forgotten, though
certain effects of light or sets of wind brought to mind, for
an instant, his memory and the memory of the Third Rome.

This began to happen when my first contacts with Russian
Communists compelled me to note there is something about
Russian Communism and Communists that makes both
radically different from Western Communism and Communists. In those days, too, Russian Communists, after observing me narrowly, used to say sometimes: "You are a
peasant, simply a Russian peasant." I used to resent this
then because it seemed to question my Communist orthodoxy,
to reject me arrogantly from the club. But I had presently
to note too that it worked out in quite an opposite way. Far
from implying a rejection, the charge of unorthodox peas-
antness seemed, on the part of Russian Communists, to bind
me to them with peculiar closeness. And it is this that I felt
for those aliens, and they appeared to feel for me, that special
closeness that begins at a point beyond all that which commonly impedes human relationships—all those things which
do not have to be described, explained, defined because they
are already understood. I do not know why this was so. I can
only say that it seemed so.

Later on, during World War II, the Third Rome recurred
again because I thought I saw, as a consequence of the War
and the Post-War era, the onset of its triumphant course, and
I wished the West to block it. Then I began, consciously
but at random, to read into the history of the vision of the
Third Rome. For in it I sensed the secret both of the special
quality of Russian Communism and of the future.

Still later, it was as if I looked up one day, as Slon used to look up from his thoughts, and saw the outlines of the Third Rome clearly looming out of darkness, as Slon's peasant saw Moscow. I did not snatch off my cap or do reverence, not only because the towers and crosses were now gone, or completely overshadowed by a most forbidding modern architecture. The Third Rome had changed its form, but not its inward meaning. I saw now an empire of some 800 million people. It was organized as a giant cartel, without counterpart in history, commanding millionfold armies and efficient energies of modern scientific and technological power, together with the brains to imagine, make, and use these. Commanding, too, the productive power of millionfold workers, working of necessity for subsistence wages. Commanding, too, by reason of its messianic energies, the power to recruit the allegiance of others in all the lands of the earth. And all that complex of power at every level was guided by collective mind, one board of directors—the Presidium of the Soviet Communist Party and its technical boards, sitting in Moscow and abetted by the subsidiary directors of Soviet China and the Soviet satellites.

In the whole world there was only one other energy mass which could match or offset that one—the United States of America. What man could doubt that the history of the rest of this century and much of the twenty-first century would be lived in terms of the powers of attraction and repulsion between those two planetary masses? This must be true whatever forms attraction and repulsion took. But here I must state dogmatically my view that coexistence is a child's dream—a dream of the childhood of the West, in part because the people of the West are hopeful and good in the way that children are; in part because that childhood of the West is a second childhood. But for Euro-Asia coexistence is not a dream; it is a part of the necessity imposed by the state of weapons (offensive weapons are once more stronger than defensive weapons; this swing is recurrent in history). Necessity takes other forms too.

Two such masses of clenched power can never coexist peacefully. Proximity, the forces of attraction and repulsion, are always at work in the effort of each mass to reduce the other, to reduce what each feels as the threat of the other. Even peace is only one of the forms in which that effort at reduction works. It may be expected to work more successfully for the one that is most conscious, knowing, and deliberate about the stakes involved.

Thus, late in life, I found myself unexpectedly close to a climax of that view of history which I had begun to hold at the age of twenty-two, and which I have never had reason to change essentially through the radical changes of my life. It was unexpected chiefly because I had not expected to live to see it. History had outrun my timing of it. It was unexpected for another reason. While I, like thousands of others, had foreseen history's main lines of force and their probable interaction, few, if any, could have foreseen the details in which that interaction would work out; few would have tried to. For history had outrun in frightfulness anything that anybody could have dreamed of in 1923.

Two journeys it is necessary to have taken in our life, in this time, to experience the meaning of what has happened: The Rhine Journey and the Steppe Journey—the journey into the heart of Europe, and the journey into the heart of Russia.

I began with the Rhine Journey. It was by way of the ruins of Europe (I do not mean only the physical ruins of the West) that I entered into that further journey to the Communist steppes.

The Narod

Henry Adams was a historical seer such as few peoples
have produced. He made the kind of sweep through Russia
that Americans since have made by the score, and have
written books about.*

---

* Most of those books can be filed for reference, chiefly factual,
where not openly or secretly biased. An exception: *Russian Assign-
ment* by Vice-Admiral (Ret.) Leslie Stevens, our naval attaché in
Moscow shortly after World War II. To a degree beyond any handy
classification we can make of it, Admiral Stevens has a sensitivity to
all things Russian, beginning with a command of the shades of meaning of the language, exceptional in any non-Russian. He is what every
true observer should be and seldom is—first of all a sharer. This rare
quality is most evident in his more casual comments. Here, the oneness of what is seen and the man who sees it are so complete that such
passages seem all but random, though, of course, they cannot be. But
such moments, together with sharp insights into character and motive
which are those of an American man-of-the-world, add up to a total
evocation in which the vastness of the Russian land (glimpsed as
swift alternations of beauty and squalor, and viewed under the special
effects of Russian sky and light), and the special quality of Russia's
people (their multiplicity in unity, their profound religiousness side
by side with that quality of *khitrost*—a cunning that is animal without specific animus—blend into a total mysteriousness, which is, never-

But the comparatively few lines that Adams wrote about Russia must, it seems to me, be read and re-read, not as final truth but as a clue to truth, insofar as truth about Russia can be refracted through an American mind. Whoever wishes to understand Russia must, perforce, begin with Henry Adams' comments, though he may, in time, leave them behind, amending some, rejecting much. For Henry Adams had a temper of mind uncommon anywhere. That kind of mind seldom if ever dismisses or disregards anything it sees. But it peers through to reach the principles of force that make what it sees, what it is. It gropes for meaning, which will be lasting, under the visible forms which are constantly fleeting or passing away.

This is what Henry Adams saw in Russia: "From the car window, one seemed to float past undulations of nomad life—herders deserted by their leaders and herds—wandering waves stopped in their wanderings—waiting for their winds or warriors to return and lead them westward; tribes that had camped like Khirgis, for the season, and had lost the means of motion without acquiring the habit of permanence. They waited and suffered . . . Their country acted as a sink of energy, like the Caspian Sea, and its surface kept the unity of ice and snow. One Russian, kissing an ikon on a saint's day, in the Kremlin, served for a hundred million . . . The Russian people could never have changed—could they ever be changed? Could inertia of race, on such a scale, be broken up or take new form?"

Henry Adams' lifetime overlapped my own by eleven years (he died in 1912). The forces that would answer his questions for him were just coming into play, beyond his field of vision, when he put his questions. It was Lenin and

---

theless, a reality). No other American (to my admittedly limited knowledge) has felt, or communicated, this peculiar understanding with such full or casual art. That is why this book, of all books about Russia and its people written by Americans in our time, is to be cherished.

his co-conspirators who would act upon that Russian mass "to lead them westward" again, not by changing their inertia of race "on such a scale," but by re-directing that inertia in such a way as to change it from an inertia of rest to an inertia of motion, liberating thereby the momentum inherent in such mass.

Adams was much too good a head to stop with a question. The Russia he saw in 1902 acted upon his intellectual nerves like a historical shock. He left it in a kind of flight. He escaped to Scandinavia, which he found more tidily like his native New England. There, at that frozen limit of the world, in the eerie White Nights of sub-Arctic Norway where burned, nevertheless, the power of "an electro-magnetic civilization," Adams peered back at what had shocked him in Russia and drew certain conclusions from what he had seen. "The image was that of the retreating ice-cap—a wall of archaic glacier, as fixed, as ancient, as eternal, as the wall of archaic ice that blocked the ocean a few hundred miles to the northward, and more likely to advance. Scandinavia had been ever at its mercy. Europe had never changed. The imaginary line that crossed the level continent from the Baltic to the Black Sea, merely extended the northern barrier-line. The Hungarians and Poles, on one side, still struggled against the Russian inertia of race, and retained their own energies under the same conditions that caused inertia across the frontier . . . Germans, Scandinavians, Poles and Hungarians, energetic as they were, had never held their own against the hetero-geneous mass of inertia called Russia, and trembled with terror whenever Russia moved."

"Adams," said Adams, "had never before met a *ne plus ultra*, and knew not what to make of it." So he made this of it: he foresaw that the decisive moment of our history would be reached when the energy of Russian inertia met American nervous energy. He foresaw, almost at the same moment, that if Russian inertia should overspread China, the little drama of history would end in the overthrow of our clumsy Western civilization. He set an approximate date for the event: 1950.

What Adams did not understand (after all, he could not know everything) was the degree to which Russian inertia was embodied in a particular force—the cult of the Russian people, including certain mysterious beliefs that that people held about themselves. He did not understand, either (how was Henry Adams to know about what revolutionists were thinking in Russian cells and cellars or in dingy rooms in half a dozen Western cities?), how, by manipulating history, men would manipulate those mysterious beliefs. It is that cult of the people we must now turn to, for it is one of the motive forces of the Third Rome. It is well to remember, too, that the words "cult" and "beliefs," if vague, are still too definite to describe what we are dealing with here—something so intangible yet so effective that it suggests more properly what physics would call a "field of force."

Somewhere, in a passage which retains the power of anything truly seen, Max Eastman describes the singularly arresting quality of Russian faces. He tells how, in a crowd, on a bus, the eye is suddenly caught and stopped by the face of some old man or young woman, who except for their faces appear no different from anybody else. The arresting quality of those faces is that they look as if the people they belong to were capable of walking calmly up to the mouth of cannons. For those in the West, where experience does not, in general, include walking up to cannons, this is something difficult to understand and possibly even to believe. It has the romantic ring. Yet Eastman is reporting literally. But he is writing of Russia in the period following the 1917 Revolution, so that he sees in such faces the revolutionary type at its best. He is not mistaken about that, either. Variations of this type occurred among terrorists, nihilists, anarchists, especially (in our time) among Socialist Revolutionaries (the party of the peasants). They occurred even in the ranks of the Russian Communist Party up to the Great Purge. It was precisely that type that the Purge was intended to kill off because it was a type on which conformity cannot be enforced—Communist conformity or any other. So it is natural that such types should have occurred especially among worker-Bolsheviks, those of proletarian or peasant origin, and that they should have been found largely first among the anti-Leninist, then among the anti-Socialist Oppositions.

But this type of face is not simply a revolutionary type. Among Russians it is a type common to a degree quite unimaginable in the West. It is the type of the best of the *narod* (the people). With whatever special firmness the revolutionary experience may have shaped it by way of discipline or devotion, basically the type is shaped by a prior experience which results from the profoundest feelings of the Russian peasant at his best. Those feelings are best expressed, however inadequately, in the form of two beliefs: the Kingdom of God is within you; a reign of righteousness and justice is possible on earth. And amidst injustice and suffering, the peasantry guards this secret within itself. One day, the earthly reign of righteousness and justice will be realized; and the peasant has been put on earth to bring it about. This is the deepest meaning of the Third Rome, underlying and surviving all the corrupt earthly form in which the Third Rome seeks to assert itself. Such, to echo the Russian phrase, is the promise. This bears directly on the peculiarly Russian cult of the *narod* as the God-bearing part of mankind; for that peculiarly Russian concept, God-bearing, Russian has a special word: *bogonosets*. In Russia, the peasants are felt by other Russians to be God-bearing in a way that sets them apart from the rest of mankind. The Russian peasants feel this themselves. When it is remembered that at the turn of the century 75 per cent of Russians were peasants (and that this ratio probably persisted in this century), it is clear why the peasants in particular are felt to be the people, the *narod;* although it is almost as difficult for the mind of the industrialized, rationalized West to imagine a vast empire, 75 per cent of whose people are peasants, as it is for the West to imagine anything as vague or unlikely as "God-bearing" applied to peasants who as often as not were illiterate, sometimes in rags, sometimes crawling with vermin. Still, it is necessary to try to get at the nature of these strange people who now confront us, subtly transformed as they are in terms of historical force. It is necessary to try to grasp, so far as words and imagination can, how it came to be as it is, how it feels about itself.

"We are 'the dark people,' " Russian peasants used to say about themselves. "We live in 'the dark villages.' " *Tyomnu narod* (the dark people), *tyomnu cyelu* (the dark villages). There is a strain of sadness about the word *tyomniem,* dark, such as most of us feel (if we think about it at all) at nightfall; and a strain of fear, which "the lights of an electromagnetic civilization" have flooded out of the Western mind. Yet most of us felt the sense of that Russian strain as "a child's fear of the dark"; and this, I suppose, is not only because darkness takes away for a time our safeguarding sight, but has its roots, past discovery, along a racial memory of a time when the onset of night was literally terrifying because night swarmed with beasts of prey (animal and human) whom only a fragile fire before a cave mouth kept at bay. Perhaps it goes back farther, to a time when each nightfall stirred a little panic in the hearts of primitive men; but this was a return of a universal darkness—Milton's "Chaos and old Night"—against which the creative command, "Let there be Light!" might not prevail.

But there is a deeper strain, too, in those words "dark people," "dark villages." It derives from the strength that almost any life feels from settling firmly close to its roots. There is a sense of mystery as a fastness, and of village as fastness—a stronghold planted in the soil it rests on from which those within peer out, or swarm out. Russian peasants do not speak of their farms, lands, holdings, as Europeans or Americans do. These words are alien to the Russian mind which instead speaks of "the village," *cyelo*, where we might say "farms" or "countryside." The Russian peasants do not live in separate farmsteads, but in villages from which they go forth to work their fields. That village life was instinctively collective long before Communism, so that to Americans, Russian village life (and even Russian city life) seems uncomfortably like the clumping together of tent caterpillars in a web. This collectivity is also felt as a fastness, a communal stronghold.

"We are the dark people, we live in the dark villages," the peasants used to say. They also used to say: "We are the Orthodox people." They did not say, "We are the Russian people," because their religion, rather than any political term, was felt to be the mark of their nationality. It was as the Orthodox people that they thought of themselves—a nation whose oneness in faith, blood, and soil set them off against all comers. In this they were more like a horde in the Mongol sense than any European nation, but a horde peopling immense distances beneath a crushing violence of extreme cold and heat, and crushing human violence. And the distances distilled their own kind of silences. Silence and distance, and the kind of soul shaped by them and capable of enduring them—this, too, is part of the Russian oneness. Horizon is another. This is, to the Russian eye, not only a horizon of the swallowing steppes (by no means all of Russia is steppe). But it is also a sense of space, receding continentally— "whither eyes look"—north to the Arctic ice, east to the Pacific Ocean, south until sight is lost against the barriers of some of the world's highest and wildest mountains—always an infinity of distance matched by a perpendicular infinity of sky. Anton Chekhov said that the best description of the sea he had ever read was written by a Moscow schoolboy: *"More bolshoi* (the sea is vast)." Euro-Asia is vast. And this vastness, now somnolent, now violent, is drained by great, somnolent Russian rivers or the sometimes violent rivers of Siberia. It is crossed, too, by other vastnesses where mind and eye lose themselves—barrens like the Barabinskaya Steppe, deserts shrivelingly hot in summer, petrifying with winter cold, belts of conifer forest, silent taiga which is permanent swamp because sunlight cannot penetrate the trees to dry up the forest floor—beyond that tundra where vegetation stunts or dies away toward the annihilating north. Only to the coast is distance blocked and infinite vision checked by the comparatively puny caps of Europe. This is a block more effective than the Asian mountain walls. Europe forever challenges, fascinates, and repels Euro-Asia. But Euro-Asia does not look toward Europe except sporadically. Europe is alien.

Euro-Asia looks elsewhere. Those perspectives of space are matched by a perspective of time and history toward which the Russian eye has peered since it became aware of history. It is a horizon as alien to the mind of the West as the West is alien to Euro-Asia. Only the scholars or certain artists of the West peered that way. The West is not at home there. On that strange horizon, the Russian eye sees, flaring in imagination, the domes and minarets of the Second Rome—Byzantium (Constantinople, now Istanbul), by which Christendom and culture reached the steppes. It is a legendary vision, and the Russian does not call it Byzantium. He has his own special word for it: Tsargrad—the Imperial city, city of the Tsar (Tsar, the Russian form of Caesar). The depth of the special Russian feeling for Byzantium is perhaps suggested by the fact that Tsargrad, alone, or almost alone, among the names of foreign cities, is declined through all nine of the inflections of the Russian noun; is treated as a

Russian word. The Second Rome is more real to Russians than the First Rome even in its latter-day form, though his Orthodox faith came to the Russian from the Second Rome before it broke away from Catholic Rome.*

But while the Russian eye is directed toward Tsargrad, the Russian often by-passes Byzantium. For his deeper religious affinity strains across the Bosporus, out of Byzantine Europe into Nearer Asia. The sources of Orthodox faith, the shrines of its spirit, and many of its vagaries strained toward the oldest provinces of the Christian Church, those first won for Christendom and earliest lost, submerged by the onset of Islam. Russian history is criss-crossed with the pilgrimages to those lands of simple peasants or priests who were themselves peasants or peasants' sons. Politically, Russian governments have long asserted a protectorate over all Christians in those submerged lands. But that political assertion reflects a feeling that saturates even the peasant mass—a feeling that its spiritual home lies by way of Byzantium and the Greek Orthodox monastery of Mount Athos through Syria to Jerusalem, and beyond Jerusalem to the Christian residue of Egypt. This feeling embraces the outlying provinces of that eastern Christendom, the Christian peoples of Transcaucasia—Georgians, Azerbaijanians, Armenians—peoples whom the West feel to be more mysterious, more alien, more unknown than the Euro-Asian Russians. Russian Orthodoxy looks to Christian Asia and that fringe of Europe which the channels of the Bosporus and the Dardanelles divide from Asia. It looks past Catholic Europe, which it encounters chiefly in the guise of its traditional enemy, Poland, the only other great nation in which religion and nationality are so much at one as they are among Russians. Russia looks to the East. But not in this sense (as is

---

* From the Roman Catholic viewpoint, the Russian Orthodox Church is schismatic but not heretical. That is, its sacraments are efficacious but unlawful because Russian Orthodoxy is not in communion with Rome.

commonly supposed) to the Farther East—that is more as an expression of political and expansionist energy. It is to the Nearer East that the Russian soul looks, and the dream of a Russian Constantinople, Russian control of the Bosporus and Dardanelles, is only the political form of the much deeper impulse.

All this the Russian *narod* feel, in one degree or another, even though their feelings do not reach the form of clear ideas, as might be expected to happen in the West. Outwardly, the Russian peasant mass is Orthodox, its life is saturated with piety side by side with the superstitions that derive from the point where its darker roots reach into the soil with a feeling that is essentially pagan. When Marya Timofevna (in *The Possessed*) mentions "our great mother the damp earth," she is reaching back to cults of the Great Mother, the fertility goddess, who from the dawn of time has swayed the minds of the peoples of the Eastern Mediterranean shores. That, I think, is why she says: "Believe me, Shatushka, there is no harm in such tears."

To Western eyes, the Russian soul is chiefly a Russian paradox. Among its more obvious features is "Russian fatalism" broken by outbursts of a maniacal savagery. Russian fatalism is a patient endurance by millions of a massive, interminable outrage that would move the men of the West to fighting fury, resisting with teeth and nails if they had no other weapons in their hands. Russian fatalism includes an endless patient suffering, as if suffering were itself a secret virtue.

With this goes another paradox that baffles the West: that boundless Russian capacity for a compassion whose purity and volume takes us back to a simple compassion of which the Gospels speak to us most singularly. Yet, side by side with that compassion lurks again that berserk impulse

to ferocity whose fury seems to cancel even the idea of compassion. There is, too, an arrogance taking the most primitive and brutal forms (what Westerner who has known
Russians has not known this?), side by side with something
of which the West is less aware is a sense that in life, all, all
are guilty of everything because guilt is fated; at the heart of
life lies a core of irrational evil, no one knows why, but which
all suffer in their individual degrees, lifting that suffering to
virtue (there seems no other way), by the patience with which
all suffer and the meaning they give to it in their lives. Of this
sense, that overwhelming Russian compassion is one aspect. It
takes other forms, utterly bewildering, even abhorrent, to the
West. Among them is an impulse to public confession of guilt,
which is felt, at its deepest level, not to be personally debas-
ing, because in no other way can the mortgage of general
guilt be lifted; while the sense of tragic suffering as a fixed
condition by which life is to be borne wraps the sufferer in
its tattered virtue. More than a little of this sense played
mysteriously through the confessions of the Moscow Purge
trials, and not only on the part of those confessing.

We glimpse it, dramatized historically, in the confession
of Ivan the Terrible. Ivan, after perpetrating crimes that
seemed to alienate him from mankind, struck his son in a fit
of rage and killed him at a blow. The Tsar then called together a *semski sobor*—an assembly of all ranks of the Russian people. To them Ivan confessed his crimes in detail and
declared himself unfit any longer to rule them. Whereupon
they fell on their knees before the penitent and demanded
that he, and only he, continue to rule them. Political shrewdness on the part of Ivan IV? Perhaps. The leaders of the
Twentieth Congress of the Soviet Communist Party confess
Stalin's crimes, and thereby their own. Political shrewdness
on the part of the Communist leaders? Certainly. But that is
only part of the point. The shrewdness could have no effect
if something else did not exist to which it makes peculiar

appeal, something that the West does not feel, without which the appeal would be inconceivable, and the politics of such an appeal impossible. That something is the point where the Russian feelings of suffering, compassion, guilt, and penitence fuse in what we can only call religious force.

The play of that religious force is most clearly visible in Russian writing. In the last half of the last century, Russian genius produced a literature of incomparable power. Most of it is rigorously realistic. Its unsparing insights charm the rational and secular Western mind by anticipating the insights of its most surgical psychologizing. Yet that realistic Russian writing is saturated with religion. Those psychological insights are specifically religious. They pierce through the outward cast and illusions of the individual man to lay bare the form and motives of the soul, always with sentimentality, but with a compassion that precludes judgment because all are sufferers by reason of the fact that they live; and the guilt of one differs only in the individual form it takes from the guilt of all the rest.

In *The Brothers Karamazov*—perhaps the greatest, certainly the most religious of all novels—father Zosima, the saintly monk, suddenly turns to Dmitri Karamazov, the embodiment of the average sensual man, whose passions, moreover, have got beyond his power to control them. In silence, Father Zosima bows before Dmitri Karamazov. He makes the low obeisance from the waist to the earth which Russians call the *zemnoi plakan* (*zemnoi*—to the earth). Father Zosima is bowing to the suffering which he foresees Dmitri's sensualism will cause him.

That suffering is a constant condition in Russian life—and the compassion before it is symbolized in Father Zosima's silent bow to the earth. With Russians it is an instinct. It touches on religious awe—a reverence before the fact that in the creature, man, should lodge mysteriously a soul, of which the heights presuppose corresponding depths. The Western mind says with Descartes: "I think, therefore I am." The Russian says: "I am, therefore I suffer." The consequences in action which follow from those different attitudes, even when unconscious, mark a difference among breeds of men. The energy with which that difference is embodied in the Russian, the energy of his compassion before the suffering that all endure, is the same energy that informs his outbursts of ferocity. Both pass beyond what the West feels to be natural limits of feeling and of action.

It would be pointless to try to impose upon such manifestations a rigid pattern of meaning. Yet we can glimpse how the promise of the Third Rome has its roots in this "black earth," this true *chernazem* of the Russian mind. For the Russian not only feels acutely his organic difference from the West; where the West feels that difference to mark an inferiority in the Russian (who is acutely aware, too, of this feeling in the West), the Russian feels his peculiar superiority to the West. He feels in himself a mysterious power that is missing from the outer world and is a promise of its salvation. He feels the West to be old and ill, from too much living, too much history, exhausted by time. He feels his fellow Russians to be the last great pool of untapped energy on earth which is therefore called to revitalize the West—a force of which the origin is unknown and inexplicable. His patient endurance of suffering is at once the token of his secret power to redeem mankind, and the sign that he is called to do so. It is a promise once whispered to him which he is one day to enact and fulfill. Through ages of endurance and death, the Russian has clutched that promise to him. It is because of this that he is able to endure and suffer; and if he must die, he dies in the knowledge that the promise lives.

In the cult of the people, Orthodox religious saturation blends with those other peculiar properties of Russian energy (or soul). That mass of the peasants, who by reason of their lot in life suffered most, in some mysterious way became the bearer of a mysterious merit. Their merit was exclusive; no other group possessed it. This was felt to be true by the peasants themselves and by other Russians who could partake of that merit only to the degree to which they identified their lives with peasants, dedicated themselves to the peasants. For it is in the sense of this secret merit that the Russian peasants (therefore, the Russian people) are God-bearing, and cannot move into history without extending salvation in such terms to all other classes, and to the rest of mankind.

From this sense followed certain other developments highly puzzling to the West. There is the sense that, by contrast with the God-bearing quality implicit in the people, culture as it is known in the West is evil and perhaps Satanic. This is the meaning of the whole later life of Count Leo Tolstoy, who dramatized it in an ordeal watched by the whole world, though the West only dimly grasped what was at stake. This is why Tolstoy repudiated the works of his earlier genius— *War and Peace*, *Anna Karenina*, etc.—and why he took to writing little religious parables, like *How Much Land Should a Man Own?*, or violent denunciation of all human culture, like *What Is Art?*. That is why he sought to dress, work, and as much as possible live among peasants, particularly peasant religious pilgrims. Hence his exclusive reversion to the Gospels, the voice of the Christian Nearer East in its purest, most primitive form.

But another consequence, big with meaning for all of us, also followed from the view of the Russian peasants as a chosen people. This was the belief that the peasant collectivism represented a form of life higher than the society of the West whose hallmark was secular individualism in all fields. In turn, and in time, this passed into the belief that the Russian peasantry, the people, would carry Russia to a new height, and thereby redeem all mankind by skipping entirely the historical form known in the West as capitalism. It is this belief that Lenin (translating his theory into Marxist terms) set at the center of his doctrine not only for Russia, but for all of Asia as well. The same belief lurks as the rallying impulse behind Stalin's "Socialism in one country." In this sense, the Russian people are almost organically anti-middle class. In Russia the word *borjui* (bourgeois) did not have to be learned as something theoretical, as it did in the West, particularly among Americans. In Russia, the word *borjui* was simply a handy term for an ageless reality and an attitude which was thus conveniently verbalized. In John Reed's *Ten Days that Shook the World* there is recorded a conversation between a peasant- or working-class Red Guard and a bourgeois who is trying to make him mend his ways. To all the bourgeois' arguments, the young Red Guard has only one invariable answer: "Comrade, there are two classes. . . ."

What is being dramatized here is the timeless belief that the people are inherently the force of salvation.

It cannot be emphasized too strongly: this feeling by the Russian mass, about its inherent mission, is a feeling—not a theory. It is a religion and a historical impulse, and when in this century the largest of Russian political parties, the Socialist Revolutionaries, tried to make theory out of it, the result was a good deal like a clot of wet paper. Every attempt to politicize the impulse ended preposterously. In the 1870s, the *narodniks* (men of the people) proclaimed the slogan: "*V narod!*" (To the people!). They swarmed from the cities into the countryside, as doctors and teachers, to minister to the people. But always as agitators to move the peasant mass to that revolution which would bring to power that God-bearing peasant socialism that would transform Russia and the world. The *narodnik* crusade was foredoomed. Revolution in such terms was not what the peasants had in mind; nor did they understand such revolutionists. The peasants turned the *narodniks* in to the police. A part of the *narodniks* reverted to terror, conspiring and blowing apart their victims in the name of that very God-bearing people, who intellectually were not yet equal to their mission.

But the sense of mission lived on. It was only the political form that was untimely. Russia was becoming more and more political, under the impact of Western ideas and due to its own inner tensions. In our time, the Socialist Revolutionaries, the historical heirs of the *narodniks*, won over the peasant majority. It is often forgotten in the West that the Soviet government began as a coalition government of Communists and Left Socialist Revolutionists who were subdued when they attempted a *coup d'état* against the Bolsheviks. Many Left Socialists then entered the Russian Communist Party, or supported it.*

Russia was not only being politicalized. It was being industrialized. With that development, Communism took hold. At that point, too, a subtle transition occurs: the messianic sense of the Russian people as a God-bearing force blends with the messianism of Communism in which the working class is the instrument of salvation. The blending is untraceable. It cannot be said: here it begins; here it ends. It is a living force, not a blueprint. Moreover, the very idea of God-bearing is outrageous to the Communist mind, while the peasants with their passion for landownership represent to Marxists the enemy within—the chief base of capitalism in

---

* Of these the best known in the West is probably Alexander Blumkin whose assassination of the German Ambassador to Moscow, Count Mirback, signalled the outbreak of the Left Socialist Revolutionary revolt. As a brilliant Chief of Soviet Military Intelligence in the Near East, Blumkin got in touch with Leon Trotsky who was then in exile in Turkey. For acting as a courier between Trotsky and the Opposition in Russia, Blumkin was shot by the secret police—the first outstanding Communist whom Stalin ventured to shoot. Another of the Left Socialist Revolutionists who went over to the Communists (though without becoming a Communist) was Ilyosha Ulanov (the "Ulrich" of *Witness*), last heard of (by me) as a political prisoner serving a twenty-year sentence in the Siberian slave-labor camp at Karaganda.

a socialist base. After the brief tactic of appeasement, whereby the Bolsheviks gained indispensable peasant support, Communism would declare that inner war against the peasants which is still going on at this moment.

A woman came to see me a year or two ago, a former Communist or close fellow traveller, an ordinary working woman, working, moreover, in an industry where men are the rule and women an exception. She worked to support an incurably ill husband. I had never seen her before, and have never seen her since. She was drawn here, as nearly as I could make out, not quite knowing why herself, looking for something she had once known but had lost, something of which she thought she had caught the echo in what I had written. She began to talk curiously about her earlier life in or near the Communist Party. She said: "In the old days, I could go to any city in the country, and though I was a stranger, the comrades would take me in, and if I needed help, they would help me. They would give me a place to sleep and something to eat. There was friendship and warmth. Now there is nothing. Outside it is cold. That is what *they* do not understand."

They? Who is *they?* Trotsky tells us that when, after his sensational escape from Siberia, he reached London in the dead of night, he knocked, about five o'clock in the morning, at the door of a dingy flat. Here Lenin and his wife lived in extreme poverty. The next day Lenin showed Trotsky over London, like a future monarch showing a guest over his future capital. What struck the young Trotsky was a way Lenin had of marking an absolute distinction. Lenin did not say, Trotsky reports, "This is the famous Westminster Abbey," or "These are the English Houses of Parliament." Lenin said: "This is *their* famous Abbey, those are *their* Houses of Parliament." That *their*, which Trotsky in his middle age still found memorable enough to puzzle about, he never truly understood to the day of his death, and in this lay the seed of his failure. For Trotsky was essentially a Western mind. Lenin was a Russian, and unlike most other revolutionary exiles, wherever he went was Russian. That *they* or *their* of his was simply the word the Russian peasant uses, used as the peasant used it, to mark the absolute division of worlds. "Their" fields, the peasant said, "their" manor house, "their" lives, "their" world.

A Swiss, of that general lower-middle-class order that Germans call "*Spießbürger*," told me how in the days before Lenin came to power, he (the Swiss) used to see Lenin eating in the same cheap restaurant in Zurich. "Lenin looked," said my Swiss with an almost audible amusement, repressed, however, "like the kind of working man who always takes a bath on Saturday night." Otherwise, Lenin was unpressed and seemed completely careless of his appearance. There is no doubt that the young Swiss had seen accurately; he had simply not understood what he saw: he had no way of understanding. What he saw was the man of political genius who had rejected *they*, who did not understand, and had identified himself so completely with the people that it had become second nature to him. He had taken poverty, not as a vow but as an identification with that Russian mass. He carried it with him in exile and defeat as an immigrant carries, treasured in his pocket, a coin or a pebble from his native land. Power made no difference. Lenin lived in austerity even in the Kremlin. There radiated from him an invisible oneness with the mass, which radiated its secret power back to him.

Lenin's closest colleagues did not understand, as their comments richly reveal. They were Communists, men of a particular doctrine which explained all life and history in a way that completely satisfied their minds. Lenin was the most brilliant living exponent of that doctrine, and the most audacious. Yet here were those curious differences. Socialism absolutely rejected terror as an instrument of policy. Communism shared that rejection (though it would later make use of assassination for limited ends). But Lenin, the master Marxist, held up to his comrades the memory of those *narodniks* and Socialist Revolutionists who had practiced terror in the name of the people. As late as 1924, Grigory Zinoviev would recall (in his speech at Lenin's funeral) how deeply Lenin revered particularly those working-class terrorists "who went with bomb or revolver against this or that individual monster."

This Marxist, the moment he returned to Russian soil and was in direct contact with the Russian mass, spoke with the voice of Russia. "We don't need any parliamentary republic. We don't need any bourgeois democracy. We don't need any government but the Soviet of Workers', Soldiers' and Peasants' deputies!" His own comrades could not understand. "Lenin," said one of them, "has just announced his candidacy for the one throne in Europe that has been vacant for thirty years: I mean, the throne of Bakunin [the arch-anarchist]. Lenin, in new words, is telling the same old story: it is the old discarded notion of primitive anarchism all over again. Lenin the Social Democrat, Lenin the Marxist, Lenin the leader of our militant Social Democracy—that Lenin is no more!"

That Lenin had rejoined his people, from whom he had separated himself by distance only for personal security and the freedom to work out that organization and that strategy which, once the historical wind of their energy had blown down the flimsy structure of Tsardom, would enable him to return as warrior once more to lead the Russian tribes outward in every direction. Lenin's theory of party organization is what divides him absolutely from the Menshevik mind. The Mensheviks, members with the Bolsheviks of one party until 1908, are Russian Marxists whose intellectual brothers are the Social Democrats, Socialists, and Left Liberals of the

West. This is not the place to detail Lenin's organizational theory beyond noting that in practice, in the organization first of the Communist Party and then of the Soviet State, it amounted to a socialist Tsardom, shaped to meet modern conditions, with the top-flight Party circles replacing the Court, the Tsar's personal chancery, and the council of ministers; with a Communist bureaucracy replacing the ranks of the *Chinovniki*, the Tsarist administrative officials, buttressed by a secret police narrowly resembling Ivan the Terrible's *oprichniki* and the later Tsardom's *Okhrana*. But the Communist Tsar was not hereditary. His power was evolved or ravaged in a process of the most brutal Darwinian natural selection: first Lenin (by right of personal superiority and political craft), then Stalin. A collective leadership (such as Stalin vanquished and such as we now see again) is always evidence that the process of natural selection has not yet evolved a Tsar strong enough to assert his autocracy. Currently, this is the condition of Nikita Khrushchev. On the other hand, even an autocrat does not rule alone. History, I am sure, will one day show (though how far off one day may be I should not venture) there was a give and take and difference of opinions in the Political Bureau which quite makes nonsense of the popular view of the kind of dictator Stalin was. He simply had a habit of killing off dissenters when they threatened his autocracy. This lethal action to safeguard the autocracy is seen repeatedly in the murder of Sergei Kirov and Andrei Zhdanov and the late, sudden and long mysterious disappearance of Nikolai Voznesenski, who we now know was executed. The logic behind this shocking process is blurred for the West by reason of its peculiar Russianness and (in Stalin's case) because of his conspicuous or personal baseness and low-grade malevolence. Understanding is scarcely furthered by the fact that much of our knowledge of these events is filtered through and colored by minds of Russian Menshevik immigrants who see these matters in terms of Western socialist mentality instead of seeing them as manifestations of Russian power. So, too, the West listens (insofar as it ever listens) most raptly to these Westernizing Mensheviks (or their intellectual kin) because the West feels them to be most like itself, most like Euro-Asia, which continues, however, to remain an enigma wrapped in a mystery.

The mark of Lenin's genius is often expressed in terms of his statesmanship. Lenin, it is sometimes said, was the one statesman in a monkey cage of chattering doctrinaire revolutionists. It may help to bring Lenin into focus if we note that he was indeed the only statesman of such stature then alive. For he alone was knowingly engaged in bringing to birth, in bringing to reality, a new age of history. His associates were not a lot of chattering monkeys; among them were brains enough to run any empire, even one in chaos, as events proved. Some of his associates, moreover, had from the first a piercing insight into the special hazards and problems of creating a socialist state in a peasant land. Only, their prescience was pedantic. They were right in terms of socialist theory, or of any plain social and economic survey. But in this sense they were doctrinaire. For this was not a simple case of social and economic theory; and that is what Lenin saw, or sensed. It is here that the word statesmanship falls short. Here, statesmanship passes into political genius, which like any other genius, literary or artistic, works and creates by intuitive grasp.

For this was the point at which the messianic impulse of Communism was wedded to and surcharged by the elemental messianicism of the Russian mission. At the moment when Lenin said what must have doomed Karl Marx to a second death, "Soviet power plus electricity equals Communism"— at that moment the Third Rome re-entered history in its twentieth-century form, a form which Stalin would bring close to completion, amidst an agony of death and suffering such as even the Russian people had never known. At that point, the mystical merit within the peasants blended with the historical merit ascribed to the working class as the redeemer of human history and reached out to the merit of the masses in all other lands. In the name of a force (Communism) which denies God, what was felt to be God-bearing in the Russian people (who for the most part, it must be remembered, remained religious) rallied itself for an immense redemptive mission whose energy was felt as of old but was now manifested and expressed in wholly different terms. That redemptive sense had become "the world revolution." This is what Lenin saw, and what marked him off from the men around him.

Sukhanov, a non-Bolshevik, listened to Lenin's first public words to the armed sailors who surrounded his railway coach on his return to Russia—words that not merely echoed the clichés of Marxism, but announced an apocalypse that was Russian by inward force. "How extraordinary it was!" Sukhanov recollected. "Lenin's voice, issuing straight from the railway carriage, was a 'voice from outside.' Upon us, in the midst of the revolution, broke—the truth, by no means dissonant, by no means violating its context, but a *new* and brusque, a somewhat stunning note . . . Lenin was undeniably right, not only in announcing to us that the world socialist revolution had begun, not only in pointing out the indissoluble connection between the world war and the collapse of the imperialist system, but in emphasizing and bringing to the fore the 'world revolution' itself, insisting that we must hold our course by it, and evaluate in its light all the events of contemporary history."[*]

These are the accents of history on one of its turning points, and it is noteworthy that this voice of Sukhanov (not himself in any sense a great man) is struck from him in response to

---

[*] Sukhanov, whose real name was Nikolai Nikolayevich Himmer, was the author of the seven-volume *Russian Revolution 1917*.

something elemental in Lenin's words, as like vibrates to like throughout nature. Until Lenin spoke, the revolution had been a democratic one, an inner Russian affair. Now it was to encompass the world. It does not matter that *factually* Lenin was wrong. He saw the beginning of the "world revolution" in the German revolution, which did not break out until about a year later and then petered out. What mattered was that Lenin had touched, in socialist terms, the redemptive promise in the Russian mind. This marked him off from most other revolutionaries and rejoined him to the people.

They repaid him, as peoples always repay those who touch, however roughly or inadequately, their inmost souls. They repay in the only way they can. Those long shuffling lines that wait, muffled in winter cold or sweltering in Moscow's summer heat, inching their way along to catch a glimpse of Lenin's face in the tomb or on the Red Square—nobody marshals them there, as contingents are rounded up for the May Day demonstrations. They come of themselves, they wait of their own volition to see not a man whose hard and brilliant intellect most of them could not conceivably grasp. They wait to see a man who was peculiarly and mysteriously their own. Often they weep at what they see. Those tears tell more about his mystery, and perhaps about history, than the most profuse facts, the weightiest arguments and analyses that learned minds can contrive.

Slon did not tell me any of this. But I have had a good many years since in which to think about that sidelong glance with which Slon mentioned the Third Rome to me. I have had years, too, in which to learn that when a man reaches Slon's age, he scarcely expects much that he says to be understood, or greatly cares. At most, he peers about, more curious than expectant, for one or two who might one day understand. If he supposes that he has found one such, he lets fall what is in his mind, thinking: "*Now* he will not understand. But in ten years, twenty years, he may remember. Then he may understand; or he may not."

I think now that Slon did me great honor, in that sense, in mentioning the Third Rome. And he was right: I did not understand. But I did remember; and when, in the fullness of time, I began to catch up with Slon and to see a little more clearly, as his peasant glimpsed morning Moscow from the Sparrow Hills, that horizon toward which Slon's finger carelessly pointed, I was ever after grateful. In the Third Rome, I came to believe at last, Slon had disclosed to me a clue to one of the meanings of our time.

An old Russian peasant tale tells how Prince Ivan mourned his wife, Vasilissa the All-wise, to whom, while intending to do good, he had done a harm, so that she flew away from him in the form of a swan. For a whole year, the story tells us, Ivan longed for his wife. The next year he made up his mind. He asked his Tsar-father's permission and his mother's blessing, said his prayers to God, bowing to all four horizons, and set out "whither eyes look." That is a Russian way of saying that he did not know where he was going. At last, Ivan met a little old man who said to him: "Good health to to you, dear lad! What do you look for and whither do you go?" Ivan had to tell him that he really did not know. The old man fumbled in his rags and brought out a little ball. "Here is a little ball for you," he said to Ivan. "Toss it ahead of you. Wherever it rolls, follow boldly." Ivan did so, though the little ball led him through some wild woods and strange adventures before he reached the ends of the earth and freed his wife from Koshchei the Deathless, who is death itself. Deathless, because of all changing things in life, death alone is changeless. All of us daily live our deaths, and may hold ourselves fortunate only if we suppose that we have wrung something from the experience so that in the end we are not left as at the outset—with empty hands.

To me, Slon was a little like Ivan's old man. Met briefly,

he fumbled in his rags and handed me a little ball. It led me across that quaking bog, through that unlikely, shadowy wilderness which Russians themselves call *russkaya dusha* (the Russian soul), to that end of experience where the Third Rome stands, its uprooted turnips catching a triumphant light, though whether it is sunup or sundown, no one knows for certain yet. For that is the secret, and for some the ordeal, of the next fifty years.

General Kutepov

One day in the early thirties, General Kutepov was walking down a street in Paris when he completely disappeared. One moment, the General was there, a martially dignified man, old but still physically powerful, walking in the sunlight down a quiet street in a capital of civilization. The next moment the General was not there, only the sunlight was there, and nobody who could be kind to him, or in any way help or pity him, ever saw General Kutepov again. I do not know whether the General was a good or a bad man, as we reckon these matters with our little human ready-reckoners. I incline to think that, on balance, he must have been more good than bad by measurements quite beyond our power to make, because at the instant of final need and horror in General Kutepov's human experience, God was so extraordinarily good to him. Of course, the form God's mercy took may seem, again by our little human measuring sticks, somewhat drastic. But what else was possible at that point? And, as Karl Barth has told us: "Man cannot define God by talking about man in however loud a voice. *Gott ist ganz anders* (God is wholly otherwise)." But why drag God into the disappearance of a White Russian General on a Paris street? Besides, all this is speculation, and the enlightened mind of this age feels at home chiefly with nuts and bolts—with facts. Relevant fact here is that for many years, I supposed that I was one of a comparative handful of men who knew what had happened to General Kutepov on that peaceful Paris street.

At the time the General disappeared, I was simply a raw young Communist recruit. I was simply interested in the General's disappearance as mystery. Years would pass before I knew that such mysteries, that sudden disappearances, abductions, murder were mere commonplaces of the operation of history in our time, that they go on around us constantly, and that the belief that we live in a civilization still orderly and tranquil is a fiction maintained chiefly by shutting our eyes very tightly to the contrary evidence.

At the time, I was sure of only one thing: that the rumors that Communists had had something to do with General Kutepov's disappearance were lies. For, in those days, I knew that while people like General Kutepov and his White Russians were quite capable of kidnapping and murdering Communists, it was inconceivable that Communists would use such methods. And this despite the fact that I knew quite well that in terms of their own doctrine of war and power—those were exactly the methods that Communists must use.

Soon enough, I "guessed" that the truth about his disappearance probably lay somewhere in a spate of little news reports that General Kutepov had been seen with "his mistress" in Buenos Aires, in Tokyo, and other distant parts. Perhaps it was never explicitly said, but the implication was strong that the General had disappeared for reasons of his own connected with a private scandal. It would not have occurred to me that Communists had systematically planted these lies. Nor would I have dreamed these far-flung lies were part of a systematic derogation following a rule set down by Sergei Nechaev, a Russian revolutionist, in his *Revolutionist's Catechism* written about 1865: "It is not enough to kill an adversary. He must be first dishonored."

It was an officer of the Red Army who told me what had happened to General Kutepov, some years after his disappearance. The officer was, in fact, the tank commander of the Leningrad Military District, though I knew him only as "Herbert" or "Otto" or "Karl." We were sitting in an apartment in New York City. I no longer remember why we were there. His conversation about General Kutepov was one of the only two conversations of length I recall having with this man. For I scarcely knew him, yet I liked him. Among all humans, including Communists, there are always a few whom we think of instinctively as the "good men," the decent men, those who will stand for right as long as circumstances permit, and perhaps a little longer; those who will play fair in their human relations so long as it is humanly possible, and again, perhaps a fraction longer. And in that fraction is the little dust of their human merit. I felt instinctively that Herbert was that kind of a man.

It was toward the end of the day. The light was already failing. Suddenly Herbert said: "Do you know what happened to Kutepov?" I did not even know why he was asking me. Nor for some time did I know why he was telling me what followed. I suppose he was midway in his story before I said to myself: "Horror—it is horror that is making him tell me this." Today I would say: "It was a retching of the soul, a spasm of the soul in its effort to throw off poison, not much different from the spasm by which a stomach tries to throw off a poison."

Of course, we forget that Communists are men with souls which in certain cases, much more numerous than we dream of, continue to torment them long after they suppose they have cured themselves of the fallacy called a soul. Nor is it always easy to see in the midst of these retchings that it is a soul

which is at work. Recently, Vladimir Petrov, a former Soviet
diplomat and secret police officer in Australia, told us about
the jailers and the executioners in the Soviet prisons, how
many of them are brutes to begin with and how their duties
further brutalize them. "Yet," he added, "they are men, so
many of them drink heavily." Perhaps even Petrov did not
know what he was saying; so how should others see that that
drinking, so unsoulful in itself, signals in fact a stirring of
the soul—perhaps its last feeble stirrings which will take the
sufferers to drink but no farther; and, indeed, circumstances
are not favorable to much more.

Both Herbert and I would have denied the reality of the
soul, not simply as an article of faith, but as a matter of intelligence, and without heat, since one does not become heated
about what is self-evident. So, at the time, I merely sensed
that Herbert was unburdening himself of a gnawing horror,
and I felt a stir of pride because the fact that he was unburdening himself to me, a callow novice whom he scarcely
knew, could mean only that his instinct told him that at core,
I, in my wholly different way, was of the same breed of man
as he was.

This is what he told me. In Paris, in the 1920s, General
Kutepov headed an organization of White Russians driven
from Russia by the Communist Revolution, and extremely
active in plotting against it. Their purpose was to overthrow
the Soviet government, and to this end they promoted and
maintained relations with the intelligence sections and other
agencies of the German, French and British governments.
Moscow decided to liquidate General Kutepov. This presented certain difficulties since the act must be committed in
a foreign country. But the Soviet secret police were accustomed
to overcoming difficulties. A plot was set afoot whereby General Kutepov was to be lured into surroundings suitable for
his execution by means of the seductions of a popular singer
who was also a White Russian. But progress was slow.

Meanwhile Moscow itself took a new tack in the Kutepov

affair. A wholly different problem was posed. Moscow's directives were explicit: under no circumstances was General Kutepov to be killed. He was to be kidnapped and taken to the Soviet Union alive. For in his head were the secrets of his anti-Soviet plans and all his connections with foreign governments. And it was these that the General was to be made to disclose. Only afterwards would he be shot. This was, of course, an even more difficult project than killing General Kutepov in France. Great rewards were promised those who would deliver the General safely—cash premiums, advancements in rank, and long vacations in rest homes in the Crimea or the Caucasus.

The project began as such projects usually do—with a close surveillance. This proved rather simple. It developed that General Kutepov was in the habit of walking from his house to his organization headquarters. He always took the same route and part of it led through a quiet side street. Perhaps it was just the orderly quiet of that street which appealed to that old man who had seen so much, revolution, civil war, defeat, and exile. "This old Hindenburg" (the phrase was Herbert's) always marched straight and never glanced behind him.

The conspirators succeeded in renting a room next to or above or below General Kutepov's room. There, they installed listening devices so that they even heard him sometimes worrying about how he was to pay his rent. "And do you know," said Herbert, "it is strange to hear a man worrying about the rent when you know he will never have to pay it."

On the basis of this surveillance, further details were elaborated. Two or three secret agents, outfitted as fishermen (they are almost as common as grass along the Seine) began to explore the right bank of that river far below Paris. At last they found a fairly secluded spot where they could sit fishing. Beyond, the water was deep enough so that a cargo ship could anchor. From it a small boat could put ashore to take on the kidnapped General. Am I only imagining that the Soviet ship selected for this mission was named the *Maria Ulyanova?* I am no longer sure. Ulyanova was Lenin's sister, and if the ship was not named for her, it bore some other legendary name of the Russian Revolution.

The center of the plot was the Soviet Embassy in Paris, though, as usual in such cases, under no consideration must the Embassy be connected with the affair. But the plotters held somewhat gloomy sessions in the Embassy. For there was one detail that defied solution. General Kutepov, while aging, was a vigorous man. How were they going to get him into an automobile in order to kidnap him? Before they could overcome him even on a quiet street, he would cause such an uproar as was quite unthinkable. On this point, the whole plot stalled. It stalled so completely that Moscow sent out one of its trouble-shooters to take over. He proved to be one of those ferocious little monsters who are rather common among the Communist secret services. I have met and dealt with one or two. He listened while his agents reviewed the steps in the kidnapping and explained their difficulty. "Fools!" he burst out at that point. "You don't force Kutepov into a car." But, he then explained, it was perfectly simple to get him to enter one. A *gendarme* simply walks up to him on the street, and ever so courteously with ever so many apologies deplores the necessity of having to request the General to accompany him to the nearest police station due to some trifling matter about his residence papers. Residence papers trouble every non-citizen in a strange land. The *gendarme* would hail a passing taxi, and General Kutepov would get into the cab with him. Once in the cab, the General would be chloroformed by a saturated handkerchief pressed over his face.

From there on, things moved fast. The French Communist Party supplied a comrade taxi driver, a *gendarme*'s uniform was found and someone to wear it. It was arranged that a

second car, driven by a Soviet agent, should closely follow
the taxi. During the first stage of the attempt, the second car
would serve to block pursuit if any should develop. Later,
General Kutepov would be transferred to the second car
for the dash to the riverfront below Paris. The roads were
explored and re-explored to establish the exact time required
for the trip which must synchronize nicely with the short time
that the *Maria Ulyanova* stood in to take the General aboard.
It had to tick like watchworks. The hour was set. The day
came. "The old Hindenburg" marched for the last time down
the quiet street. The *gendarme* stepped up and made his
courteous request. The taxi passed and was hailed. General
Kutepov got in, followed by the gendarme. The cab pulled
away. The second car followed. Finding another man already
in the cab, General Kutepov began to struggle. But the chloro-
form rag was ready and he subsided abruptly. Everything
had been foreseen—everything but one thing. When the
handkerchief was removed from his face, the General was
not breathing. What had not been foreseen was the condition
of the General's heart. In his extremity, it had rendered
him his last service. By God's mercy, General Kutepov was
dead.

The effect of this on the two secret agents in the cab, and
presently on the third one in the following car, was appalling.
In an instant, all those golden hopes—bonuses, advancement,
vacations with their families—had crumbled to much worse
than nothing. The agents were certain of recall to Moscow,
degradation, punishment, if not something more extreme.
In the panic that ensued the driver of the car which contained
the General's body made a wrong turn and lost his way.
Hopelessly mazed, and in terror of being stopped for some reason, the agents parked at a little distance while one of them
went to ask directions at an inn. The driver got his bearings,
but the innkeeper followed him outside, despite his pleas not
to put himself out. All of the secret agents thought that the

innkeeper looked suspiciously toward the parked car and its one immobile rider; and this increased their panic.

At last, they arrived at the rendezvous. But they were at least one hour late. The captain of the ship, or whatever crew member was the secret agent responsible for picking up General Kutepov, had evidently panicked too. The *Maria Uly-anova* was moving far off to sea.

If there had been panic before among the General's bearers, there was now something like dementia. For they had now to dispose of the body. One of them was for simply dumping it in some suitable ditch along the road. The others shouted that this would be madness. At last, another of them faced it: they must take General Kupetov's body to the Embassy and there dispose of it. At first blush, it seemed too preposterous to be true. But we think of things as preposterous in terms of more or less ordinary circumstances. This was by now quite extraordinary. So it was probably the most sensible proposal. For where else could they go?

That did not save them from the maniacal fury of their ferocious little leader who also felt the clammy chill of failure close around him in some of its most dismaying possibilities. To his cries were added the cries of the Ambassador, who saw a prospect of scandal, which reduced him to snapped nerves. There followed a truly Russian scene, a scene of shouting and out-shouting over the General's inert body dumped on an Embassy floor, such as only Russians, among emotional peoples, can sustain at quite such pointless length or stridency.

In the end, the little monster took control. He sent the quivering Ambassador about his business, and ordered his broken-spirited agents to lug the body into the Embassy base-ment. Then, into the night, three or four of them set about dismembering General Kutepov with a view to burying him compendiously in quicklime below the basement. But in order to prove to headquarters that General Kutepov was at least dead, it was decided to cut off his head and hands and dispatch them to Moscow in the diplomatic pouch. This happy thought stirred in one of the agents a last flash of zeal. Perhaps he thought to recover a last shred of his professional competence. Should they not, he suggested eagerly, along with the head and hands also send Moscow the General's heart? The little monster fixed the questioner with a freezing stare. "What do you think we are?" he said slowly through clenched teeth. "*Boyars?*"

That was the end of the story. It had grown dark while Herbert was talking. Suddenly he said: "There is only one truth—if you push a man hard enough, he will die. That is all."

The People of Riva

I have had this curious personal experience. I am a man who has twice deserted from Communism to the West. But—this is what I call curious—though each time I found Communism insupportable, I nevertheless felt within its ranks a sense of basic well-being, a sense of being at one with the purposeful unfolding of history, a sense of fulfillment that goes far beyond personal matters and amounts to all that we commonly bracket in the word "hope." On the other hand, each time that I have lived the life of the West, I have experienced a feeling held at bay only by an effort of the will. For this feeling I shall use the word "despair," though the term is inaccurate and I shall presently try to make it more exact. I have found that the mood of Communism (despite its atrocious features) is a mood of hope, while the West (despite its gracious features) promotes a mood of despair.

Before an aroused readership rends me for that statement, let me make two points about it: 1. You have nothing to fear from the former Communist who tells you what he feels;

you have only to fear the former Communist who does not; 2.
The important point is not that somebody feels this way;
the important point is to try to discover how such a feeling is
possible.

The nature of my breaks with Communism I reported in
detail in *Witness*. I must recapitulate them here briefly. The
first break occurred around 1929, and was a break, not with
Communism, but with the Communist Party. It was a reaction
to the first impact of Stalinism on the American Communist
Party. No doubt, it marked the culmination of something
much less conscious, maturing over a long period. I mean a
final reaction to all that is grubby, squalid and preposterous
in the physical environment of Communism, and sterile and
killing in its intellectual and spiritual climate. From this,
life outside the Communist Party came with a sense of vast
relief and release. Yet, in a short while, that life seemed so
smotheringly hopeless that I returned to Communism with
a far greater sense of relief and release, resolved to obey
absolutely its harshest, most fantastic and irrational demands
(even while my conscious mind knew them to be fantastic
and irrational), provided only that Communism would let
me collaborate in its central effort. For I found in Communism
a rational and dedicated purpose. I held that Communism
would one day work out of its squalor, folly, and beastliness
in the course of working toward that purpose. The West, I
found, could only work itself deeper into a purposeless futility.

My second break with Communism occurred in 1938. This
was an utterly different kind of break. The first break had
been, in a sense, a break about tactics. The second was a
break about principle. Intervening years of intensive Communist experience, inflamed by the great Russian Purge and
Show-trials, and much else that I had seen or experienced,
compelled me to make a rigorous re-examination of Communist belief. That scrutiny led me to draw the conclusion that
my first reaction had stopped short of, namely, that the

squalor, folly, and beastliness of Communism were inseparable from it. They were not, as I had supposed, the clutter and excreta incidental to a phase which time and circumstance would outgrow. They were inevitable manifestations, inherent in one form or other whenever men consciously reject God as the central fact of life; reject, that is, something infinitely greater than themselves, and seek to organize life in terms of their own fallible intelligence, which ranges from an intolerable shallowness to extravagant brutality. With this in sight, went an experience which I have also reported in *Witness*, though only glancingly, in part, because language fumbles at this outermost range so that even the great mystics leave us with a sense of failure to communicate in words what they have felt and known; in part, because an insurmountable reticence bars us from sharing what is most precious and mysterious to us. This does not imply a suspension of the thinking mind. The mind that has suffered this experience cannot thereafter fail to thank God for the gift of life. I do not understand why, but it becomes impossible. At the same time, the same mind cannot but be perplexed (like the thinking minds of all ages) by the paradox that this gift is given to man in a garden infested not by the affably tempting Snake of Genesis, but a garden where under every flower and leaf swarm live cobras and pit vipers. This paradox we phrase as "the problem of evil." There are only two main answers to it. One is that resignation which is at the heart of every great religion ("In His Will is our peace"). The other is the foreclosure of the problem itself by the rejection of God, which is Communism's solution. Of course, this solution is not a Communist monopoly; the same effect is produced by that indifference which is much more widespread in the West than Communism, even among nominal Christians. This problem torments millions of minds, even of a kind which we do not easily describe as "thinking," people who are, in fact, scarcely or only intermittently conscious of what troubles them. The rejection of the problem in bulk is one of Communism's most subtle appeals, again even though the rejection may not be thought about in any specific way, but simply as a relief.*

Perhaps I should note that there must be many Communists who do not accept in full the orthodox Communist view of religion. There are millions of Communists in the world and they do not differ greatly in human traits from millions of anybody anywhere else. People everywhere have all manner of tacit reservations, qualifications, little private exceptions about the faith they publicly profess. It would greatly help the understanding of the West if it could give up the habit of imagining the Communist as something finally and unalterably complete in himself, or as a stock character in a play who is always predictably the same, a villian, or as we like to say, "Communist gangster" or "Communist bandit." Communists are exactly as different one from another as anybody else. The point is not that the Communist is always the same man or type of man, as we know the moment we stop to think about it. The point is that an immense diversity of men have been moved by the promise of a single faith and doctrine, and by certain historical factors that make them susceptible to it. I greatly doubt that the number of Communists who really enjoy liquidating people differs much from the sum of such people elsewhere; there are always some brutes. The motives for Communist atrocities, like Communist conversions, are not to be found in textbooks of psychiatry; though that is where the West, in its unwilling-

---

* It is argued by many, both Right and Left, that the rejection of God is not the starting point of Communism. I can only say flatly that these people have never understood what Communism was about, and refer them, without waste of words to Friedrich Engels' *Ludwig Feuerbach: The End of Classical German Philosophy*, and Karl Marx's *Theses on Feurbach*, which are usually included with Engel's essay. Both are fairly brief. Any literate mind can understand them without undue effort. For those who shun original texts, there is Father Henri de Lubac's *Drama of Atheist Humanism*.

ness to come to grips with the root problem, repeatedly looks for them, and of course consistently fails to find an answer.

It is twenty years to the month since I broke with Communism. At that date such breaks, whatever their various circumstances or the particular forms they took in each individual case, always occurred in reaction to a single historic development—the extermination of the revolutionary generation of 1914-1917 (and certain older survivors) by Communism as a necessary precondition to its petrifying into a permanent dictatorship, totalitarian and bureaucratic. By the generation of 1914-1917, I mean that part of it whose horizon was defined and whose mind was shaped by the First World War and the Russian Revolution. In general, such men and women, in despair before a world in despair and massive dissolution, turned revolutionist as the only effective course they found in the historical disaster, and turned to Communism as the one force in being which offered, in the vast vacuum, meaning and the possibility to act with purpose. The Communist experience, a man's turning Communist, was always primarily a historical experience, a direct reaction to history felt as entrapment under the debris of all kinds of a collapsing society, vividly enacted in the toppling walls of its cities—Madrid, Nanking, London, Berlin, Nagasaki, Hiroshima. That is why attempts to explain the Communist experience primarily in personal, psychological terms (a popular pastime among us) explain almost nothing and chiefly multiply mystification. That is why, too, the circumstances of such breaks that strike the general interest—the lurid flight and pursuit by the police of both sides (Communism and the West)—were not what was most important for those who broke. All this was real enough, terrifyingly, sometimes fatally, real. But these circumstances were of a kind best distinguished as "trying." What was lastingly important to those who survived such breaks was that their lives were henceforth stripped of meaning and purpose. They were doubly stripped. Henceforth, the sorry fugitives would hold with themselves a daily colloquy much like that between the Mayor of Riva at the bier of the Hunter Gracchus in Kafka's parable.* As I remember the story, grossly stripped down:

"Are you dead?" asks the Mayor.

"Yes," answers the man on the bier, "as you see."

"But you are alive, too," says the Mayor.

"In a way," says the man on the bier. "In a way, I am also alive."

In life, the man on the bier explains, he had been known as the Hunter Gracchus. Hunting one day in the Black Forest, he slipped among rocks and broke his neck. "Then came the mishap." He found himself neither quite dead nor yet living. "My death boat went off its course. A wrong swing of the helm, a moment's inattention on the pilot's part, a deflection due perhaps to some longing of my own for my wondrously beautiful native land—I do not know what it was. All I know is that I remained on earth and my boat travelled earthly waters. So that I, who wished only to live among my mountains, travel, after my death, through all the lands of the earth."

"A terrible fate," says the Mayor on reflection.

"Nobody," says the man on the bier, "will come to help me. For even if people were given an order to help me, they would stay in the houses with all the doors and windows shut. All would take to their beds and pull the bed clothes over their heads. The whole world would be like an inn closed for the night. And that makes good sense, too. For nobody knows about me. And, even if anybody did know about me, he would not know how to take me, how to help me. The very thought of helping me is a sickness that can only be cured by taking to one's bed. I know this, and so I do not cry out or call for help,

---

* Franz Kafka, *Parables and Paradoxes*. New York: The Schocken Press, 1947.

even though at times—when I lose my grip, as just now, for example—I think strongly of doing so."

"Extraordinary," says the Mayor of Riva, "extraordinary. And now do you think to remain with us in Riva for a while?"

"I think not," says the man on the bier, and smiles. But, to soften the little irony of that smile, he touches the Mayor of Riva placatingly with his dead hand.

I used to keep the book in the top drawer of my desk at *Time* magazine, together with three other small books: Edmund Burke's *Reflections on the French Revolution*, my father's pocket-sized volume of *Coriolanus* ("Rome and her rats are at the point of battle"), and Dostoevsky's *The Possessed* ("Nations are built up and moved by another force which sways and dominates them, the origin of which is unknown and inexplicable; that force is the force of an insatiable desire to go on to the end, though at the same time it denies an end. It is the force of the persistent assertion of one's own existence, and a denial of death").

Often, in the months before the Hiss Case broke, I used to take out Kafka's little book by way of a break in the tedium of my own writing. Almost always, I found myself reading "The Hunter Gracchus." I do not remember that this was due to any fancied resemblance between the Hunter Gracchus and myself, at least not beyond the point where the Hunter Gracchus stands for all other men. The little parable runs only to seven short pages. I read it for the wonder with which, in words as deceptively simple as the conversation of children, Kafka evokes a riddle of man's existence. I did not think I understood the meaning of the riddle, or that Kafka thought he did. His purpose was to pose it.

Some time after the Hiss Case had formally closed, certain of my effects, including Kafka's *Parables*, were sent back to me from *Time*, somewhat as the effects found in the pockets of a man who has met a fatal accident—his wallet, driver's license, social security stub—are mailed to his relicts. But like the Hunter Gracchus, I was there to receive my own effects. Again, I read Kafka's little parable noting inescapably, with a certain amusement, that it now suggested certain personal meanings which ran deeper than the surface fact that I had, in one sense, survived my own life.

A year or two later, when after a tedious convalescence from a heart attack it was decreed that I was once more equal to holding a book in bed, and equal to the excitement of reading, I again read the seven pages of "The Hunter Gracchus." Now my thoughts about it ranged far beyond the personal and I had lots of leisure to labor them. They went something like this.

We live in a revolutionary age. The whole world is unsettled by revolution because, for the first time in human history, the whole world is enmeshed in the same civilization —the technological civilization of the West. It is really one world, which everywhere suffers from the same sickness and disorder whose original focus of infection was the West— that is, Europe and North America.

The revolutionary forces are inherent in the cell structure of the West. We call these forces variously socialism, communism, fascism, materialism. But those are only the names men give to some revolutionary manifestation—to classify, vivify, rally, or promote it. Each is the name of a system by which men seek to order and control the revolutionary upheaval. Each is the name of a solution offered for it. What we commonly overlook, perhaps because most of these movements are directed against capitalism, is that capitalism is itself a revolutionary force.

Here and there the revolutionary crisis has called forth a number of counterrevolutionists. They have been of many kinds and breeds. Some were monstrous by any ordinary standard. Some were rather lovable and human insofar as a leader of anything can ever permit himself to be so, since he must daily sacrifice his humanity for the sake of an overriding purpose. What is curious is this. The more monstrous these counterrevolutionists were and the more clearly their counter-revolutionary character partook of revolutionary strains, the more the West showed a tendency to deal with and appease them. On the other hand, the more the counterrevolutionists resembled the ordinary types of the West and the more they invoked its tradition, the more furiously the West condemned them. One and all, monsters or otherwise, the West has de-stroyed them, either in alliance with the forces of open revolu-tion, or in connivance with them. Or, in lesser cases, the West has destroyed them itself, by discrediting and silencing them. This has been true whether the counterrevolutionists were the heads of states, generals, or senators.

"And this," as the Hunter Gracchus says, "makes good sense." For each of those who has stood up to defend the traditions of the West against open revolution has been marked by some personal flaw. It is as if each carried in him-self, like an open wound, some ailment of the threatened tis-sue which he was seeking to save. Each has been undone by stressing or exaggerating that weakness. It makes no differ-ence that all men have such flaws. All men do not offer them-selves to combat revolution. It can be stated as a rule with few exceptions that whenever in the twentieth century a man has stood up to defend the West against revolution, he has been destroyed by those whom he meant to defend or destroyed with their tacit approval or through their passivity.

General Drazha Mikhailovitch spoke for his kind to the Communist Yugoslav court which condemned him to death: "I wanted nothing for myself . . . I had against me an or-ganization, the Communist Party, which knows no compro-mise . . . The gale of the world carried away me and my work."

How futile is the eloquence which even its closeness to death cannot lift above pathos, as if a simple savage in his

ignorance were to try to move an intercontinental ballistic
missile to compassion by mentioning goodness and great purpose. And how apparent becomes the fatal flaw in General
Mikhailovitch's character when he supposes that the Communist Party was the revolution that he had against him.
What he had against him was the deepest failing of the
West, which let him die without raising a hand in his defense.
What he failed to understand was that the West is itself revolutionary, though the nature of its revolutionary thrust
takes forms different from that of Communism. But, at heart,
the West was closer to Tito than to Mikhailovitch who was
merely a parochial Serbian a patriot in a nineteenth-century
sense, traditional and religious, a general but not otherwise
much different from a peasant.

The West believes that man's destiny is prosperity and an
abundance of goods. So does the Politburo.

I awoke one morning to a surprised sense of a vast, relaxed
peace, and also to the realization that I was surfacing from a
dream in which I had been singing. In fact, after I was awake
but before I fully surfaced, my mind continued to sing through
a stanza of the song. It was in German:

> Brüder, zur Sonne, zur Freiheit,
> Brüder, zum Lichte empor,
> Hell aus der dunklen Vergangenheit
> Leuchtet die Zukunft hervor.*

You may have heard it, though without knowing what it
was. It is a Communist marching song, an unusually good
one. I had marched to it several decades ago. Yet for years,
I had not heard it, nor had it even, I think, passed through
my mind. Out of what depths had it come, and how had it

---

* Brothers, to sunlight, to freedom,
  Brothers, upward to light,
  Bright from the darkness of the past
  Beacons the future.

brought along that exceptional sense of great ordered peace? My dream was so recent that I seemed less to recapture it than to dream back into it. In my dream, I had found myself walking at night across a bleak square. It was enclosed with dark buildings and filled with masses of people. They were not crowding. They were drifting about aimlessly, alone or in little groups, because (I do not know how I know this) they had lost the sense of human cohesiveness. They had no direction; they were not going anywhere; they had no hope, but they did not know they had none. Do not ask me how I knew what touched me with bleak pity. But at the same time, I felt something joyous—not exultation, but a joy of life, a confidence of being alive which I wished to share with those sufferers. I turned to the shadowy figure, walking beside me—my brother, who has been dead many years. I asked him, nodding to the aimless people: "Shall we show them what to do?" At that instant, we were marching across the square. I realized I had a banner. For though I could not see it, I felt the wind take it and spread it, and felt the same little twist of resistance and pleasure in my shoulders as in the past. Then the song began. For though I was singing it, I could not be singing it; I have a very bad voice. The music simply came out of me and filled the square with the courage and joy of life:

> *Brüder, zur Sonne, zur Freiheit,*
> *Brüder, zum Lichte empor....*

So marching and singing, we crossed the dark square to its edge, when I awoke with the song still running on in my mind, and still trailing into the waking world that deep sense of peace which I had meant to bring to the people on the dark square. In puzzling over this strange dream, it seemed to me that, somewhere under the waters of sleep, I had again swum abreast, for a moment, of something that is a commonplace in the Communist world—purpose.

• • •

Through the convulsions of history various stoic postures have come into play. The great poet of history in this time sketched one such posture for us in one of the age's two great defeatist images, *The Twilight of the West.* (The other was *The Scholar Gypsy.*) Spengler wrote: "We are born into this time and must see it through to the end."

Those of us who became revolutionists in this time set our faces like stone against that image and staked our lives against the meaninglessness of history. In general, our act took the form of a decision against suicide. For who would consent to live a meaningless horror? Therefore our act, however mistaken in the consequence, will always seem to us a moral act. Some, demoralized by their disaster, will deny this. Some, you may force to deny it as a price of life (almost anything can be exacted of those who wish to live on in this world). But whatever they say, it is unlikely that in their hearts they are convinced. In their hearts, they are unconvinced: they hold that in its time and place, theirs was a moral act. They believe that in one of the few ways then evident to them, they bore witness to the spirit of man against historical meaninglessness and chaos. To become a revolutionist in this time is always primarily a historical experience, one enjoined by history and an attitude to it.

Later on, some of these even discovered that in opting against suicide, they had opted for murder organized under the name of Communism. And never were men more horribly undeceived. Albert Camus has paraphrased their dilemma in a notable passage. (Camus himself was a former Communist, former activist of the French Resistance.) He writes: "The question is to know whether innocence, from the moment it decides to act, can prevent itself from committing murder. We can act only among the men who surround us in that moment which is ours (*i.e.,* the century's historical crisis). We know nothing unless we know whether or not we have the right to murder that other before us, or to have him killed." This is what those men perceived too late and much less clearly under the pressures of the moment than it can be seen in calmer hindsight. A few—pitifully few, it is worth noting—found the strength (again combined with geographic luck) to act against their commitment to murder. This act, too, seemed to them a moral act. Of the two acts it seemed the higher, if only because it was so much the more difficult. The difficulties were of two orders, one of which, the more important, is little thought about. In breaking with Communism, these men had to expose themselves to the proper justice (or vengeance) of a society against which they had deliberately acted. All was novel, too, and untried. There were no charts. Nothing quite like this had happened before. And almost all were alone; almost all had acted alone, drawing their conclusions for themselves, drawing their strength to act from themselves, sealed in a lonely initiative that did not dare to share its thoughts with any other. Many, too, were carried to extremes by the force of reacting to something, a force which was an imperative to act at all. (Look at any line-up of captives. There may be philosophers among them. You will not easily find them under the dirt, the unwashed rags, weariness, and uncertainty. But these things could be borne, outlived, or personally succumbed to, which would dispose of the problem.) The more important difficulty was something else.

They were back where they started. The whole ordeal had been action against meaninglessness. They were back in a West without meaning, a West that is unable to find in itself a meaning equal to the crisis that besets it.

A Man
of the Right

The letters that follow were written over a period of about four years. I selected them from scores written in that period because they show Chambers struggling to define his political position. (He voted straight Republican tickets, but uneasily.) The first letter refers to an article Fortune *asked him to write describing his idea of the "Conservative Position." He began the article but never finished it for reasons that will become apparent. The other letters were to William Buckley, Editor of* National Review, *and Willi Schlamm, like Chambers an ex-Communist and then on the staff of* National Review *—written before and after Chambers worked for that magazine.—D.N-T.*

Dear Dunc:

Let's talk about the article on the Conservative Position. I do not see how you could be anything but distressed by my slowness in writing it. At the same time, I am putting everything I have into it. Everything I have is far short of the burst of stamina that used to carry me over the hump in past times. But I still have a good deal. Besides, there is on my shoulder an editorial touch much less patient than yours. It is a bony touch and its peremptory command is to finish while there is yet time . . . One has the sense of inditing an epitaph, an obit for the morgue, against the deadline of the patient's foreseeable demise. Or, it may be a kind of ms. found in a bottle to be washed up, chance serving, on some unimaginable shore after bobbing in what unimaginable sea of time. So much for climate.

The problems of writing are themselves very great. This is not a problem of waving some sparklers or touching off some rockets in memory of the Middle Ages or the Venetian

Renaissance. They provided their own arsensal of fireworks. The problem here is to make people *want* to read what most people ordinarily never want to read about and what in general others have found so resistant and unrewarding that few have wanted to write about it; and have come off for the most part, even the best of them, rather poorly in their infrequent attempts. To make readers want to read it—that is operational problem No. 1. But that scarcely take us across the doorsill.

The heart of the greater problem is, what makes the Conservative position so unappealing? What makes this great central position of mankind so much a skeleton of dried bones? Why, to put it simply, has the Right scarcely a voice that speaks for it with authority or conviction—or without the curse of faint apology? These are facts that must be thought through to the truth that makes them formidable. But these are merely the negative outworks that must be forced by the man who would explore and explain the central position. For there it towers, everlasting, I would say. But it is very difficult to excite people about what is everlasting.

No one is of much help in the matter. Those who have sought to deal with the riddle in the past have, for the most part, it seems to me, largely encrusted it with all manner of distracting error. We must give Russell Kirk an A for effort in *The Conservative Mind*. But looked at coldly—what confusion is brewed by slamming into one pot John Adams, John Randolph, John Calhoun, James Russell Lowell, Henry Adams, and George Santayana. Informed the book is; worthy it is—a worthy master's thesis. And, *faute de mieux*, we do well to push it. But if you were a marine in a landing boat, would you wade up the seabeach at Tarawa for *that* conservative position? And neither would I!

That is why I am trying to write a conservative position that will make sense to, that will not enrage, a marine as he steps waist-deep into the gunfire at Tarawa. No other is any good or any use. If it can't be done, there is no defensible conservative position—for the conservative position is not merely an acquisitive position. In my gropings and strugglings through the outworks, I think I have gone beyond the conservative position. I have found that behind it lies something much more steadfast—the conservative spirit, or, if you will, the conservative principle. Ages change, politics shift and slither—the conservative spirit does not change. It adjusts— because it is a summation of human wisdom, and in a sense organic, it looks from the fastness of life, and bends or yields to what is passing, but maintains, as the light shines in darkness, what is everlasting because it partakes of it itself.

But all this, of course, is only the backdrop to what must be stated. I hope this will give you some idea of the degree to which I am involved in this task. It is difficult to set logic to music. But logic which does not sing is only more of the same old mouse cheese. I am trying to make it sing so that others will sing it. For if you could excite a boy of draft age with the conservative position as now generally presented, it would be proper to suspect that the young man was a prig or a dud. And not the least of my problems is your businessman, a non-reader.

As ever,
Whittaker

April 2, 1954

Dear Dunc:

It is not just a question of reading books; after all, we have all read a book. The businessman despises the mind because it constantly threatens to complicate or subvert a few functions of the intelligence which are all he has use for. But he also fears the mind: for the mind is the host of the spirit. His functionalism is anti-spirit. He would like to liquidate it in the interest of efficiency. But it always eludes him. So he does the next best thing. He derides it. Now the spirit is taking vengeance.

Oswald Spengler says that if businessmen did read books, they would not be doers. I think he has a case. The businessmen's own instincts are right. The mistake is to ask them to be what they cannot be. Spengler quotes a Latin tag to make the point: *Navigare est necesse; vivere non est necesse:* "navigating (perhaps one should say: shipping) is necessary; living is not necessary." These men and their forebears built (and run) this technological civilization because they are this kind of men, and this kind of civilization requires them and merely tolerates others—thee and me and Joe Doaks.

Hence the implacable fury of the intellectuals—the excluded—now that they have learned to translate their fury into terms of political action. But at this point the businessman's illiteracy is his own nemesis. For those who have made this technological civilization by stripping from their lives everything except the will to power in those terms, who are what they are because they will not read—those captains no longer have left the minds to cope with the new sets of factors that their achievement has set in motion. At that point, not to read, not to think, becomes their fate. In the terse phrase of the masses whom their efforts have called forth: they never knew what hit them. Literally, they will never know what hit them. Reflex has replaced intelligence. Almost without exception the great businessmen are charmed and impressed by the great Communists whenever history (or trade) has brought them together face to face. They find they speak the same language, *i.e.*, the language of power and action stripped of intellectual baggage. But fate is glimpsed grimly in this fact: though the great Communists fool and baffle the great businessmen, the great businessmen are no puzzle to the great Communists who see straight through and beyond them.

I remember the outraged groans—oh, many years ago— when you laid down *The Decline of the West.* I do not believe that you ever read a briefer (104-page) book of Oswald's titled *Man and Technics*. Permit me to quote from the last two paragraphs as altogether the cheeriest bit of writing about our times:

> The history of the technics is fast drawing to its inevitable close. . . . Already the danger is so great for every individual, every class, every people that to cherish any illusion whatever is deplorable . . . there is no question of prudent retreat or wise renunciation. Only dreamers believe that there is a way out. Optimism is cowardice. We are born into this time and must bravely follow the path to the destined end. There is no other way. Our duty is to hold on to the lost position, without hope, without rescue, like that Roman soldier whose bones were found in front of a door in Pompeii, because, during the eruption of Vesuvius, he died at his post since they forgot to relieve him. That is greatness. That is what it means to be a thoroughbred. The honorable end is the one thing that can *not* be taken from a man.

Of course, Spengler wrote this in 1931 so that he did not live to learn that new techniques would develop whereby even the honorable end can be taken from a man. And, of course, he did not even hear of the A and H Bombs. You can see that Oswald's cold was worse than mine—I wish somebody could take that away from me.

Let me know when you get down to the country. Perhaps by that time the grandchild (yours) will be here. Ours only casts its shadow before—and what a shadow! My poor child.

Our love to all of you,

Whittaker

P.S. For no better reason than the fact that I was reminded of it last night, let me close with an irrelevant story which I find amusing. After the Hiss trials, I attended my first Quaker meeting in two years. I found myself the only man in a group of women Friends. We sat as usual in a circle. Facing me was

Mrs. XXX who might have modelled for one of the Helen Hokinson ladies. For an hour, the silence was total, rather than rewarding. Mrs. XXX herself ended it. Emerging from the mystic depths, she glanced across at me and asked: "Does thee feel that Dean Acheson must go?"

August 5, 1954

Dear Bill:

I no longer believe that political solutions are possible for us. I am baffled by the way people still speak of the West as if it were at least a cultural unity against Communism though it is divided not only by a political, but by an invisible cleavage. On one side are the voiceless masses with their own subdivisions and fractures. On the other side is the enlightened, articulate elite which, to one degree or other, has rejected the religious roots of the civilization—the roots without which it is no longer Western civilization, but a new order of beliefs, attitudes and mandates.

In short, this is the order of which Communism is one logical expression, originating not in Russia, but in the culture capitals of the West, reaching Russia by clandestine delivery via the old underground centers in Cracow, Vienna, Berne, Zurich, and Geneva. It is a Western body of belief that now threatens the West from Russia. As a body of Western beliefs, secular and rationalistic, the intelligentsia of the West share it, and are therefore always committed to a secret emotional complicity with Communism of which they dislike, not the Communism, but only what, by the chances of history, Russia has specifically added to it—slave-labor camps, purges, MVD *et al.* And that, not because the Western intellectuals find them unjustifiable, but because they are afraid of being caught in them. If they could have Communism without the brutalities of ruling that the Russian experience bred, they

have only marginal objections. Why should they object?
What else is socialism but Communism with the claws re-
tracted? And there is positivism. What is more, every garage
mechanic in the West, insofar as he believes in nuts and bolts,
but asks: "The Holy Ghost, what's that?" shares the substance of those same beliefs. Of course, the mechanic does
not know, when he asks: "The Holy Ghost, what's that?"
that he is simply echoing Stalin at Teheran: "The Pope—
how many divisions has the Pope?"

That is the real confrontation of forces. The enemy—he is
ourselves. That is why it is idle to talk about preventing the
wreck of Western civilization. It is already a wreck from
within. That is why we can hope to do little more now than
snatch a fingernail of a saint from the rack or a handful of
ashes from the faggots, and bury them secretly in a flowerpot
against the day, ages hence, when a few men begin again to
dare to believe that there was once something else, that something else is thinkable, and need some evidence of what it was,
and the fortifying knowledge that there were those who, at
the great nightfall, took loving thought to preserve the tokens
of hope and truth.

Sincerely,
Whittaker

September 14, 1954

Dear Dunc:

I have developed a rule to compensate for my blindness
about domestic politics. First, you set up the general situation
in which the U.S. is, for us, the important factor. Then you
estimate what is needed to meet that situation in terms of
leading men and maneuver. Having done that, you dump it,

except as a guide to what will not be, in the reasonable, firm faith that the American electorate will do just about the opposite of what reality indicates. The hazards of this method are obvious. Moreover, the premises are unfair because they imply that the American should act after the fashion of civilized Western man; as if he were what Europeans have always held him to be, though not always saying so as frankly as some Britons, namely, a colonial appendage of the West. And he isn't. He is a radical break with the West. He is something new (value judgments are secondary here). That is what most American intellectuals, and almost all Europeans, have failed to grasp. It is only at this point—that point of the American break with the West—that American history becomes of interest; that the American, as a type in history, becomes of interest. This is the point at which he is incalculable in terms of the mind of the West. He doesn't react according to plan because he isn't part of the plan. Henry Adams knew a good deal about this. He knew, in the form of a family catastrophe, that Andrew Jackson was a catastrophe, not merely to the initial American dream, but to the civilized West; and that Jackson presupposed Ulysses Grant and O. Henry's "Gold Bugs" and Jay Gould, just as they presupposed Dneprostroi and Magnitogorsk, whose underlying forces he presciently prefigured. But neither did he sniff at Andrew or Ulysses or Gould as forces of history. He merely said that they disproved Evolution. Henry preferred Chartres and the Virgin—a civilized preference. But Henry's greatness lies in the fact that he never mistook his preference for his historical reality, or let it get in the way of his extremely cold-blooded discernments. . . .

Of course, it is the duty of the intellectuals of the West to preach reaction, and to keep pointing out why the Enlightenment and its fruits were a wrong turning in man's history. But it *was* a turning, and, within its terms, we must maneuver at the point where to maneuver is to live. Hence the diehard

Republican position is not merely foredoomed; it is unintelli-
gent, for it does not understand its own logic in terms of
history. It still supposes that Senator Taft was a conservative
instead of what he actually was: a balky revolutionist who
was trying with his bare hands to stop the great wheel of
revolution from turning beyond the point which he and his
like found proper and comfortable. Actually, the Senator was
much clearer about the situation, at least his intuitions were
surer, than his camp followers. That is why he claimed, quite
correctly, that he was not a conservative but a liberal. So he
was—but a liberal on an escalator serving the Tower of
Babel. His objection was not to the Tower or the escalator,
but to being carried too fast past the twenty-ninth floor. He
also saw pretty clearly that there was no roof on the Tower
and that the escalator led into the wild blue yonder. But I
think it is only playing with words to suppose that the Senator's balkiness about the point he was trying to stop at was
conservatism. It was much more due to the fact that, as an intensely (even narrowly) practical mind, he understood what
Lenin understood when he said that he who says A must also
say B. Senator Taft saw this point from hither Ohio, after his
own dry fashion—that is, statistically instead of dynamically
—and he declined to say Bu-Bu-Bu-B. But he knew well
enough that nobody in Cincinnati was conservative in the
sense that he was going to get up and shout: "Farmers, back
to horses and the hand plough; smash your tractors and buy no
more." Instead, he very sensibly shaped the Taft-Hartley Law,
essentially a liberalizing measure, as he well understood from
where he stood on the escalator; but essentially also a counter-
revolutionary measure from where Labor stood since Labor
wanted to reach the thirtieth floor fustest with the mostest.

A friend claims that the archetype of the intellectual is
Don Quixote, and that his justification (perhaps his absolu-
tion) for being is to tilt against windmills. Good enough as
far as it goes. But I hold that the logic of that position is

enforced not by the intellectual, but by the martyr. That is why the political leaders of the Right are so futile and so fatuous. For there are no more solutions by argument of the loyal opposition. There are only martyrdoms, which are never solutions but pyres whose flicker is addressed, not primarily to the present, but to a posterity that has not yet cohered out of chaos and old night.

What I think my friend does not understand is that, not Quixote, but Joan [of Arc] is its effective assertion. Not words, but the play of fire seals man's hope and faith that there is a reality beyond and above the merely worldly reality of the turning wheel of history. Yet the wheel is real, the wheel is logical. Hence in periods of change like this one, it is only those who will throw themselves against it, in full consciousness of the cost and consequences, who can justify a defiance of its logic by certifying man's hope that a greater and better logic is conceivable. It is only by that scale that it is permissible to know that the midges are midges. But the same scale also tells us that Don Quixote has hair in his eyes. Dostoevsky, too, held that Don Quixote was the greatest creation of the human mind, or something close to that. But Joan has always held the center of my mind. Don Quixote was mad. But Joan was not; she was in all real affairs much more realistic than the professional realists of her day, who like those of our own day, were seldom realistic beyond the tips of their noses. But she also had hold of a deeper reality. For, of course, her voices spoke to her. We know this because otherwise nothing could have happened at all. The events, not the legend, would otherwise have been impossible.

The *New York Herald* or the *New York Tribune* used to publish with its Sunday edition uncolored prints of paintings which were certified great at least to the extent that they hung in some museum. I remember Bastien Le Page's well-known painting of Joan of Arc. We see the Maid, standing in the orchard at Domremy, listening to the voices of the saints.

This print I kept and put away between the pages of a great dictionary from which I took it from time to time to study and brood on it. I thought then that this was great art. My standards have since changed somewhat. I remember the disappointment with which, perhaps two decades later, I came upon the original, and was struck as much by its ostentatiously vast dimensions and anemic coloring as by a diffuse sentimentality which sent me shying back to Giotto or Fra Angelico. Today I believe that my boyhood response was wiser than my youthful superiority—I think that Bastien Le Page's Joan, for all its faults as painting, belongs to what George Orwell, in a penetrating essay on Kipling, has called "good bad art."

For, of course, what fixed me as a boy was the sense that I was in the presence of a great mystery. Joan had not as yet, I think, been solemnly acknowledged as a saint, and I was much too immature to articulate the implications which I dimly sensed. Still I knew that I was in the presence of mystery, a great mystery, one of those moments when a human creature has intruded, beyond any possible calculus of the mind or its imagination, into the process of history and has changed its course. The impact was the greater because here it was presented in terms with which I was perfectly familiar. Here was a sturdy milkmaid not greatly different from certain other husky milkmaids whom I knew. One of them, who used to deliver our family milk, was so much an amazon that my father was in the habit of referring to her as "that man, Mary." Here stood this instantly recognizable type in the orchard of an instantly recognizable farmstead. Moreover, the religious implication, which was deeply present—in fact, it gave the picture its whole meaning—was completely undisturbing. For the faces of the saints had been worked out and had to be looked for in the pattern on the apple boughs. It had the same fascination as that boy's puzzle in which what at first glance looked like a barnyard scene, turned out on

closer scrutiny to include the head of a pony or the face of a
cat dissembled in the lines of a barn roof or tree branches . . .
After Joan had been officially canonized, and as part of
our propaganda for France during World War I, a heroic
statue of her was unveiled on Riverside Drive in New York
City. I could never look at it except with dislike. This was not
Joan of Arc. This was the silly attitudinizing and trappings
in which the human mind invariably seeks to screen from its
knowledge the mere dirt and blood, weakness and suffering
that go into any acts like Joan's.

For me, Joan remained, even after I was old enough to
make the necessary qualifications, the peasant girl of Bastien
Le Page. She remained so until I came upon the photograph
of a statue of Joan in *Great Saints* by Walter Nigg. This was
a dumpier Joan, and though in armor, completely unheroic,
less peasant than lower-middle class—at least a peasant of a
family already on the highway to shopkeeping. This Joan,
the image closest to that of her own age, was probably the
closest to the physical facts. It divested her of nothing of her
sanctity. It merely rooted it more firmly in reality, and thereby
made it more wonderful.

Even as a boy, I had been least impressed by the obvious
mysteries of Joan's story—her unerring recognition of the
Dauphin though he was disguised as one of his own courtiers,
her knowledge that the sword would be found buried under-
neath such and such an altar. These merely raise the question:
How? It was other facts that impressed me always—the fact
that when wounded in the neck by an arrow she had screamed
and lost heart; the fact that in prison she had tried to kill
herself by throwing herself from the wall; the fact that she
had signed a partial recantation. These to me were always the
authenticating points of Joan's history even before I could
formulate my thoughts about them as firmly as I suppose that
I now do. Those made her human, were the evidences that
her mission was indeed divine because whenever she lapsed

from it she was precisely human. But Joan was a product of the countryside, not of cities. . . .

As always,
Whittaker

September 1954

Dear Willi:

History tells me that the rock-core of the Conservative Position, or any fragment of it, can be held realistically only if conservatism will accommodate itself to the needs and hopes of the masses—needs and hopes, which like the masses themselves are the product of machines. For, of course, our fight, as I think we said, is only incidentally with socialists or other heroes of that kidney. *Wesentlich*, it is with machines.

A conservatism that cannot face the facts of the machine and mass production, and its consequences in government and politics, is foredoomed to futility and petulance. A conservatism that allows for them has an eleventh-hour chance of rallying what is sound in the West.

In the matter of social security, for example, the masses of Americans, like the Russian peasants in 1918, are signing the peace with their feet. The farmers are signing for a socialist agriculture with their feet.

Next Friday, eight of my neighbors, including one of my close personal friends, go on trial in Federal Court in Baltimore for various violations of the crop-control laws. Emotionally, I am with them to the point of fury. Yet, from a realistic viewpoint, their position is preposterous. First, because, by and large, the nation's farmers have voted for socialization in this form. Second, because even these farmers themselves are not invincibly against subsidies in the form of support checks. What they are against is Government inspection of their crops to check the grain allotments.

But if you have voted for subsidies, or accepted $ checks, you have also voted for supervision. Who says A must also say B. Third, even if they were opposed on principle (as some are) to both subsidies and inspection, their position and reality have nothing in common because, in hard fact, in battling the Government, they are battling a Boyg, a mirage. It is only in the second instance that they are battling the Government. What, if they grasped reality, they are really battling is the 40-horsepower tractor, the self-propelled combine, the mechanical cornpicker, the hay-drier, and 10-20-20 fertilizers which make possible those gigantic yields and that increased man-hour productivity whose abundance spells bankruptcy and crisis—or controls. This is not theory. This is what a man knows when he stands before the wheat harvest in the brimming granary bins, and knows that the grain he runs through his fingers is his contribution to an unsalable surplus—this terrene wealth, this bounty of his sweat and acres—which, uncontrolled, spells not wealth, but his undoing. Few farmers voted for socialism as such, or even the program of the Farmers Union or the ADA, which, by and large, they loathe. They voted for a curb on their own incontinent productivity for the same reason that a fat man takes to diet—ultimately, to prolong his life.

The machine has done this. But every one of my indicted neighbors has sold off his horses and rides his tractor, and sends soil samples to the state college to learn how to up his yields. And not one of them has the slightest intention of smashing his machines or going back to horses and moderate yields—because machine farming is one reality that he can see and feel. Moreover, each knows how absurd it would be for him alone to buck the trend—he would be ploughed under by those who would not go along. The mass of farmers will keep their tractors, and milk more and more cows, until they drop of heart attacks. Only, they will not cut back. Therefore, the machine has made the economy socialistic. The

Government has only enacted one aspect of the fact into law. A conservatism that will not accept this situation must say: "We are reactionary in the literal sense. To be logical, we must urge you farmers to smash your machines (not sell them off, but smash them, and buy no more). For, otherwise, you will always get what you wanted; while what you do not want (restrictions, the end of the private domain) will be the literal reaping of what you sowed." But a conservatism that would say that is not a political force, or even a twitch: it has become a literary whimsy.

I loathe rural socialism. That is why I stopped growing wheat several years ago, and corn last year. I am trying to shape a workable farm economy that will slip around the socialist shackles; coexist with it in, as John Chamberlain once said, "the interstices." But I am not a farmer in the general sense. I am the exception, not the rule. I prove nothing unless the possibility that a few men can still live amiably by by-passing, not by kicking against the pricks. I have by no means proved it as yet. Meanwhile, let the Government men measure my fields and yields to their hearts' content. The very sight of them enrages me. I usually begin by treating them with formal courtesy and end by telling them to their faces that they are useless parasites. But, at worst, they stay only for a few hours, like a flock of crows; and, as I do not hunt crows when I am too busy with other things, though their clatter and marauding exasperates me, so I do not "run" (take a gun to) the Agriculture inspectors, as some of my neighbors have done. For I know that the crows will be there so long as the corn attracts and feeds them. And, unlike the crows, the inspectors are better armed than I am. I will simply not plant corn though I have no illusion that that is more than a postponement. If it isn't corn, it will be some other crop.

As you know, most factory workers are farmers *manqués*. Moreover, they flocked to the factories in the first place because even the industrial horrors of the nineteenth century seemed preferable to more than ten hours of haying in a shrivelling sun, or cows going bad with garget. I worked the hay load last night against the coming rain—by headlights, long after dark. I know the farmer's case for the machine and for the factory. And I know, like the cut of hay-bale cords in my hands, that a conservatism that cannot find room in its folds for these actualities is a conservatism doomed to petulance and dwindling—first unreality and then defeat. Let the conservative fill barley sacks behind the moving combine for even eight hours in a really good sun, and then load them, 100, 150 lb. bags, until midnight, and he will learn more about the realities of rural socialism (and about the realities of conservatism) than he could ever glean from the late, ever to be honored Robert Taft.

Naturally, it is not so simple as I have sketched it above. I know, too, that the 40-horsepower tractor is only one turn on the road that leads to the H-Bomb and beyond. If I were a younger man, if there were any frontiers left, I should flee to some frontier because, when the house is afire, you leave by whatever hole is open for whatever area is freest of fire. Since there are no regional frontiers, I have been seeking the next best thing—the frontiers within, John's interstices. But I have no notion that my antics have a validity for anybody else except a handful of similar escapists. Escapism is laudable, perhaps the only truly honorable course for humane men—but only for them. Those who remain in the world, if they will not surrender on its terms, must maneuver within its terms. That is what conservatives must decide: how much to give in order to survive at all; how much to give in order not to give up the basic principles. And, of course, that results in a dance along a precipice. Many will drop over, and, always, the cliff-dancers will hear the screaming curses of those who fall, or be numbed by the sullen silence of those, nobler souls perhaps, who will not join the dance.

Tell your wife that I am not really cavalier about toadstools. I am bold, but fairly prudent as in: *Sei kühn, sei kühn, aber nicht zu kühn*. But it is as well to learn to know poison when one sees it: the noblest minds have found it a blessing at need.

What a harangue.

As always,
Whittaker

September, 1954

Dear Bill:

I have long feared (have sometimes cautioned) that you suppose me to be something which I really am not. At the risk of offending you, I am going to try to rough out crudely the situation out of which I think the trouble comes. First, you stand within a religious orthodoxy. I stand within no religious orthodoxy. The temptation to orthodoxy is often strong, never more than in an age like this one, especially in a personal situation like mine. But it is not a temptation to which I have found it possible to yield. Forgive me for saying this, but we must get ground under our feet.

You also stand within, or, at any rate, are elaborating, a political orthodoxy. I stand within no political orthodoxy. You mean to be a conservative, and I know no one who seems to me to have a better right to the term. I am not a conservative. Sometimes I have used the term loosely, especially when I was first called on publicly to classify myself. I say: I am a man of the Right. I am a man of the Right because I mean to uphold capitalism in its American version. But I claim that capitalism is not, and by its essential nature cannot conceivably be, conservative.

This is peculiarly true of capitalism in the United States, which knew no Middle Ages; which was born, insofar as it was ideological, of the Enlightenment. Hence the native effort to rest in the past always makes us a little uneasy, seems merely nostalgic, antiquarian, futile, and slightly fraudulent. England was the first great power in which capitalism seized the State apparatus; begun in 1640, consolidated in 1660. France was the second. In both powers, the medieval vestiges, which had slowly to be assimilated or co-existed with, formed a conservative continuity that was valid, and persists even into 1958.

America was the first capitalist power that started from scratch in a raw continent. We are something new under the sun. Only the American South sought to persist in the past, as an agrarian culture, resting on slaves instead of serfs. To wipe out this anachronistic stronghold, above all to break its political hold on the nation as a whole, the emergent capitalist North fought with it what amounted to a second Revolution, that took form in what was (up to that time) the bloodiest (and first) of modern wars. Here, for the first time on such a scale, were used the products, turned into weapons, of Northern industrial capitalism—railroads, telegraph, machine guns, submarines, armored ships, etc., etc. In sum, the South lost because it could not match the North in those products whose fabrication it scorned in the name of a superior culture —the fatality of history. You know the rest. From the ruins of war, in direct consequence of war's industrial needs, U.S. capitalism burst into such growth as the world had never seen before. Moreover, as the contending capitalism of Europe (and Japan) later destroyed themselves in war, American capitalism grew massive as the unassailed arsenal. At the same time, with the favorable trade balance, it freed itself from Europe's financial grip and became itself the guardian of the hoard whose symbol is Fort Knox.

There is in this history not one single touch of conservatism. How could it be otherwise? Conservatism is alien to the very nature of capitalism whose love of life and growth is perpetual change. We are living in one of its periods of breathless acceleration of change. Science has been, from the beginning, the ideological weapon of capitalism, and is now asserting (even though it may not be interested in doing so) an exclusive dominance. I am saying that conservatism and capitalism are mutually exclusive manifestations, and antipathetic at root. Capitalism, whenever it seeks to become conservative in any quarter, at once settles into mere reaction —that is, a mere brake on the wheel, a brake that does not hold because the logic of the wheel is to turn. Hence the sense of unreality and pessimism on the Right, running off into all manner of crackpotism. Hence, on the other side, the singular manifestation (or so it seems) of prime capitalists (a Rockefeller, a Harriman or Mennen Williams) turning, as we say, Left. In fact, whatever political forms their turn cloaks itself in, they are chiefly seeking to pace, in order to continue to dominate, the new developments to which the logic of capitalism itself is giving rise, now at tremendous rates of speed. I, too, am a fly, clinging to that violently turning wheel, in the hope of slowing it by what a fly's weight is worth. But I am pro-capitalist; I would only retard for an instant, seek to break the fearful impacts of change, hold back lest the rush of development (in a multitude of frightful forms) carry us to catastrophe, as, in fact, seems almost inevitable. But, above all, I seek to understand what the reality of the desperate forces is, and what is their relationship in violent flux . . . We are in the middle of a universal earthquake. If we survive it, then there will be something to reflect on. It is perfectly clear that we may not survive. At that point, I lose interest.

Forgive me, if you can, the primer history lesson, the discursive superficiality of all this, from which so much is left out. So much that is relevant. But, poor as it is, I think I owe it to you as a crude chart of my view.

We look forward to your visit.

                                        As always,
                                        Whittaker

How to Look
at the Gorgon's Head

Son:

You asked me recently: "What becomes of me if socialism
wins everywhere?" As I glanced at you during the seconds
while I was groping to decide whether or not I had the right
to answer you directly, you may have thought that the image
in my mind was simply one of you, sitting beside my desk,
adding gravely: "I have to think of my life in terms of twenty
or thirty years." In fact, there were two other images in my
mind. Both rose from whatever cells we keep such recollec-
tions capped in to rise only to the top at a question like yours.
One was the image of a boy standing motionless at night beside the sheep barn, leaning on his rifle. It was you a few
years younger. The other image was the ruin of a wall receding swiftly across a wide plain.

The images rose together because your question provided
a link between them in my mind. I shall deal first with the
image of the boy, standing silent, holding your gun by the
sheep barn on a night when raiding hounds had awaked us.

You called quietly to make sure that, in my surprise, I did not fire. Neither of us knew that the other was up. Each had simply responded, independently, in the same way, to the same alarm. I looked at you with as deep contentment as a man can know. But all I said to you was to go back to sleep, that I would watch alone for awhile. What filled my mind was that sight of you standing, self-summoned, in the shadow of the barn. It touched in me something which, I suspect, most fathers are given to feel at some moment—the feeling of any man that with his son beside him he is never any more a man completely alone in the creation. It gave the simplest reassurance craved by any man, who, toward the end of his years, must begin to lean a little into that region of space which is freezingly cold and dusty with the debris of so many shattered or encrusted molds that he is leaving behind him in this one son, leaning on a rifle, to shield his own by night. That was the image of the boy.

The other image was wholly different. It begins with myself when I was only a few years older than you are now, when I was twenty-two. I was travelling alone by train from Brussels to Paris. At one moment, in northern France, everybody crowded to a window and pointed. There stood in the distance, which the train swiftly diminished, a wedge of jagged wall: St. Quentin. The train was crossing the still-raw battle lines of the old Western front. The wall was what was left by the shell-fire of World War I, which had ceased not quite four years before. In itself the broken wall was not much different from the wall of any house partly dismantled to make way for a housing project. But to me it was not so. I had recently come out of a Germany where closing in every waking hour, on me as on everybody else, there were the pressures of something for which nothing in my experience had prepared me—the pressures of the collapse of a world. I had never before witnessed mass desperation. But I was not too young to read its signs in the lines of every other face I passed more explicitly than in the words with which some tried to convey it to us. I did not know the meaning of what I was witnessing. There could scarcely have been set loose to view at first hand one of history's great turning points a young American more ignorant than I of its realities. I did not know that all around me, as I went my silly way, the Communists were stocking arms and drilling men for what was to be, a few months later, the aborted revolution of 1923. I was as ignorant as a foreign correspondent of what a Communist really was. But even I could not quite escape the vertigo that goes with paying something like thirty thousand marks for the morning's rolls and coffee (inflation was at its height). And, as I left that despair-haunted German nation, I came out through the Belgian, English, and French armies occupying the Rhineland. All I sensed, and the ruins at Louvain did nothing to diminish it, was that one fact: that I was present at the visible collapse of a world. Its dismaying impacts came together against that wedge of wall left standing in the plain. So that its simple ordinariness made it ever after the unifying symbol of all I felt but did not then understand. It raised to a new power the question which was forming in my mind—the question of which yours is a current version. I put it differently in keeping with that so much earlier stage of our ordeal: "What is happening to us?" I spent the rest of my life trying to answer it. The difference in the question measures what has happened to us in the distance we have come.

These images, which take so long to tell about, converged for a few seconds only in my mind. Your question focussed them because, when I was just five years older than you are now, I came to believe that it was my lot to live at the end of an age such as occurs once in a thousand or two thousand years. Such an end does not consist merely in violent change. It implies a radical transformation of all reality—first of all, of men's view of the world and the meaning of their life and death in it. The wedge of wall stood close to the center of the earthquake, shaken down by the first shocks, irreparably. Your question told me how far, in my lifetime, the shocks had spread. They had reached you in this quiet land at the outermost edge of the disturbance. They had reached you at a stage as different from that stage in which I first felt them as age is from childhood. What had puzzled my mind was to you a possibility verging on finality in personal form: "What becomes of me if socialism wins everywhere?"

You meant, by socialism, just what I should mean (since we have talked over these things before). That is, you meant, by socialism, all those related political manifestations, including Communism and a good deal of what in America passes, for reasons of political expedience, by the name of Liberalism; that have common origins in the historical insights and (to one degree or another) in the doctrines of Karl Marx and others; that share at least two beliefs—the necessity of internationalism and of planned economies; and that differ chiefly about the problem of violence or coercion, how it is to be applied in the socializing processes, in what amounts, at what point. In other words, with similar ends in view, one body of socialist thought (British socialism, for example) would change traditional society lawfully by using the conventional machinery of government to bring about its radical change. The other great body of socialist thought (Communism) would make the change unlawfully by smashing the conventional governmental forms at the start, and improvising the new socialist society from scratch.

Like me, you could not seriously use either word, socialism or Communism, as an epithet, recognizing that neither of these is merely a product of human mischief, but that each of these great movements is a name for a political form in which a deep-going conflict of forces within our age is reflected and enacted. Like me, you must feel, too, that the success of either of these revolutionary forms faces you, not so much with a problem of choice—that is, whether or not, by compromise and inconspicuousness you could manage to exist, drag out some kind of crippled existence under either form. Rather, it faces you with a much more ultimate problem, that is, whether or not it would be physically possible to endure the daily suffocation which socialism must mean to you in everything that makes life worth living to a free man. Ultimately, that is what your question implied. And that made it extremely difficult to answer.

Because I sat silent for a few seconds, you probably thought that I was groping for an answer or words to put it in. Instead, I was groping to decide whether I had the right to answer you at all. You probably thought, too, that the image behind my eyes, as I watched you, was simply that of you sitting beside my desk, adding with the awesome gravity of your age: "You know, I must think of my life, now, in terms of twenty or thirty years."

Do you remember the Gorgons, the three beautiful and deadly sisters, on their seaside rock in the moonlight? You will recall that, in the Greek myth, Perseus was sent to slay one of the Gorgons in the belief that they would unfailingly slay him, and thus thriftily relieve the world of that tiresome young man. We remember his name much better than so many more important ones in the intervening thousands of years because Perseus managed not to be slain, and because, around that mythical feat, the Greeks, as usual, managed to condense certain indispensable wisdom about experience more crisply than anybody else, and more simply.

The sleeping Gorgons were not terrifying, of course, because their heads were uncomfortably crowned with snakes instead of hair. Their terror lay in the fact that any man who dared to look them directly in the face was turned to stone. Yours was a petrifying question that raised the problem of the future in the form of which, for me, it is most acute and personal—in the form of your life and your sister's.

So I remembered that when Perseus cut off the Gorgon's head, he did so not by looking her directly in the face. He studied her reflection in a polished shield at the moment when he poised his sword and struck. For part of the wisdom of this fable is its warning that it is not always (or often) well to look reality too steadily in the face lest it turn our wills to stone.

So I chose not to answer your question, then, judging that it was unfair to you to hasten the time when, as my son, you would certainly have your chance to face the Gorgon's head even in a polished shield. For I could not answer you with that saving indirection which we call tact and which we use to spare those who, for one reason or another, we feel are not equipped to meet the impact of reality. I could only answer you, as my son, with the literal reality, as I see it.

History, it seems to me, is now beginning to move with great speed toward a showdown. I believe that socialism already holds important beachheads here. You know, too, that I hold that the winds of history need blow only a little more keenly to disperse a lot of willful fog and illusion that now shrouds the true meaning of these beachheads, not only from the mass of people but even from many of those included on the beachheads.

Again, I am forecasting what most people will consider a sickly nightmare. That is, a world in which Communism may have so far extended its power that the United States will be islanded and outnumbered so that the questions of the day will be whether the last fringe war is to be fought in the United States and how to avoid it. That is where, I am assuming, the socialist beachheads come in. They will provide the mediating forces with Communism. For the socialists most resemble, share in their own terms the Communist objectives, just as they share the basic Communist view of the world and what man should try to make of it, and therefore speak a dialect of the same language. Hence, it is to socialists that Communists commonly speak first in consolidating their advances. These advances have, in general, been made with much more practical meaning and patience than the West has noted. For Communists understand, in its most cold-blooded form, the art of ruling, that is, the art of exercising power. This is precisely what, in general, socialists have never understood for reasons that go deep into the real differences between socialist and Communist, but which this is not the place to examine. Thus, socialism almost always enters into coalition with Communism, dragging along a whole flutter of people who are not even as well defined as socialists. These are the vaguely humane and progressive, sometimes articulate, as a rule, intellectually and politically rather genderless people that perhaps every civilization in collapse breeds as a symptom of waste product, and this one certainly does.

This pattern of eleventh-hour socialist coalition with Communism has become almost traditional. We saw it in 1919 when the socialists, then the government of Hungary, went into the jails and there made a deal with the Communist leaders by way of a coalition in which the Communists were the dominant power. We saw it again in Poland in the 1940s where the Communists first ruled in coalition with the socialists. We saw it again in Czechoslovakia as part of the softening-up tactic whereby the Communists seized power in that country by a *coup d'état* in 1948. The same kind of pattern was trying to assert itself in the fall of China, though there the socialist-liberal groups within the Nationalist framework were small; and unfamiliar to most of us, so that, curiously, we can observe their temper, and the traditional pattern, much more closely from the American end where it operated with decisive success to confuse and paralyze the will of this nation about the China crisis. And, of course, Communist power in Italy rests on a coalition with the powerful Socialist Party led by Pietro Nenni. I think we may expect to see something like the same pattern repeat itself in the present German situation, though the German socialists (Social Democrats) long blocked the path of Communism, in part because the 1919 Revolution made the socialists the government of Germany so that they became actual rivals of the Communists for government power. Why does this pattern repeat? Obviously, both socialists and Communists are social revolutionists, agreeing closely in general purpose, differing chiefly in certain methods—that is, differing about the use of violence to achieve power. But there is often, too, a strong emotional affinity that persists beyond all other differences. This affinity, I think, Mr. Hugh Dalton has expressed most tersely. Some years ago, this former minister of the Crown was exhorting his colleagues at a meeting of the Labor Party to pursue a more sympathetic policy toward the Soviet government. Mr. Dalton put it this way: "The Left understands the Left." I take it that here is only one rational reading of this remark and that Mr. Dalton meant that socialist sympathy is of its nature closer to revolutionary forces, including the Communists, than it can be to the traditional forces within a nation. This is perfectly logical, and I, for one, am grateful for the candor and the simple clarity.

Socialists commonly make coalitions with the Communists only in the desperate clinches of history, which are, of course, becoming more desperate and more frequent. No doubt, certain of the socialist leaders, those perhaps who by temperament of expediency hold closest to the Communist pattern, suppose that through coalition they may achieve real power. It is not even necessary to read into the word "power" a selfish or narrow meaning, but simply to take it as it may appear to such people as a means of putting into effect certain doctrines and projects which they deeply believe to be for the common good. Yet the mass of socialists are moved at such times, I think, by other motives. They see themselves acting as the only effective brake left upon Communist extremism, as the one moderating force left in an endangered nation. In this they must seem to themselves to be acting in the name of reality and common sense. And so they must seem to millions of others, too, who are not socialists but who must come to look upon the socialists almost as saviours, since there are no others. I am not sure but what common sense, in such terms, may not prove one of the gravest forces of our undoing. And this pattern might one day be repeated here so that millions of Americans, awaking at last from the great complacency, turn to the socialists (in America, read "liberals") and cry: "You alone can talk to these people, and, in fact, they will talk to no one but you. In the name of common sense, do whatever is necessary to save us."

As your father I must tell you that your question implies another much more rending. It is: whether you would choose to live at all in a world where socialism had won everywhere. It is a rending paradox of our time that history is atomic. But the mass of men lags far behind. Thus, they seldom know what is happening to them, or even what has happened to them. In most ways, they contrive to exist in the age of Queen Victoria, seeing the world and seeking to act by the standards of that quieter time. If, by any chance, they catch, out of the tail of their eyes, the shadow of the Gorgon's head, they close their eyes tightly and lapse back with all the inertia of unconscious will into an illusion which reality has not yet shot from around them.

Unhappily, my son, you cannot shut your eyes. You have to see that this age is not Sir Winston Churchill's "sunny uplands." It is a battered beachhead where, even for masses of men, the decisions reached will be life-and-death decisions. They will be reached, moreover, with none of the spacious margin for choice of easier times. In this age is being decided what terms life is worth living on. This is the point of conflict beyond all words like socialism which are merely names for the political forms in which the conflict is reflected or enacted.

What you will have to face, the genius of an English mind

and speech has put in final words into the mouth of Brutus, surveying the lost field of Philippi:

> Thou seest the world, Volumnius, how it goes;
> Our enemies have beat us to the pit:
> It is more worthy to leap in ourselves,
> Then tarry till they push us.

A sudden acceleration seems to have set in so that history has begun to run out with awesome urgency. I have little to leave you but my reading of the meaning of what is happening to us.

The Sentry

My son walked up the path on the summer day, and did not look back, which is the way he and I like to keep our important partings: short and simple. The path was the brick path from the house to the barns that his mother had laid down in more carefree days, so long ago that he probably could not remember a time when the path had not been there. It was shaded by the English walnut trees and the locusts that had been growing before he was born so that they were part of the permanent landscape of his boyhood. He would return in an hour or so. Yet we both knew that this was an important parting. He was walking toward one of the invisible divides of our time, and must walk toward it alone. He was driving to Westminster, Maryland, to register with his draft board. By answering some routine questions, by filling some blank spaces in an official form and signing his name, he would begin to march, at the lowest stage, in the lowest rank, directly into the history of his time.

My son and I seldom talk solemnly about anything. By

choice, we have lived our lives together chiefly in work clothes. We think we know that life, where it counts for us, is best dealt with in work clothes, and its meanings, where they count for us, are best dealt with in workaday words. Where such words will not serve, we prefer humor. Where humor will not serve, we prefer silence.

But, before he left, my son had been restless. I suppose that most are at such a time. And I suppose that I was much like any other father in wanting somehow to reach what I took to be the cause of his restlessness—his chilling sense that his life, which until then had been free as only young American lives are any longer free, was about to harden into one more serial number on the endless dog tags. I thought that I must try to make clearer to him a wider reality under the simple formality he was about to go through.

So I told my son that only in the strictly legal sense, was anybody summoning him anywhere. He was, in fact, going to register certain claims of his own. By registering for the draft, he was, for the first time, registering his claim to be a man and citizen by claiming his right to bear arms in defense of his land. Further, he was claiming his right to fellowship among his people in the only terms that finally seal that fellowship—his right to offer his life, at need, for all the rest, all those other lives known and unknown to him, the mean just as much as the generous, the weak just as much as the strong, the foolish just as much as the wise, which make up the millionfold mystery of a nation. This was the saving point of knowledge, to be lost only at the risk of personal disaster—that a man always gives his life just as much for those whom we loosely call "bad" as for those whom we loosely call "good." This was the knowledge that, in any job lot of humanity, sorts the men from the boys, together with the specifically Christian knowledge that it is by sacrifice, or the willingness to sacrifice, that any man snatches life from the blur and smudge of death and gives it meaning while he measures himself. We understand each other well, my son and I. He understood that I spoke at all because that was the utmost point to which I could go with him on the march that he must take from there alone.

But our sons are also our children. At eighteen, my son tops me by several inches, and must glance down a little when he speaks to me directly. Few fathers can have brought that much boy so far along the turns and spins of life without feeling a simple pang as they watch him walk away. For, from that moment, we know that the most familiar everyday path, from any house to any barn, now dips beyond our sight, and that it is there—at some point where we no longer have power to see or help—that the veiled figures of necessity and of chance wait motionless.

Any father who, in his thoughts, has reached that point, reaches, at the same instant, a blank wall in which the single gate is barred by a sentry with a braced rifle. If, in his thoughts, the father should ask the face beneath the depersonalized helmet: "Who are you?" the sentry will answer: "I am the man who stands beside your son because I am the personification of all men's sons."

If the father asks: "What are you guarding?" the sentry will answer: "An ageless knowledge—the knowledge that at least once in his life, life allows every man to know what he is capable of. It allows each to give the answer whose meaning is always the same, however it is given."

If the father then asks: "What is the answer?" the sentry will say: "A resistance fighter gave it once in two words. A stranger asked him: 'What do you do in the hills when you are seriously wounded, without medicine or water, you cannot crawl away and you know no help will come?' The fighter answered: 'We die.' "

If the father asks: "Must that be the answer?" the sentry

will say: "That is the answer—the same from the birth of
the race to the fall of the Hydrogen Bomb. That is what a
man is capable of. We die—that is, we do not surrender.
We die that life may live. That is what enough men have
always known. And that is why no man, father or otherwise,
can spare any other man, son or not, his right to give at
need that answer, which he never gives for himself alone.
He gives it for all others. And whenever any age, nation, or
enough men in it, have lost the instinct to give that answer,
there is only one question left to answer: 'How long?' For
they will have lost an instinct necessary to live."

If the father then asks in his torment: "Why must the
answer be given?" the sentry will say: "Because someone
has always died that you may sit quietly in your lamplight
of an evening. Think that one over. For generations like yours
have become very cunning in taking cover from it, or in
confusing it."

If the father objects: "But all that is heroics," the sentry
will answer: "We laugh at the word 'hero.' We laugh till we
are sick. Because the first time a man sees a body bloating
in a ditch, he knows that there is nothing heroic about death.
But we know, too, that any man who denies that the least
man alive is capable of heroism, curses life. Turn back, old
man, you clutter the space you stand on. Your job is to wait,
and to try not to remember. But remember this: The same
answer will also be required of you, in your own way—and
of every other father—in part every moment that you are
waiting, and in full if the moment comes when your son
claims his right to give that answer in full. Go, and do not
come back to this point, even in thought, unless life and
death send for you."

My son's car crept up the slope and out of sight around
the end of the barn just as simply as everything that ever
matters in life, in the end, simply passes out of sight. My
son was the being for whom the last years of my life were

largely lived, and without whom it was scarcely conceivable
that I should have made the effort to live them. He was not
the only being with such claims upon my life. His mother and
sister had equal claims, or greater. But as a son and, therefore, in this century inevitably a soldier, he had a particular
claim. Simply by being, he posed for me the question which
I prayed that life would never bring him to put to me: What
have you done? For, when I was scarcely older than my son,
I had shared the view of certain revolutionary circles that,
for those who could foresee what the history of our age would
be like (and thousands did foresee it), it was better not to
breed children to suffer it. Nevertheless, I had given my son
life. Now life and history were interacting. By 1955, the
main sweep of history differed from what I had expected in
1925, chiefly by being on a scale of havoc so much vaster and
more various than any man would have dared to imagine
thirty years before. Through the radical changes of my
individual life, my view of the forces shaping the history of
our time had scarcely changed at all. What had changed
was my view of how a man conducts himself in face of those
forces.

The underpinnings of the world give way—will continue
to give way so long as there are lines of structural weakness
to crumble, inducing pressures great enough to crumble
them. They will continue until the unsettled crust of the
world achieves a new pattern of stability in a new balance of
tensions.

By the age of twenty-four, I had begun to surmise that
the history of the twentieth century was to be the history of
an earthquake whose successive shocks, the result of causes
working largely out of sight, would take form in world wars,
civil wars, and less readily classifiable dislocations. My observation, and that of others, told me that the world of our
time was shot through, at every level, with lines of sagging
structural weakness, against which grinding pressures were

at work, and that the shocks would continue, taking little
account of the thoughts, hopes, plans, strategies, and even
the life and death of millions, until the process had worked
itself out to the end, until a new adjustment of reality had
been reached in a new balance of tensions.

Thirty years later, at the age of fifty-four, I had only to
open my country newspaper, or turn the knob of a radio, to
learn clamorously that the earthquake was still in full swing.
As usual, even in an earthquake, masses of people who had
not felt its full shock went busily about their personal affairs. And, as usual, those who make a virtue of their failure
to think, feel, or act forcefully by calling it "moderation,"
were assuring the rest that much the most sensible course
was to suppose that the shocks could be contained; we might
even learn to coexist with them.

It was into a late, if not the last, convulsion of that historical
earthquake that my son was marching. I was troubled that,
like most of his generation, he seemed to me to know so little
about the reality of the forces which, one way or another,
must shape the rest of his life.

My son thought that he was marching, ultimately, toward
a third world war. I thought that he was marching into a
worldwide revolution of which the two world wars had been
chiefly the most conspicuous claps. I thought it at least extremely unlikely that there would be a third world war.

My son thought that he was marching against Communism, that Communism was, in fact, the revolution. I
thought that Communism was only one manifestation among
others, though a malignant and aggressive one, of a revolution that included the West quite as much as the Communist
world.

He thought that Communism had caused this crisis of
history. I thought that the historical crisis existed independent
of Communism. Communism had not invented the crisis of
history or even that phrase, which was merely a shorthand

way of lumping the action of all the unsettling forces of our time, too cumbrous and complex to deal with in detail. Communism inflamed this crisis by promoting a solution that it offered for it.

My son believed that the Communist solution was unworkable, and, under its brutish and homicidal manifestations, preposterous and often comical. He believed this, in large part, because that was what was being said in the world around him. I, on the contrary, held that the Communist solution was a workable solution. At least, after some forty years, it was still menacingly at work. It was a solution, by our standards, of a very low order. By any practical experience known to the West, it was grossly primitive, inefficient, and wasteful. In any human terms shared by us, it was evil and hideous. But the fact that it was horrible and inhuman did not prove that it was unworkable.

Nevertheless, my son also believed (for he had picked up this paradox too of our popular thinking) that the strength of Communism, and its menace to us, lay chiefly in its military, technological, scientific, and conspiratorial power. I thought this view much too easy to fit the observable facts.

My son believed this because he thought of the West as a unit distinct from Communism, standing wholly apart from it, and, under all the shifts and twists of governments and parties, opposed to Communism. I held that the West was no such unit, that it was, in fact, deeply, if not incurably, divided against itself—and not chiefly along national lines.

"Honey! Honey! Honey!"

Ritual is, of course, a ceremony whereby we celebrate and give form to some of our deepest beliefs. Often we do not know exactly what it is we are giving expression to because we do not know exactly what it is we believe. Ritual speaks for us without our having to and gives us a common language whereby to express a body of feeling, of otherwise formless hopes, fears, desires. Sometimes, therefore, ritual itself becomes more important to us than what it expresses. When that happens, and when the ideas that ritual give form to (for there are rituals of opinion as well as rituals of belief) no longer correspond to the reality around us, we feel a vague discomfort that most of us succeed in repressing. Sometimes, too, we find ourselves saying things which are completely at odds with what we do. Between acts and facts a curious discrepancy sets in. We are scarcely conscious of it.

I was sitting in one of our training camps—one of those vast military cities—thousands of sun-baked, bulldozed, almost treeless acres, thousands of cubic housing units, painted identical olive drab and laid out with that geometric bleakness whereby technology imposes simple order on its own complexity. Here men, structures, life are regimented, disciplined, stripped to the irreducible function of preparing for modern war, so that even the post's nursery school and beauty parlor are painted olive drab.

From behind me, on a drill field that stretched from a horizon I could not see to a horizon that lay beyond a dip I could not follow, came the thud of footfalls—five hundred or a thousand men marching, and the drill sergeants commanding the step: "Hup, two, three, four! Hup, two, three, four!" The men began to sing—five hundred or a thousand voices lifting the words,

> Five more days and I'll be out,
> Honey! Honey! Honey!
> Five more days and I'll be out,
> Honey! Honey! Honey!

It was funny, strictly in the American style, which shifts gears on an unbearable longing to make it bearable by making it funny. It was sobering, too. For if there is a sound sadder than that of soldiers marching or singing as they march, few parents have heard it—especially when it has been heard three times on a scale without equal in history within the life span of a middle-aged man.

But, above all, the words of the song were frightening. In themselves they were nothing, but they did not come from nothing. Those who sang them scarcely gave them conscious meaning. But they had a meaning. They were not accidental. They echoed something extremely widespread and deep-rooted throughout the Western world. They echo ourselves—not what we commonly say, but what we deeply feel. They go to the heart of our most cherished unrealities.

Hope and fear alike have turned the West into a vast drill field. And as all of us—all of us—go marching, sergeants barking the step, from a horizon we have turned our backs on to a horizon that eludes us, we think even if we do not say it:

> Five more days and I'll be out,
> Honey! Honey! Honey!

The worst of it is that some of us believe it.

Amanita Muscaria

The fly amanita (the *Amanita muscaria*) grows in Siberia—
and also in our American woods. It is one of the most
beautiful of mushrooms; its yellow cap is usually covered
with what look like tiny flecks of white scale. It is also one
of the more poisonous members of a mushroom tribe that
is generally deadly to man. Americans who eat it from
ignorance, unless they take quick countermeasures, expect
to die. Countermeasures are not always successful because the
poison principle is akin to the principle of rattlesnake venom;
it breaks down the red cells of the blood. In parts of Siberia,
the fly amanita is left to soak in vodka. This decoction is
then drunk; no one dies. Instead, it lifts the drinkers above
what we commonly call "drunkenness" into a kind of madness
which is most nearly described in the Greek word *menis*, the
first word incidentally of *The Iliad*, the root of our word
"mania." That madness enables those who risk it to survive
the monumental cold of that country, the winters of almost

unending night, its desolate distances, unpeopled, savage, tundra and taiga, the perpetual silence of those thousand-mile evergreen forests where even in summer, the sun never penetrates to the forest floor, which is therefore a swamp. The strength of poison is required to enable some men to endure the pressures of such reality.

Yet, too, as the ice recedes in spring, ducks return and fly in wedges above the reviving land. Here is found the frail Siberian iris, which, transplanted to our gardens, we call, because its color is deeper than imperial purple, "Caesar's Brother." Here blooms the martagon, the most delicate of lilies and perhaps the only purple one. A Rumanian woman, a Communist, once said to me: "Who has not seen the sun rise on Lake Baikal and the mountains"—she hesitated for words to convey something tremendous, and added—"will die without having seen the world."

And once I met a Russian, a gracious, slightly melancholy man, slowly dying of a heart condition. In his youth, he had been an anarchist and had passed some time in Siberian exile. As the realization grew on him, a little incredulous that I grasped not only his words but meanings which the words only partly represented, he drew out of some dusty heap something that he wanted to show me. It was a photograph of himself taken in Siberia, an old-fashioned photograph, not rectangular but round like the camera lens. It showed a young man with the dreamy, idealistic face common to the anarchist type. He wore a Russian blouse, the *rubashka*, and was sitting in a Siberian hut beside a window filled with potted plants. The older version of the young exile, the man close to death, began to speak, choosing his English words slowly (he spoke five or six languages and I suppose it was difficult sometimes to sort out the right words in the right order). He said: "The Siberians are not a mellow people, like the Great Russians. But, you see," (here he pointed to the potted plants in the photograph), "there are flowers in the window. So there is something good and gentle about those people, too."

The poison, amanita, and potted plants induced madness and the distance of desolation.

Let me try to turn over this thought and look at it from quite a different direction. The strangest American I have ever known once told me something I could never forget. He once found himself closeted perforce with a small group of lawyers who were bent on crippling or perverting his integrity and truth. This was not because they were enemies of truth. It was because they passionately held certain other things to be true, which this man's truth seemed to them to threaten or destroy. To get him to pervert or seriously qualify his truth, they had, therefore, to break down his will to resist. There was no possibility of violence but all kinds of subtle shifts and pressures were in play. It was much like what, when Communists use it, we call "brainwashing." As the process went on for several days, my man began to fear that he could not endure—that from physical and psychological exhaustion he would surrender too much. He was experienced and he drew upon all the resources of such experience which were, in fact, rather slender. He tried to meet unrelenting pressure with elasticity to give, or seem to give, in details and nonessentials, while giving nothing on his central truth. There is a naïve belief abroad in our peaceful world that truth is its own shield and lance; truth is enough and has only to be true to itself to prevail. In long haul, we must still hope that this is so. But in close combat, it is not so; and American prisoners of war, if they brought back nothing else from their dreadful experience in North Korean prison camps, brought back that knowledge. "There is only one truth," as the officer of the Red Army said to me, "if you push a man hard enough, he will die. That is all." The strongest man alive can be destroyed without ever a finger being laid on him; and the truest truth will be destroyed with him, at least for the time being, and that for the moment is perhaps all that counts. This happens with statistical certainty unless the victim has some secret talisman from which, at the moment the enemy is pushing him hard enough and his strength is at last gasp, he can draw a secret strength. That is the meaning of a report about the U.S. POWs in Korea which indicates that those who held out against Communist pressures were chiefly Catholics, Orthodox Jews, and Fundamentalist Protestants. It was the tangible talisman of those faiths that these men drew strength from in their weakness, and so did not succumb. The others' pockets were empty.

Different men, different extremities make use of different talismans. My man told me that he had survived his ordeal because, after the first day, seeing what was in store, he provided himself with a vial of poison. He was determined to use it if, through weakness, he felt himself liable to betray his truth, or if, through weakness, he let the others seriously pervert it. He wanted not to use the poison; he wanted to live. But if the others were determined to force a lie, he was determined to give them a death. He kept the vial in a trouser pocket. When he felt the pressures becoming unbearable, he would slip his hand in his pocket and finger the vial of poison. He said that from that touch of death, he drew the strength to live.

Fly amanita, a vial of poison, in some such way as this the secret of the Third Rome serves the Russian. In agony, in suffering and defeat, he silently reaches for it. From the touch, he draws the strength to endure. In any case, he may die. That changes little. For what he has drawn from his secret is a certitude that transcends his own life. It is the certitude that in him, the will to go on will go on after his life is done. It is greater than he is.

"Through all the
terrors and the
distances . . ."

Jonah

_____

About Jonah, we are told at first only that "the word came unto" him. This is carrying terseness pretty far. Yet we see that it could scarcely be otherwise, since this extraordinary book of the Bible, which speaks to us in mid-twentieth century exactly as if a voice from among ourselves were speaking directly to us but with a wisdom we have lost and a humanity we have largely laid aside—this book is hardly six pages long. In those six pages, better than in thousands of others more recent, we instantly recognize ourselves, our plight, our problem, our dismay; and, in the end, our anger. No judgment is pronounced. If there is a judgment, it is implicit. Who can judge suffering—that is, unless he is prepared to incur in turn a judgment of those who suffer by it? In this book, God Himself tacitly suspends judgment. No doubt there are books of the Old Testament which are, as we say, "greater." None is more compassionate.

About Jonah, his family life, his business, his likes, his dislikes, faults, merits, we are told nothing at all. We learn

only the name of his father, which means nothing to us or
means something only to a few scholars, if, indeed, it means
anything to them. About "the word" we learn only that
Jonah knew it to be a command of God (we are not told
why Jonah supposed this to be so), and that the word commanded him to go up to Nineveh, "that great city," and "cry
out against" its total corruption. In short, Jonah is nobody,
that is to say, everyone. This is particularly clear in his
reaction to that summons. Jonah, the sensible man, the
sensible everybody, is appalled. He hurries to the coast as
fast as he can and buys passage for Tarshish, at the opposite
end of the Mediterranean Sea. He means to put as much
water as he can between himself and that outlandish business
of luring voices and that bizarre business of shouting through
the streets of a big city. This has all been pretty exhausting.
Once aboard ship, he falls asleep. What a narrow escape!

But is there ever any escape? While he is asleep a storm
whips up, the ship begins to founder, the sailors, super-
stitious like so many men dwarfed by the silent or tumultuous
universe, remember Jonah and haul him up on deck, and
demand his credentials. He tells them: "I am a Hebrew." It
is like asking to be lynched. "A Hebrew"—a Jew, a man
different from the crew, a man to whom clings a mystery
since he is one of a nation to whom clings a mystery. We
fear mystery—the unknown—never more so than in a storm
at sea. "Take me up," says Jonah, "and cast me into the sea.
For, it is for my sake that this has come upon you." But that
is not what the sailors do. How marvelous it is because how
human. Among those plain men, who are also everybody, that
compassion and simple justice stirs that constantly lurks
among men in the mass, ennobling them as, with a strong
gentleness, it tempers the harshness of their daily lives. They
suppose, in their ignorance of meteorology, that a sacrifice is
required to calm the sea. But they do not simply pounce on
that Jew, Jonah. Instead, practicing the rough and readiest
justice they know, they draw lots to determine which one

shall die that the rest may live. "And the lot fell on Jonah." We do not know what became of the crew. Presumably, the ship made it to Tarshish, and its company retold the curious incident in the dockside taverns.

But we know what happened next to Jonah. He was promptly swallowed by the whale, which scholars tell us was really a "great fish," and which everybody has so much fun with. In its belly Jonah made the return trip to the Middle East. In that clammy, fishy cavity, he made, too, those comments on God and men (that is, everybody, himself), which sound from the darkness like the surging of the sea above, and in the space of a few lines make this brief existential book one of the supreme statements of the human quandary: "All the waves and the billows passed over me. . . ."

Thereupon, the great fish "spat" Jonah out, obligingly, on the seashore. He was back where he started, as everybody else is every so often. And at the second command of God he went to Nineveh, that great city—in no very patient mood, I should think. "Why me?" he must have asked himself. "Why just me?" But what else was there to do. Obediently he shouted his news of disaster in Nineveh's streets. Then the most extraordinary thing of all occurred. Jonah was heard, and what is more unbelievable, believed. The whole corrupt city, from king to slave, put on sackcloth, repented and reformed. Was this historically true? Certainly, the modern temper inclines to doubt. We may scarcely doubt, though, that if this was historically true, it is the only case of record in which a great people on the brink of disaster listened, looked into itself, judged itself, and found salvation in humility. In any case, seeing this wonder, God revoked His doom.

Nothing makes all this so credible as Jonah's reaction to it. It was completely human. He was deeply chagrined that God had not carried out his prophecies. He got out of redeemed Nineveh as quickly as his legs would take him. All those long and fruitless travels, sea miles, land miles. Jonah sat down and basked in the hot sun. God sent rustling up a vine to shade the misguided man. Again Jonah took refuge from too much wakefulness in sleep, and while he slept God sent a worm to eat up the vine. And when Jonah woke to find even the vine gone, he was bitter past remedy. Then God asked: "Do you well to be angry?" Jonah answered in the extremity of humanity pushed too far: "I do well to be angry, angry enough to die." God's voice is understanding in a way quite uncommon in His Old Testament. "Are you angry," He asks, "about a cucumber vine which came up in a night and was devoured in a night? And would you have me destroy Nineveh, that great city, in which are more than a hundred and twenty thousand souls that cannot tell their right hand from their left, and much cattle besides?"

That is all. That is the end of this little book. Like Jonah regurgitated on the shore of Palestine, we are back where we started. We are back with that "word" that came to Jonah in the first place. We may surmise, among other surmises, that that "word" is spoken again and again, throughout history, at many times, in many tongues, and that those who utter it are as unlikely, and sometimes as unaware of what it means, as those who hear it.

Agee

There is always a certain presumption in publicly claiming close friendship with someone whom we have long felt to be greater than ourselves, especially when the world, or a part of it, has belatedly discovered that there was greatness in

him, and when he is no longer here to say of us: Yes, that is
how it was; or: No, I felt about it a little differently. I am
speaking about James Agee, who died in 1955 of a heart
attack. I want you to know that I recognize the presumption
and I shall risk it anyway . . . What I shall say is my tribute
to my friend, whose grave on his quiet farm I have not seen,
and may not get to see, but approach in this way.

In fact, life had separated us for several years before. I
was engaged in certain well-known events. Later, I was con-
fined about two years, writing a book. Jim was in Holly-
wood, working with John Huston. Then came two heart
attacks in quick succession. From his sick room came, too,
seven- and eight-page letters, pencilled in the minute, slant-
wise, beautiful script which was a personal cipher that took
hours to decode. In the spring of 1952, we both happened
into New York. Jim came unexpectedly to my hotel, and we
walked down Fifth Avenue together—very slowly, he could
only inch along now, so that I saw that he was taking his
last walks. He stopped before a show window in which
cruelly elegant mannequins in exaggerated posture swam in
a sickly lavender light. He stared at them for awhile. Then,
"It's a pansy's world," he said, looking at them and at the
city around us. We laughed. It was a summing up. Later,
I bought two chocolate Easter eggs for his little girls. And
that is how we parted. It is my last vivid memory of the
living man. A few months later, I was in a hospital with a
heart of my own. At Christmas, Jim sent me a dwarfed pear
tree which somebody planted for me. When I could get
about, I helped it to live under some adverse conditions.
Those days all run together in weakness to form a blur. In
that blur Jim died, and his death became part of the blur.

Multas per gentes et multa per aequora vectus,
*Venio, frater, ad has inferias.**

---

* Carried through many people and over many waters,/I come, my
brother, to these [sad] rites of death.—Catullus

For me the blur passed into an upland spell and then again into blur. In the autumn of 1955 I was unloading a truck load of hay bales—the last load of the year's last cutting of alfalfa. It was a foolish thing to do. But the day is what the day is: we do what needs doing. Before half the load was off, a heart attack.

Then the long weeks in bed while the cold came, the earth hardened, it was winter, and at last a new year. During those long silent days I read a good first novel, *Your Own Beloved Sons* by Thomas Anderson. It was about the Korean War. There was the usual misery of the front line in winter —a hardened landscape of snow not too different from that outside my window. There were familiar types, too. There was the sensitive, callow, bookish soldier named Littlejohn, and, by a stroke, nicknamed Little John. There was the crude non-com. Little John was cooking and the non-com grabbed his book. Little John tried to get it back. The book was James Agee's *The Morning Watch*. The non-com tormented Little John by suggesting that it was sex stuff. Little John felt this as a violation. He tried to explain. It did not make sense. But then he said it: "It's about religion, but it's not a religious book." Yes, that was it, that was absolutely it.

I laid the book on the bed. It seemed to me that, for the first time in years, Jim came walking toward me across a frozen field. I could see him as we can so seldom wholly visualize the dead. And, as we met, the little nod of the head, casual but so oddly reserved, and the hands clutched against the stomach in a gesture of pain, and on the face a grimace of pain—a mocking grimace. Anybody who knew Jim well knew that gesture and that grimace.

A heart attack sets the mind to living naturally with the possibility of a sudden end. As the swift and unexpected image passed, I smiled. Its place was taken by another, humorous and rather solemn one. It was an image of myself at the Judgment, with God the Father bending a little to press a little grimly, and asking me: "Will anyone speak for this man?" Then from the seraphic side lines Jim would step out—unshaved as nearly always, work shirt, work-men's shoes, corduroy trousers, as usual—and stand in silence beside me. And God the Father would half smile with the little gesture of the hand that means: "What can you do?" As we step back into the crowd, from the vault and from the depths, the choirs would sing in those pure tones. In all that throng, Jim, I thought, would be the only one who did not know that they were singing about him.

A sick man's thoughts about a dead man? Yes. Of course. Jim drank too much—in the end he largely drank himself to death. He was savagely unconventional, and, in most practical matters of life, belligerently irresponsible. Certain things—rudeness, in particular—moved him to violence. He once drove his fist through the door of a Fifth Avenue bus, which its driver had insolently refused to open for him. He was not a religious man, not in most senses understood by the Westminster Confession, which was Jim's. But he was, among all men I have known—telling them over carefully in my mind—the one who was most "about religion."

A Footfall

There are men whose lives, on the face of them, seem to have nothing to do with ours. Nevertheless, they do. We may feel this chiefly as a vague annoyance. We are completely unlike that other. We have nothing of importance in common with him because what each of us calls important is utterly different. We have no wish to know the other, or to know much about him. Presumably, he feels much the same about us. Yet we are reminded, every so often, that the other exists, is somewhere off there. Sometimes, the reminder is merely a mention of his name in conversation, or brief news about something he has done or has not done. It is no more than a recurrent awareness—one pebble suddenly noticed again among others as a thin current passes over it before sliding on. But recurrently, too, the life of that other actually brushes or crosses our own, though only for a moment. If this happens often enough to make us reflect on it, we become aware, in general reluctantly perhaps, that that other life touches ours in the realm of meaning; has some meaning for our own, even if it is one so slight, so fortuitous, that we resent having to take account of it.

In fact, both of us, that other and ourself, are in forced flight through an interminable night and waste—a flight without true rest and a waste without water. That is the condition that equates us. In that night, we do not see the other, and the flight leaves us no energy, even if there were any wish, to make the effort. But we hear him at times, drawing ahead or dropping behind, out of sight, at a little distance. In that night and flight, the other is reduced to a footfall, or a stumble and a mutter. Yet if he falls before we do, and in such a way that we cannot help but hear the thud, he makes upon us, simply by the act of falling, an undeniable claim. It is the claim on the living to bury the dead, to stop long enough in any flight to scratch out a hollow in the sand, and to fill it in again. The claim implies a little more. It is a claim to mumble a few words about the meaning of this ended life such as we mumble over the least whom we forget as we consign them to the earth. The meaning we mumble is not necessarily the right one. But if we do not attempt it, if we reject the claim, simply glance at the fallen and hurry on,

we feel (we might be hard put to it to say why) that we
incur a portion of damnation. It is only a little portion, perhaps. But we feel (and again we may not quite know why)
that that damnation is righteous.

In the last days of 1957, Howard Rushmore shot and killed
himself with his revolver. But first he shot and killed his
wife. The shooting occurred in a taxi cab in Manhattan. It
was a clear night and very cold. A murder and a suicide—in
the press, it made lively copy; a little livelier because Rushmore was a former Communist. Perhaps you read the story
for its "human interest," and then, with a certain distaste,
turned the page. Distaste and the privilege to turn pages are
a relaxation in which not all, in this time, may indulge.

In life, Rushmore crossed my path more than once. I
did not like him. I imagine that he did not like me, and that,
furthermore, both of us settled this point at first glance. On
my side, it had little to do with anything I knew about him.
In fact, I knew almost nothing about him and never felt
enough curiosity to inquire closely. The fuller details of his
life, I first learned from his obituary. Our feeling was of
the kind we explain as "temperamental." The first glance tells
two men that each is a creature of another species, and that
species are happier apart, if they keep to their own flyways
or small animal runways through the grass and thickets of
this life. Such differences, as we know, are often more
sundering than differences about much weightier matters.
By contrast, the fact that Rushmore and I had once been
Communists was scarcely more relevant to either of us than
that sometime in our childhood, each of us had probably had
measles.

Yet for almost two decades, I felt a small, secret, painful
tie to him. "Tie," is a literal word. We are forever tied to
our failures; and Rushmore was one of my failures—a failure

of simple humanity on my part. Perhaps it is more accurate to say that such failures are tied to us. We wear them invisibly around our necks like so many albatrosses. Happy is he who can suppose that he has not exceeded the lawful "bag." For a certain number of them are lawful in the degree to which extenuation ever extenuates. Man is, at best, a combat animal. He exists in a permanent condition of combat, is, in his quietest life, hunter and hunted by turns, however elaborate the conventions whereby he disguises a condition which he did not in any case elect but is always born into. Fear is combat's healthy instinct. Never more so than in an age like this one whose exigencies have embroiled us all to the point where we must ask, first and foremost, of almost any unfamiliar man who turns to us: "Who and what is he? Who and what stand behind him and make use of him, wittingly or not?" Often, if those questions cannot be quickly and clearly answered, there is no time to wait before fear arises. And the mask of fear is inhumanity. That is what happened between Rushmore and me, and cinched that little tie. Rushmore became a man who could say to me: "I asked you for bread and you gave me a stone." He never did say it. He did not need to. He had only to look at me, and I said it for him. The real Judgment, I suspect, consists of the number of such eyes that have cause to rest on us such silent glances, to which, under self-judgment, we must make such silent answer.

The story with Rushmore is this. The year was probably 1940. I was working on *Time*. I was struggling desperately to hold a job, which meant much more than economic security for my family; it meant my passport to a new life. I was struggling desperately because I had a great deal to learn, and to learn very quickly. I knew I was slipping, and that made me struggle more desperately, and that desperation made it more difficult to learn. Into my office one day walked Rushmore, unannounced, and came up

to my desk. I had not seen him before and did not particularly like what I saw now. He was a tall man, younger
than I, ill-dressed, somewhat shambling (from embarrassment, I soon saw). His face was long and, as it seemed to
me then, hard: a few strokes of the pen would have turned
it into the rat-trap caricature of a western sheriff. Even then,
I took in that the eyes were different. There was something
gentler in them, a kind of furtive sensitivity, which did
nothing to reassure me. I found it shifty, and the difference
between the lower face and the eyes incongruous. Besides
he mumbled almost incoherently, and what he mumbled, once
I made it out, was in no way reassuring, either. Its sense
was this. A day or two before, he had broken with Communism. He had been a minor employee of the *Daily Worker*,
and had walked out after a dispute about a story. Could I get
him a job where I was? He also told me his name then. I
had never heard it before.

That a man of whom I had never heard, a man a day or
two out of the Communist Party, should know who I was
and exactly where to find me, filled me with an instant cold
rage which is one of the forms that alarm takes. In those
days, I supposed that Communism, if it could arrange
favorable circumstances, would find it well worth its while
to destroy me physically. (In the light of experience, Communism must have wondered sometimes why it failed to.)
I thought Rushmore was lying. I thought he was a scout
sent by the Center to make sure that I was, in fact, occupying
such and such a desk in such and such an office. I do not
remember what I answered him. If not brusque, it was
certainly chilling. If he could have overcome his embarrassment, if he had broken out of himself long enough to say,
perhaps with anger: "You have been through it too. You
knew the night. You know what it is to crawl under the
charged barbed wire. You have heard the trailing dogs
yelp and the footfall. Help me!"—if he had said something

like that, it might have been different. That was not what
he had known, and, besides, he was not the kind of a man
who could have said that. It would have been out of character.
Instead, a look of defeat came not only over his face, but
over his whole body. He turned away and walked, stooped,
to the door. I watched him walk away, still harshly and
narrowly measuring his purpose, still questioning it. But
as I saw that stoop, I thought even then: "Can I be wrong?"

I was wrong. Rushmore had broken with Communism,
once for all. The break was perhaps the least of his troubles.
For I surmise that he was one of Communism's transients,
one of those who have nowhere else to go and find in Communism four walls, a bed, a chair, a little fellowship. So Rushmore, if I am right, got used, like others of that kind, to his
bare room, got in time a little better one (two chairs), learned
the geography of the halls, doors, windows, other rooms, other
residents—the appearances of things. Then he stayed put for a
time (it kept out the weather). One day, the bleakness out-
weighed the sense of shelter. He did not make up his bed the
way the overseer required. One thing led to another. Just being
in any one place too long gets to be a bore. He was fed up. He
walked out of the night lodging. The exit was final because
he knew nothing but the doors, halls, the rooms. He knew
they were seedy and that there were better rooms. He knew
Communism as a well-kept lodging. Communism as a reading of history, a force and an anguish of history, manifest
in millionfold armies or in millionfold suffering and death—
of that side of Communism he knew nothing.

It is unlikely he knew such a Communist (they were once
fairly common) as Vasso in Manes Sperber's *Burned
Bramble*. So it is unlikely that he ever heard Communism
disclose one of its meanings in Vasso's words: "What you
say about our pity for the unfortunate is cockeyed. My old
man knows more about it. We are men in revolt. We despise
the poor man who asks us simply to pity him. We want him

to rise up along with us. Pity may perhaps make Social
Democrats. But can you destroy a world with pity? Can you
construct a new world with pity?" If Rushmore ever had
heard a man say such things, it would not have mattered.
For he would not have known what the man was talking
about. That was why, in his brief ordeal in my office, he
could not break through to me. He could not communicate.
He was not a man reversing the course of his life or defying
in personal agony a central agony of his age. His need was
exactly what he said it was: a job.

He soon found one. Naturally, I made inquiries at once
about so ambiguous a visitor. Once I had established that
Rushmore was authentic, and not a figure in a planned
pursuit of me, that he had a job with a newspaper chain, I
lost further interest. He had a by-line. He wrote chiefly of
Communist matters and occasionally I read something he
had written. It had nothing to say to me and, in addition, in
those days I was suffering a revulsion from Communism so
organic that even news about it was emetic. Rushmore was
concerned with news, news as a deposit of details, whispers,
facts. I was concerned with meaning of which such news
was a local manifestation or excrescence.

Then in 1948, I became news myself. I do not know what
Rushmore wrote in those days. At some point, I became
aware that out of the throng of newsmen who daily beset
me, the tall figure of Rushmore was looming. My recollection
is that he seldom asked me a direct question. I remember him
as standing usually on the edge of that questioning circle,
chiefly watching. It was then I read into his eyes the un-
spoken comment: "I asked you for bread and you gave me
a stone." I read into his eyes a passing ironical sense that
he, after all, had managed better than I. I did not believe
this, but I believed he did. I read into his watchful eyes, too,
an unconscious sadness. That was better than personal
sympathy, for it seemed to me to imply a knowledge that

in my unlikely person, in that narrow focus, the issue of two irreconcilable worlds had been joined which might one day be decided in the onset of millionfold armies. Of course, I allowed for the possibility that as a former Communist, he found it expedient to hold himself aloof from another with whom the indiscriminating world might crudely link him.

I do not believe I ever saw him again. But we brushed again. Some years later, the American Committee for Cultural Freedom invited me to become a member and I accepted. This group was prevailingly liberal. Among its members were men and women whom I had known slightly and respected for many years. Active among them, too, was one man, highly literate and intelligent, who had certainly been no friend of mine during my time of troubles. This man's attitude had perhaps worked some definite mischief. To Rushmore this seemed to make my joining the American Committee for Cultural Freedom the more unpardonable because X had once frequented at least the edges of the same circles as Rushmore and I. Actually this seemed to me to explain X's motivation. He seemed to me in such revulsion at the past that he was, by a kind of necessity, blacking out of his mind all recollection of it even to the point of denying those others who could not do so. I regretted it, but I found it humanly understandable. Rushmore did not. He wrote a column, less angry than sorrowful, asking how I might feel on finding myself seated in the same room with X, or something like that. In fact, X and I never met; health kept me inactive. Rushmore seemed to feel that in joining the Cultural Committee, I was deserting the good men, and true. I felt that Rushmore was cutting himself off from humankind, was drawing sullenly into a narrow and narrowing circle. The Cultural Committee was fighting Communism. I do not ask of the man who lets me slip into his foxhole whether he believes in the ontological proof of God, whether he likes me personally, or even whether, in another part of the forest, at another time, he lobbed a grenade at me. I am interested only that for the duration of the war, he keep his rifle clean and his trigger finger nerveless against a common enemy. I understand that that is all he wants of me.

Later, I noticed that Rushmore had resigned from his newspaper and become the editor of a scandal magazine. That seemed unhappy, but no less understandable than X's behavior. In general, the world to which the former Communist returns from Communism is not a hospitable world. It largely exhausts its good will in forgiving him his offense. It suffers him. It never quite trusts him. It may not close its doors against him; some are left generously open. But, certain exceptional cases apart, it makes it very difficult to live. So I thought about Rushmore: "He did what he found to do; he took the job he could get." It proved too much for him. At some point, he resigned though I missed that news when it happened. I learned of his resignation only when the Government closed in on that particular magazine and Rushmore appeared as one of its witnesses for the prosecution. It was now his turn to sit in a witness chair, and say: "I did so and so," and feel the shame that not only men, but many creatures feel at a certain degree of consciousness—dogs, for example. It is a kind of death, a lingering because the creature does not physically die. He may, in fact, feel that this is right and good. He dies, nevertheless.

So Rushmore reached that night between Christmas, 1957, and the beginning of a new year. So he shot, first his wife and then himself. Money troubles? Marital troubles? No doubt—nothing is simple, even the atom from which can be projected the universe. But his death moved me in quite another way. I thought after reading the details: "He could not escape meaning after all. His whole life was a flight from it. In the end, it overtook him. For him, the circle came full turn."

I meant this: for most men in the West who become

Communists, that act represents a choice which is sometimes conscious, sometimes not; the choice is between suicide and life. For life and against death. What they are seeking is meaning. Albert Camus has phrased it neatly: "They do not ask to live; they ask for reasons for living."

Rakhel

There has come into my hands, unexpectedly, a translation of a Russian official document, which at first reading I found simply terrifying. It struck me with that chill of helplessness that we feel at the touch of absolutely out-matching Authority before which we are simply ants that Authority will move a little, as it chooses, with its irresistible blunt finger, because in the rule book it says that ants are to be moved this way or that. Or the finger will simply crush or maim the ants if they do not go exactly in the line the finger pushes them along, out of fright or a panic frenzy to escape. Or the finger crushes them for no reason at all, out of absentmindedness, because it is there and all powerful, and they are there, and they are nothing. Something like this was what I first felt on reading this document. But, as I thought about its human implications, I found the document in the simple literal sense uplifting, "wonderful, causing tears." I thought that in its unintentional way it said more than all the wordy, tiresome, hortatory essays about the meaning of America. It spoke to that meaning in its basic, bedrock terms of hope and freedom of which so many have lost the reality in the familiarizing plenitude, and some few, out of uncertainty and fear, even harden their faces against.

The document is a police order, equivalent to an internal passport. It is dated 1893, and headed: "I, Tsar Alexander Alexandrovitch, Autocrat of all the Russias." This Autocrat (through his servants) then permits one Rakhel (the daughter of Reuven) and her two sons, ages eight and six, and a daughter, age five (as the document carefully notes), to leave her village in the Podolsk Province for a period of six months. If, after six months, she is not back in her village, the penalties will be invoked. I do not know, and the document does not tell me, whether the Autocrat and his police knew why Rakhel was leaving the Poldolsk Province. In fact, that document was a step in her flight with the children from the Autocracy. Tolstoy says somewhere that, in our time, the wanderings of a migratory workingman in search of work beggar the wanderings of Odysseus. So, in our time, do the wanderings of simple men and women in search of hope and freedom. They number millions. In all of human history heretofore, there has been no such wandering of the peoples as has been crowded into the last fifty years. Rakhel was one of those wanderers. She was beginning her journey to the United States, to join her husband who had come before her. She knew of it in a phrase common among such as she (and which I first learned from her): *Die goldene Medina*. The accent was not on the golden (except in the sense of some mysterious Light), but on the *Medina*—that is, the city of hope, the city of deliverance.

I can easily imagine the terrors of that journey. There were the initial uprooting (felt in the most ordinary journey); the immense unknown distances; the longed for, but unknowable, destination. There were the worry and trouble which the police always mean to the very poor. There were the desperate novelties of travel, the crossing of strange frontiers, the mysteries of converting money, of which there could have been barely enough for absolute necessities. In all her life until then, Rakhel had perhaps not been ten miles from her village ("the dark villages"). And there were the three small children. Rakhel was a small, slight woman, with plenty of native intelligence. I knew Rakhel well, loved and deeply respected her. She was my mother-in-law. Of all the people I have known in my life from the top to the bottom of modern society, few have seemed to me so worthy of instinctive respect as Rakhel and her husband.

Through all the terrors and the distances, she brought the children to America. Then followed the years of almost unimaginable poverty and hardship, but also almost unimaginable thrift and ingenuity. These were followed by the years of scarcely believable success and prosperity, which was largely the work of a child who was not one of the three on the flight from the Autocracy.

The first son of this poor family born in America studied engineering at Yale, then after World War One law at New York University, and is now a practicing attorney. When the trouble with Pancho Villa broke out, he volunteered for military service. There is a family story of his first return home and coming to show his uniform to his mother, saying with naïve pride: "Feel, Mom—all wool but the buttons." It will be comical only to the humanly illiterate. Later on, this son was gassed in action in France. The burned spots on his lungs afflict him still. Every one of Rakhel's six grandsons was a college graduate: all but one professional men; all successful. With that multiplying, prospering family in mind or gathered around her, she used to say sometimes, with a musing fulfillment in which there was, too, a kind of wholly unconscious queenly pride, that she had lived to see "children's children."

Yet my most vivid recollection of her was at the very end of her life. By then her husband was dead—the companion who, unlike the others, could remember with her the dark origins in the Podolsk Province, who had shared with her harsh years of poverty and effort, and the briefer crowning years of success. By then she was a survivor, lonely even in her fulfillment. And new darkness had rolled up and threatened. A number of her college-trained children were sitting talking in deep trouble about the new threat to freedom of the mind and life from the new dictators, Hitler and Mussolini. It was about Munich, and the conversation was heavy with an intangible fear rather like conversation about the Russians today. Rakhel was sitting a little apart, simply listening. She had never thoroughly mastered the English language. What we had not realized was that she had mastered an interior language close to what Malraux calls "the language of destiny." For, from her corner, she surprised us by asking suddenly, and with a slight exasperation about the fearful dictators: "Are they immortal? Will they not die like you and me?"

When, today, I hear much fluttery conversation about the Soviet missle lead, I think: It is necessary that we have this *harbrone* (as they call it); it is indispensable and much far-sighted care and effort must go to making sure that we have these resources. But having it amounts to little without the human resources to back it up—the hope and freedom and fortitude of mind of which, for me, Rakhel makes one instance; of whom there are millions more, similarly humble, unknown; of whose existence it sometimes seems to be our vital weakness to doubt or no longer believe in or value.

It is that faith that the old Russian police order documents for me, permitting me to smile at the eternal impotence of power before the eternal will to be free.

The Golden *Medina*—the city of light, the city of deliverance.

End of an Age

The Price Is Right

"Aaaah!" breathes the studio audience, deep from its collective diaphragm. "Ohhhh!" and (rising in pitch) "Ooooh!" they thrill, as if this were the First Day, as if they had just heard pronounced (offstage) the great words, *Fiat lux* and, peeping into the abyss, were watching the Earth take form from chaos. In fact, some kind of revolving partition has turned, or heavy curtains parted, bringing into view several acres of Oriental rug, tacked the length of a wall; or a mountainous display of silverware or of Lalique glass; or the latest model of archducal automobile.

This is a TV give-away program. The point is for the four panelists to guess the price of these rich commodities. The one who bids closest, without going over the set price, which is a secret, wins these treasures for his own. This is one of the most spontaneously joyous programs that I know; and the enthusiasm on the part of the studio audience is of the most unselfish. They take home none of this plunder. But they shout glad advice to those who may. "Higher! Higher!"

they shout to those whom they think are underpricing the wares—or (frantically), "Freeze! Freeze!" to those who seem about to go too high. It is like the anguished moment when (in the *Arabian Nights*) Hakkim Baba, having loaded his donkeys with the loot of the Forty Thieves, finds, horribly, that he cannot get it (or himself) out of the cave because he has forgotten the magic words that will swing open the rock door. So: "Open Sesame! Open Sesame!" the audience shouts in effect, in a tone between dread and laughter.

Such lavish bounty, heaped up and overflowing, crowding the mind under carpets, mink coats, mink sofas (yes, mink sofas)—the glittery smother of things. Such spastic pleasure on the part of some who win them (at times, a winner makes off, in a few minutes, with thousands of dollars' worth of goods, duly totalled for our further wonder). Such lavish good nature and good will, too; such generous participation in the good fortune of others, also heaped up and overflowing in the American way. Why, then, do I watch this program, fascinated, and each time, with a catch of dismay? Why do I wish to call out to the studio viewers, much as they shout to the panelists: "Little children, that far-off sound you cannot hear above your shouting, and your rapturous 'Ohhhhs' and 'Ooooohs'—that sound is the roaring of the sea"?

I once wrote: "Life is pain," that it is "terrible and beautiful," and that, out of the ordeal of its terror and its beauty, the dignity of man is consummated under God. Christianity, rightly understood (assuming that I rightly understand it) is a tragic faith, and must be since life is a tragic experience. It cannot be otherwise since we die; and those who venture to do more than submit, suffer more before they die. In its tragedy lies its victory. For out of the power to confront and suffer tragedy alone comes greatness of concept, life, or men. The civilization that does not know this must come to nothing in ages of truce, or go down in ages of war. But nothing can destroy the civilization that knows this truth—not even defeat.

What I have said is that the philosophy of optimism and perfectibility of man, acting under his own power, are delusions and lead to disasters. But the philosophy of optimism and perfectibility make the climate of our time, and all the Left and much of the Right share the common delusion. Hence their common fury against anyone who points to the delusion and says: *"Caveat!"*

"Life is pain" must be one of the oldest cries wrenched from man's experience. It challenges many quiet assumptions of our daily life. It does not say that man should not try to make his life on earth as happy as possible. It says that if, while doing so, he fails to know that life in its sum is inevitably tragic, he will court, at last, a judgment of disaster. That is the point perhaps on which we stand as a nation. Our happiness is taking vengeance on us, for our obsession with it has left us children in the face of the most matured evil on human record.

Budapest, 1956

These immense events in a Poland quivering just this side of detonation, and in a Hungary which we have watched slowly bleed to death, gesticulating wildly in sympathy with its screams—these are not sudden or disjointed happenings. Nor are they new in the sense that has most appalled the

West. Nothing in the way of horror has happened in Hungary which has not happened again and again within the Communist Empire, and more horribly, as those who knew have tried frantically to tell you for decades. These events, this terror and the resistance that incites it, cannot be understood simply in and by themselves. They have a long pre-history.

Thirty-nine years almost to a day separated the October events in Petrograd and the October events in Budapest. But something more annihilating than time divided them. In those thirty-nine years, in the name of the Communist experiment, there was perpetrated a human agony which no matter how vividly reported remains largely meaningless because imagination cannot cope with such multiples of suffering. The statistics of massacre are most striking. It is reasonably certain that within the past four decades Soviet Communism has killed 20 or 30 million of its subjects, while within the last twelvemonth Chinese Communists have certainly killed as many again. But death at least releases. The misery of the living was merely more protracted than that of the dead. For Communism condemned them to live without hope.

In Budapest, civilians huddled in a hallway over a machine gun—men as tense with fear no doubt as all men who have gone against out-matching Communism, not with words alone, but with weapons; and therefore, supremely courageous since they know the price at stake—man the guns. Patrolling the littered pavements, children with slung rifles and tormented faces. On the streets, youths, boys and girls, darting against Soviet tanks with homemade bomb and revolver. In the squares, the ranged bodies of the fallen, now nondescript in death and stared at by the nondescript living of a kind that always clots around the raw edges of action.

We heard the last appeal of Radio Budapest even while the Russians were bursting in the doors:

"People of the world . . . Help us! People of Europe, whom we once defended against the attacks of Asiatic barbarians, listen now to the alarm bells ring . . . People of the civilized world, in the name of liberty and solidarity, we are asking you to help . . . The light vanishes. The shadows grow darker hour by hour. Listen to our cry . . . God be with you and with us."

At that point the station went off the air and the silence was more stunning than the words.

We must remember who these revolutionists are. They are those whom the West abandoned to Communism. They are the human herd of one of history's greatest cattle deals. Unless a man's good sense is inflamed by a partisan political need to justify that deal, is there really anyone who does not know that the West traded these populations to Communism as the price of something that the West held more important than their freedom? The West called that something "permanent peace" and sought to safeguard it through the agency of the United Nations. Therefore, these populations were bound over to Communism. Under all the verbiage, that was the reason these populations were the bait with which we meant to lure Communism into the United Nations—as if anything could have kept Communism out. It is nonsense to say that this was wisdom then, and these peoples were subsequently enslaved because Communism welshed on its pledges safeguarding their freedom. A village banker would have hesitated to draw a $100 mortgage in such terms, not only because (as many knew and warned at the time) the pledges were patently worthless, but also because they were unenforceable. So, in the name of peace, the West abandoned these millions to Communism and watched them run into its pens, roped and thrown and branded with its brand.

Many a Polish and Hungarian child was too young to know that the whole course of Life on Earth had been sealed irrevocably at the moment when the wise men of the West set their signatures to that deal beside those of the cunning men of Moscow. Around twelve years later, those children knew it well enough when, in the streets of Poznan and of Budapest, they went with bottle-bomb and revolver against this or that Communist monster. They knew then that they had been abandoned by the West. And when they rose and fought, outmatched, against that fate, and the West approved and watched, they knew something else. They knew that they had been abandoned twice. "Aaaah!" the West breathed deep from its collective diaphragm. "Ohhhh!" (rising in pitch) "Ooooh!" it shrilled at the spectacle of satellite heroism. "Higher! Higher!" some voices shouted from the West. "Freeze! Freeze!" cried others.

Autumn, 1957

The opportunity had been given and it had gone. Autumn had frozen into winter. The Hungarian revolution had passed into the stricken twitchings of the general strike. The West continued to babble about it—some jumble of initials or words that meant that a second revolt might occur in the spring. What does the West know of the pathology of revolution, let alone the pathology of a revolution defeated, which converts at once into mean commonplaces of a kind that make no colorful news stories, the helplessness, grief, and induced terror of those who have had the mischance to survive fathers, brothers, sons, who have been shot, jailed, or have simply "disappeared"? Or the unheroic monotony of no food, fuel, gas, electricity; the grimy misery of cold, continual, sapping cold; and the colder knowledge, gained by so hideous a trial and error, that no help is coming from anywhere, not in time, not in any way that counts.

Most of us have heard that when the Abbé Sieyès was asked what he had done in the French Revolution, he answered: "I survived." It is, surely, the master crack of worldly prudence. Communism, slowly (and at least momentarily) mastering the satellite revolution of 1956, might also have said of it with growing grimness: "We survived." The West could say the same. Asked, "What did you do in the day when heaven was falling, the day earth's foundations fled?—What did you do in that day?" the West, too, could answer: "We survived." It is well to face this fact. For there has been much high feeling and high talk about Hungarian heroism and Communist outrage. But facts, said Lenin, facts are stubborn. Two facts stand out clearly about the Hungarian revolt, and since truth, and truth alone, enables us to burst the mistakes and failures of the past, and retrieve them in the future, let us face these facts. Fact 1: The West encouraged these people in their revolt. It matters not at all that encouragement was never phrased in explicit words. What did those radio broadcasts to the satellites mean if not revolt? They meant revolt and were so understood. Fact 2: At the point of revolt, the West could give the Hungarians one, and only one, effective form of help— weapons and manpower. But let us not condemn the West childishly because it found no way to do this. Geography itself fought against such aid. Yet geography could not be the decisive factor. If the question of such aid had been put to a referendum, how many sober men in the West, knowing what it meant—risk world war, risk the Bombs, risk your sons—how many would have voted to send aid? Perhaps not many. It is well to face this, too, with a certain courage. Yet the crushing of Hungary itself should not mislead us into supposing that this action was futile. That is just what it was not. In revolution, only that action is futile which, from motives of fear or prudence, capitulates short of resistance. Capitulation is the true disaster because it demoralizes the will, and therewith all else successively. It is because they resisted that the Hungarians command the first heights of history, the outcome of which turns on the will to survive. The Hungarians speak to this will in the West for two reasons. The first is simple enough. All other factors change or fade—the politics, economics, and their catchwords that men defied or defended. But resistance enacts a simple meaning that is always the same. It says that when man, the sufferer, rises by courage above the odds of pain, he liberates by his act the one force that brute power, destroying all else, is powerless to destroy. It lives because its example is caught at again and again by others who suffer and whom it moves to dream of resisting in their turn. This is the dialectic of hope; it stirs in darkness.

That is the first meaning of Budapest. It leads directly to the second, and in the conflict of wills that must shape the fate of the age, its relevance is twofold. It touches both Communism and the West. For if the satellite revolution has challenged Soviet Communism as it has seldom been challenged, it challenged the West in a different way. It challenged the West to reverse the history of the last four decades, which has been characterized by this incongruity, that a Communism permanently strife-torn and precarious, and long weak in most material ways beyond anything imaginable to the average experience of the West, has repeatedly stood off or scored off a West in most material ways immensely more powerful. It was never a question of comparative physical strengths. Power, on the part of the West, was never lacking. Will was lacking. And the failure of will has been matched by a failure of intelligence. In general, this has taken the form of an ageless complacency that neither knows, nor really wishes to know, the meaning, motives, or methods of Communism.

But it runs off recurrently, too, into mass delusions that Communism, if coddled, is about to change into the opposite of itself, of all that has given it power and empire, and to become something more like the image that the West cherishes of the West—something more eligible for the garden-party guest list. This, of the most implacably purposeful revolutionists in history.

It is at this point of will—the point where the Hungarians challenge the discrepant will to act of the West and of Communism—that we sense that Budapest was a battle for the world. We sense that what is done, or is not done, in consequence, will define the course of the rest of the century, and, therewith, the shape of the future—one way or the other. It is a strengthening of the West's will to act, and act intelligently, that Hungarian courage implores even in disaster.

"Thamus, Thamus, Thamus"

All that chiefly matters about Thamus is that he thought that he was called three times by name from the horizons of the sea: "Thamus! Thamus! Thamus!" Then he was given that message—that his age had reached its end.

The date was some time in the reign of Tiberius Caesar. Thus, the incident must have occurred about thirty years after Christ was born. The place was a ship heading across the Mediterranean Sea toward Italy. Thamus was the ship's captain. Presumably, somebody thought him a man practical enough to be entrusted with a ship and its cargo. These shreds of fact and inference we know only from a few lines of an obscure work of Plutarch's—the *De Defectione Oraculorum (On the Cessation of the Oracles)*. That cessation was so noticeable—all the mysterious voices, which had so often guided the great actions of the Greek and Roman age, suddenly grown small or still—that it puzzled Plutarch, who was himself born only a generation or so after Thamus.

We know nothing else whatever about Thamus. Our one glimpse of him is at the instant when his name was called. Curiously, that has been enough to preserve his memory out of millions of others who then lived without trace, so that we glimpse him yet—a little, far-off, faceless figure, riding his single plank of premonition out of the shipwreck of his world and two thousand years of history.

The voice called from all the edges of the sea: "Thamus! Thamus! Thamus! The great god Pan is dead!" Among the gods of the Roman age, Pan was scarcely even respectable. So that, at first, it seems a little surprising that the voice did not report, instead, that Jupiter (*Zeus Pater*—Zeus the Father) was dead. But to some this in itself may seem a kind of confirmation that Thamus heard rightly. For Pan, with the goat horns and goat legs, was a symbol of the rank creative force of nature. And perhaps it is always the creative energy of an age which dies out first.

"The great god Pan is dead!" In simple hindsight, we know now that that was literally true at the moment when Thamus thought he heard it. We may surmise, with a side glance at ourselves, that others besides Thamus also knew it at that time—in their bones, as we say, even if they were at some pains not to know anything so disquieting with their heads. Perhaps that is why anybody troubled to record what that obscure ship's captain said had happened to him.

Ages live by a body of beliefs (held casually, but tenaciously, by the mass of men) which offer an explanation of the meaning of their world, and men's life and death in it —men's destiny. Ages end when for any or many reasons that explanation no longer explains the meaning of the world, and men's life and death, in a way that makes sense to them in terms of their daily reality. This is something quite different from the violent political changes that commonly mark history's turning points. Those are chiefly changes of institutions. The change that ends ages is infinitely gradual, and, for a long time, largely imperceptible. It is a shift in the general angle of vision, in the way in which the great mass of men tacitly view as true the meaning of the world and of their life and death in it. The changes of institutions which this shift of vision makes possible, and in which it is embodied—they come much later. Before they come, before the shift of vision is widespread enough to be filled in new forms, reflecting the new vision, the fading of the old one is always felt first as a deepening sense of void, a sense that life has lost its meaning.

Decades before Thamus, men sensed that the Roman age was ending. Some of them sought to arrest the end by violence, like Brutus and his co-conspirators, in the name of an ideal past, in the name of the dying Republic. Others (Caesar, Augustus) sought to arrest the end by violence in the name of a realistic present, under pressure of the restive masses, and related pressures. And, in fact, they did rescue the forms of life. By means of some ponderous (and murderous) patchwork, they enabled the Roman age to rock on for several hundred years. So, as if nothing had really changed, devout pagans continued to worship at the altars of *Zeus Pater*. The great god Pan himself still leered rakishly from the shrubbery, at least in the form of statuary much in vogue in the equivalent of garden clubs at Rome, or on the fashionable country estates. Yet all sensed that something was ending. Something had simply gone out of life. More and more, they phrased that sense of something irreparably missing in those two Latin words, which, like a smog of low toxicity, drift over the last centuries of the Roman age. The words are *tædium vitae*, as those who felt it called it—the awful tediousness at the heart of life, its meaninglessness, once the common body of beliefs that explained the world and man's destiny had lost its force, and no longer made sense in line with the reality of men's lives.

Doubtless, it was not a matter for much active concern, except for occasional gifted intellectuals like Tacitus. After all, for the mass of men, reality is largely a bread-and-butter point, where, if life forces the equation ever so little, "bread" and "butter" are terms quickly convertible into "life and death." Men do not simply stop work to think: "The age is ending." At most, they sometimes catch themselves thinking: "It has all got too big. Life has got too big. Government is too big. The cities are too big. Even the buildings are too big. The problems are too vast. The solutions are too complex, and each solution breeds new complexity."

The most active (or ambitious) minds still promote political solutions, which, more and more, crowd out all else as the mechanics of public hope. But the mass of men creep for refuge from complexity, and burrow for life's meaning deeper into their private lives, which, though small, contain all the reality a man can plainly find and feel. Otherwise, men tend to turn indifferent. That, not cynicism or violence, is the true mark of the end. It is not that men reject faith; they no longer feel strongly enough about it for active rejection. It is not that men no longer feel a need for God, or that they even abandon conventional beliefs or altars. They may even, moved by a blurred anxiety, crowd them more closely. It is rather, to echo the words of Lubac, that man can no longer take them seriously. Yet men feel indifference as a gnawing hollowness. For indifference is not simply neutral or negative. Men's very indifference is a reflex of their organic reverence for truth. They will not do truth the irreverence of having it on any terms less than reality. (It is the edges of that slow-healing wound.) It is the gap between the truth men crave and the reality they live, the faith men need to live by and the lives they must live even without it, that makes the human ordeal when ages end. By contrast, external political events, however spectacular in scale or monstrous their shapes, are seen to be chiefly surface manifestations. Wars, truces, revolutions, massacres, the conflict of nations, parties, or systems of doctrine, are seen to be the symptoms of a crisis. They are not the crisis itself. They are the forms in which a deeper conflict is reflected or enacted. Thus, their interaction may change or defer situations: they do not end the crisis, which nevertheless they always promise to end. So that as each promise proves futile, men lapse into a habit of permanent scepticism that infects their view of everything.

The surmise that an age is ending is perhaps the last fact that such an age ever wishes to know about itself. Yet most men probably sense it, even if they do not grasp the full meaning of what they sense. It is as if such generations were born hearing the tolling of a bell that calls them nowhere but persists as a kind of undertone, remote, but implicit, behind all their acts and fears. It is that undertone to which the cry that Thamus heard gives explicit voice: "Thamus! Thamus! Thamus! The great god Pan is dead!"

This is true even if, in the name of the raw energy of life and of everybody's need to get on with today's job, men are moved to resist, or even to deny what they deeply sense. It is equally true if, as in an age of fission, men are sometimes moved to wonder whether the end of one age invariably implies the beginning of another.

"The Year's Sweepings"

Now that the American earth satellite *Explorer* is firmly up there, the change of national mood could almost be photographed, it seems so palpable. It is almost, I thought at first, trying to find some measure for it, like the coming of spring, which, despite deep freezes in Florida and several frozen months presumably ahead of us all, is, nevertheless, here. In midwinter, country people always know when the change has occurred which means that spring has come—and not because (as here) a few snowdrops have run up leaves and flowers, welcomed even while they are recognized as foolhardy. The change is felt as an itch, a fermenting impatience to get at the earth again in order to feel, after our winter-death, life flowing from the substance of the world into the hands that work it. The mood seems to have something to do with a subtle change of light in lengthening days. Among stockmen, there is a school which holds that it is this effect of light, acting on the nerves of the eye and so on certain centers of the brain, not well understood, that suddenly sets the most matronly of cows to behaving in ways not elemental, but businesslike. It is as if, in a big, prosperous, and well-ordered farmhouse, somebody had let the furnace go out in midwinter. This happens sometimes, even in the best run houses. There follow a great complaining, blaming, bleak shivering and fear of bursting pipes, until somebody goes down and gets the heating system to working again. After all, there was ample fuel in the bins or tanks. Will, effort, perhaps a slight adjustment of the mechanism were chiefly needed. Then warmth rustles up in the cold rooms. The chill lifts. Life revives. People go about their routine chores again. That is much more the mood, as it reaches me, of American reaction to *Explorer*. With it goes a stern mental jotting never to let the furnace go untended again—and perhaps something more. For by midsummer, if the talk is true, space should be almost as full of American earth satellites as the garden is of June bugs.

From this, we may hope, among more solid advantages, for certain incidental tranquillizing effects. Perhaps certain layers of Europeans may now get a new grip of themselves, and manage at last to check that prolonged giggling fit (half funk, half malicious glee), which *Sputnik I* brought on last autumn, and into which they have lapsed again and again, uncontrollably, at any mention of those Soviet moons and the first *Vanguard* mishap at Canaveral.

Perhaps there will be a levelling off, even in politically partisan Washington, something under its nonpartisan masks, of a post-sputnik mood that, at times, it seemed possible to describe only in Alice in Wonderland terms, as "reeling and writhing and fainting in coils." There were moments when official voices seemed to speak like leaders to a troubled people, with informed firmness, "Keep steady. Keep rank. Keep in mind that you have the productive capacity, and *they* do not; that you need chiefly fear not Soviet superiority, but fear itself."

Above all, one hopes, that Senator So-and-so (or was he a congressman?) may now rest his eyes. I mean the nameless legislator, unstrung by missile testimony before a Congressional committee, and quoted as saying that he felt as if he had been "staring into Hell." I missed the original story in the American press. But I picked up its sound effects from

London's *New Statesman*—with refinements, since here the tone of awful instancy so thinly veils "the chuckle spread from ear to ear." This is the Capitol scene as reported from London: "The evidence, it seems, was so alarming that two of the committee's members fainted, another had a heart attack."

It is a little too wishfully a re-do of the Brussels ball on the eve of Waterloo, with the dancers making madly for the exits at "the cannon's fearful roar." And I especially like that "it seems," half disclaiming, while it delivers the sneak punch. In any case, *Explorer* should revive the committee's fainting and stricken members (if there were any). But that legislator staring into Hell is more difficult, since he is less arresting for what he thought he saw than for certain questions which the suddenness of his shock raises. To wit, where had he been staring for the past forty years? And was the Hell he at last found himself staring straight into, the right Hell after all?

American post-sputnik nerves were a reaction, opposite and about equal to, the dense inertia of our complacency with respect to Communism, its meaning and purposes, and, above all, its clenched will to achieve both. It would be a pity if, as our pendulum swing of alarm settles reassured into shorter, less frantic arcs, we should confuse Hell with its fireworks, however menacing. Hell is there, all right. But, of course it is not recent or novel; and a suspicion will not down that its meaning takes in more ground than the trajectory of the most efficient ICBM can measure. Certainly, its meaning is not military only, or even chiefly.

For when we have closed the weapons gap (I have assumed from the first that we shall), and though Communism does not, meanwhile, indulge that strategy of the "first blow," shattering us at a single saturation stroke (as I am assuming —overconfidently, some assure me—that it will not), then we shall have outstripped only an immediate peril. We shall certainly not have ended the general crisis of which Hell is a symbol and of which the rocket hazard is one token, suddenly brought into view as if a revolving partition had turned or a heavy curtain parted. We shall only have caught up again with the general crisis, which, far from ending, will orbit more firmly at a new stage. It is the battle for the world that is approaching showdown. It has no counterpart in history. Nothing like it, for scale or finality, has ever before been known. In fact, the battle was joined decisively four decades ago. The new stage discloses the plunging depth and gathering intensity of the conflict. It discloses this to the degree in which the necessities of conflict have pushed science and technology, East and West, into space, to grapple there for a mastery, stalemated on an Earth become too small an arena in which to decide the issue between such fearfully warring energies.

It would be childish in the extreme to suppose, in face of this tremendous onset, that its course can be charted in conventional or reminiscent ways, or that we ourselves and life as we have known it will not be radically changed by it —have not, in fact, been changing at speeds too swift, in a profusion too complex, for the mind to keep pace—almost out of recognition of what we were or have known. The conflict itself, at the point of its leap into space, must enjoin this result even if the conflict did not mark a crisis of great, impersonal forces which shape it to this end, even as they have long been shaping all life and its relationships.

The battle is not only for the world. The battle is for the breed of man and mind that is henceforth to dominate it. The conflict selects him as every major shift in history has selected the man and mind that dominates his epoch, promotes that change, and is promoted by it. In this process the main lines of force have been clear enough for forty years. What startles is that they have unexpectedly become clearer and to more eyes. It is the consequences which are in question. Yet we are permitted to grope for some of them, if we are willing to incur that large risk of error without which the mind seldom gropes for anything. So groping, I, for one, live into each succeeding year with deepening wonder. For among the centuries, this one seems to me to be of a greatness whose meaning we cheat ourselves out of continually by refusing to let ourselves know it as a whole.

This closing year suitably (and literally) wound us round with silent and silencing sheets of heavy snow. Early in the storm, some three thousand telephones went dead hereabouts, including our own. This cut us off completely from the world, so that if an emergency had occurred—power failure, fire, critical sickness—we had no way of summoning help, which in any case could not have reached us. Secondary roads had ceased to exist. I suppose that here and there, a trunk road was kept precariously open by ploughing and re-ploughing. But the special effect of this storm was that of an eerier silence—the silence of a landscape in which, for miles and miles in every direction, almost nothing any longer moved. Thirty miles from Baltimore, sixty miles from Washington, a highly motorized, mechanized, and electrified civilization had been brought to a dead stop precisely in the degree to which it was civilized. In fact, we were among the lucky ones. Our TV channel, itself running on auxiliary power, reported that, all around us, power had failed at the source or from falling lines. Thousands of people, in fact whole communities, were without heat and water, were abruptly in the midst of disaster. While the storm lasted, our own danger was great; for we are almost completely electrified. The terror of this storm was the dead weight of wet snow. So we looked out from time to time with some interest, to see whether the power lines were holding under that weight; or listened to the crack of branches, which in falling might have taken down the lines, or to the roar, like prolonged thunder, with which the snow mass sometimes slid off the roof and, striking the porch, shook this brick house violently. What would we have done had the power failed—an impassable half-mile from the nearest impassable country road, a mile from the state road, six miles from the nearest unreachable town? Even the jeep in tractor gear could not move twenty feet in that snow.

Each building seemed a vortex of these circling waves. Through the dense whiteness, I just made out the tops of the pines on the hill, looming darkly indistinct out of the blur. We are old friends. Two or three years ago, in what seemed to me at the sudden moment to be a brush with death, I lay down on the porch floor, propping my head on a handy chunk of wood in such a way as to have these pines, then dark against the deepest blue, cloudless autumn sky, as my last image of the world on leaving it. Of course, I was ahead of myself; I was not leaving yet. But in coronary seizures that is just what we do not know, as pain (by a happy arrangement, it is quickly over, as a rule) runs, while it lasts, like a dark current, sapping and swaying all certainty. I have laid these lines in here only because what I write now is written from the far side of that moment. A friend who shares most of my disabilities said to me recently: "In his last days, a man first hears the world—the leaf, the wing, the stone. He has been listening to it all his life, but now he first really hears it." Yes, and he first really sees it, too, in his last look-around, or what he takes to be his last. Gratitude would not be too grand a word for what I felt at being permitted to have those pine tops as a last image of the world. Yet gratitude was not the form that feeling took— nothing so defined—but a diffuse, pervasive sense that all is good. Life had been good. Death was good. Therefore, frightfullness was good. For death is, of course, precisely life's most frightful assault on the mind—most frightful and most frightening. And let there be no question that I was also frightened at that moment, like every other man who has ever reached it, if only because he is bent by pain and something more for which the ancients (as usual) found the unimprovable tag: *de ignato pro terrifice* (the unknown terrifies us). That calm we so much admire in others at such moments is an imposition on that terror by the mind tautened to its utmost in the last effort to defy dissolution. Nothing like the mind in this form, at this intensity, has ever been known, been possible before. I should say, on the basis of an incomplete experience, that the effort is easier the first and second time, and becomes increasingly more difficult the oftener it must be repeated. But this is nothing beside the knowledge gained, not from hearsay, but by experience, that frightfulness, too, is good. And by "good," I mean a necessary part of life; and it cannot be otherwise while there is death.

All my adult life—that is, since I was old enough to draw conclusions and form opinions for myself (as we say with wonderful inaccuracy)—I have held that reality is the only freedom. To know truly what things really are, not what we should wish them to be; to act out of that knowledge of reality—that, I held, was freedom for the mind. There was never any danger of knowing reality too truly, for, in this pursuit the most knowing mind is, at best, a blunt instrument. But to seek to know reality and to act on it—that was freedom. And that freedom included, of course, the freedom not to act, or to act, at need, in defiance of reality, in the full certainty that to do so was to fail, a failure that could be justified only to the degree in which someone who found the effort worth making was willing to pick up failure's irrevocable tab. What the moment with the pines seemed to say was this: There is a beach—not beyond reality, while we live we cannot get beyond reality—but a narrow beach which marks the point where reality merges with all that which is unknown and which here opens up. Standing on that beach, a man first knows the world. For this is the most radical extension of reality there is. Here a man grasps that frightfulness is as necessary a part of life as joy. This is not the grand resignation. This is the steady glance which permits a man at last to weigh what he fears in the knowledge that he can reject any part of the experience only at the price of violating the whole. So Arnold wrote of Goethe:

> And he was happy, if to know
> Causes of things, and far below
> His feet to see the lurid flow
> Of terror, and insane distress.
> And headlong fate, be happiness.*

Nothing new in this, of course, except as it is new to every individual man who experiences it. His viewpoint, if he outlives the experience, is thereafter curiously changed. In a sense, he has burst the barrier of despair which each must burst for himself—no one can help him. The risks are much like breaking the sound barrier, and so are the fruits. Our world wars, revolutions, famines, and in their special feature of the time, the planned massacre by great governments of millions of their own subjects—it is unlikely that any other four decades in history can point to such an accomplishment. Each of us carries in his mind or body the incurable traces of those horrors. But which one of us would have chosen to live in any but this great and terrible century, or wish to be any but who he is? I would not.

That is what those pine tops say to me. They are no more meaningful against the most cloudless of blue autumn skies than when looming out of the whirling whiteness of this culminating year of 1957. But I see them not only from my personal beach or land's end. (I am beached in another way.) The West as a whole is beset by a sudden anxiety

---

* "Memorial Verses, April 1850."

amounting sometimes to alarm. In that hubbub of surprise, I find myself unsurprised. The lines of force were clear enough.

So it was given to me to live into the year 1957, which left as a deposit in consciousness the tremendous knowledge that man had broken through the earth's atmosphere into space. For in the flight of years, 1957 must henceforth stand, while time lasts or consciousness of it, as the year of the earth satellites and the frightful forces that launched them— the giant rockets, carrying man to new heights of mind and space. For not to see that each rocket, each time one is launched, is, above all, a specific form which the human mind has taken in this time, is to miss something. Each is a form in which the utmost that the abstract and the practical mind are capable of has embodied itself, when both are stretched in unison to their utmost tension of thinking and doing. Nothing like the mind in these forms, at these velocities, has ever before been known on Earth. A friend writes: "Put out of your mind, for a moment, if you can, all that political fiddle you are always fussing with. Is not the deeper meaning of those sputniks that they have ended metaphysics? Isn't that what is really implied in the 'crash' emphasis on training scientists, which Communism is already well along in, and which we are beginning to fumble with simply as a price of survival? Isn't that what that 'bleep, bleep' was really saying to us—that science has ended metaphysics?"

I suppose I see what my exasperated friend is driving at, though I lack competence to answer in his terms. I take him to mean that the rockets are not only weapons. They are, above all, transforming tools. He is concerned less with a world which they may transform by thermonuclear explosion than with a world already transformed to the point where it could have produced such weapons. He means that the rockets, and the conditions that called them forth, and called forth an effort of the mind at a level which could imagine and shape those forms, and the related thermonuclear forces that define their annihilative efficiency—all these together, and all they stand for, are about to transform all the relationships of our lives, and our ways of seeing and thinking about them, into something radically different from what we men have ever known before. This is, moreover, inescapable. Will and wish are scarcely in point. Much more in point is an irreversible momentum which has long been in play, but has now reached an acceleration whose rate every man can now see for himself.

Yet I cannot stop at that. My mind cannot break away from something else: Behind each rocket still stands man, who is its contriver and starting point, just as, if a rocket is hydrogen-headed, he is its target. And a man, even the least thoughtful and most brutish, is a mystery; and a rocket is not. A rocket, the most ingenious and complex, is precisely one of the most radical dispellings of mystery that there is. All that remains of mystery in a rocket is those tatters of it that we call the "bugs," which mind must mercilessly dispel before the metal mass can fire and soar and function as a rocket. This is, in part, what my friend is driving at in asking if science has not ended metaphysics. Instead of metaphysics, he might just as well have said: mystery. Precisely because, in my earthbound way, I cannot bring myself to suppose that there are not questions still to be explored at that level which my friend calls "political," but which I, claiming a larger franchise for the term, would call "the human condition"—the level of the man behind the rocket or on its receiving end. Nor do I find the implications of these questions less awesome. Nor do I believe that the two levels can be separated. I am going to turn then away from the rockets and sputniks, to less spectacular man. I wish to turn to where, in the fifty-eighth year of the century, I find

man in his human masses most meaningful in terms of the
century's total meaning.

Some of my friends charged me with overpricing the
meaning of the satellite revolt and of the human forces in
it. About this I should like to set out two points for your consideration. The first point has to do with what those forces
did and what, as a result, the experience may have done to
them. The second point has to do with their extent.

Point 1. Those miserable human forces in the satellites—
and they alone in the world first dared to rise against the
dictatorship. They—and not the immensely rich, deployed,
embattled West—dared defy and make effective head against
outmatching Communism. Now in defeat and captive still they
must nevertheless feel stirring in themselves the force of something like Lucretius' meaning: "When all mankind lay grovel-
ling in the dust, one man stood up and walked at length along
the flaming walls of the world." To feel this not as a flourish
but as a right, earned by reason of having given that feeling
effect in the reality of acts, implies an experience as transforming in human terms as are the transforming implications of science. It must, to the degree in which it is felt, set
apart the human thousands, perhaps millions, who knew the
experience, from those who did not. In fact, they were
already set apart. The West had set them apart. This is a
second fact to brood on. These millions were captive precisely
because the West abandoned them to Communism. The West
abandoned them as bait or bribe to Communism, to tempt
it to collaborate in our dream of perpetual peace. The mind
that will not face this fact is likely to be the same mind which
holds that Yalta (letting that one name stand for a great
deal more) was a disaster only because Communism did not
live up to its agreement. The notion that Communism could
be lured or bribed into peace was as wildly fanciful as the

notion that Communism would honor the terms of any agreement which it found in its interest to break. It makes no sense to say that the statesmen of the West could not forsee this turn unless we assume that the word "statesman" has no meaning. For many minds in the West who were not statesmen did forsee and warn of it. The insight required no illuminating genius; was, indeed, less an insight than a habit of pointing to Communism's invariable record. However certain opinion in the West prefers to rationalize the Yalta effect, the satellite peoples have no need to. To them it is a simple fact with which they daily live: They were abandoned.

Abandoned, the satellite throngs rose. From their depths, they rose and dared defy a power that enmeshed them in a web of force which paralyzed them at every turn in the act of rising. Still, they rose. And as the West watched admiringly those human throngs knew that they had been abandoned twice. They must at the moment surmise—at least the colder minds and steadier eyes among them—that they are about to be abandoned a third time. For a general peace settlement such as we now seem headed for, is scarcely conceivable unless one of its conditions in effect guarantees in perpetuity the captivity of the satellite nations, whatever deprecating forms the abandonment takes, and granting that in the language of statecraft there are few words whose meaning is more ephemeral than perpetuity.

From this, I draw a conclusion that to some may seem outrageous, to others paradoxical. For I doubt that this prospect dismays these captive human forces. I belong to a school which holds, as a principle of all growth, that what does not destroy me outright, strengthens me outright. I am trying to fix an effect, extremely difficult to communicate; no tools or measures exist for reckoning it, so that in this development man remains a mystery at least in the degree to which it is immeasurable. I am talking about a qualitative change in individual men under the pressure of necessity, and in those human masses which are the sum of such men. Professor Toynbee has tried to fix some semblance of this effect by calling it: challenge and response. He is speaking about man in the presence of an adversity which, if it does not destroy him, strengthens him. If man proves equal to the challenge, he first outlives and then surpasses the adversity, and, in the course of the experience, rises to a new stage of development, perhaps to a new height. My own mind, out of a different discipline and habit, sees this process and its workings somewhat differently. Yet the net effect is much the same. I cite Arnold Toynbee's metaphor because it is familiar and easily intelligible to many.

Let me try to give it substance like this. Remember the song:

> *Brüder, zur Sonne, zur Freiheit . . .*
> Brothers, to sunlight, to freedom,
> Brothers, upward to light;
> Bright from the darkness of the past
> Beacons the future.

When, during the Polish revolt against the Soviet dictatorship, crowds of five hundred thousand men, women, and children jammed the streets and squares around Warsaw's public buildings, which of us could doubt that that was the song they sang, whatever new words or tune they sang it to, or that even if they were silent, that was the meaning of their silence?

But the meaning was much more than that. A crowd of five hundred thousand, suddenly summoned out of the human mass, has the implications of a happening in Nature. Like an earthquake, it implies a radical readjustment of reality. It is the outward, visible evidence of massive pressures, long working out of sight. And, as in an earthquake, almost nothing about it is certain except that the shocks will not cease, the earth will not stop heaving, until all has settled again into a new tentative balance of tensions. But that new balance of tensions is defined, in turn, by something else. For crowds of five hundred thousand men, women, and children also mean this: Traditional power is in a crisis no longer controllable by traditional means, power is migrating from its official quarters (in this case those of the dictatorship), and is seeking to take up a new center in the human mass. At the moment, it may fail. In any case the transition process may be slow, heart-wrenchingly slow, and may work itself out in an infinity of unimaginable disguises. But its transforming effect is inevitable. It transforms the human forces that the effect has set in motion. It transforms the inhuman forces (the dictatorship) they move against. When power becomes inhuman, human action continues against it even under the appearance of inaction. For inhuman power breeds, minute by minute, the human forces of resistance to it in the very act of trying to check them. It strengthens them to the degree in which it breeds a force equal to what it struggles against. In short, I am saying that, in the satellite revolt, revolution in its Communist form has bred out of itself and its necessities the human forces which must transform it, and have no choice but to do so, since they cannot act otherwise (especially in the absence of any effective action by the West) and live and be and simply breathe as men. The alternative is extinction. Man, by the fact that he lives, is the mortal enemy of extinction. Every human life is an hourly illustration that man will suffer anything sooner than extinction. This development I find among the most meaningful for the age. I am claiming that the satellite revolt is a revolt of the order of the Russian Revolution of 1917, of which it is a phase. And this whether or not it completes its meaning. How wide that meaning is we must seek elsewhere.

Point 2. We ourselves defeat that fuller meaning constantly by seeing those human forces as limited to the satellite nations because in them these forces first were ignited, and were, above all, within sight and sound of the West. Yet, like any other great convulsion, this one had its premonitory spasms, which define its true extent. We forget (one of the symptoms of our disorder is that we tend to forget almost everything as soon as it happens) the great strike of 1953—more truly a rising—in the Arctic complex of Soviet slave camps called Vorkuta. We forget (or do not know) that, perhaps for a decade, there has existed, particularly among Soviet university youth, an anti-Soviet underground movement, calling itself The True Work of Lenin Group (*Gruppa: Istinni Trud Lenina*). These are few, pitifully few perhaps, and Communists are many. When, at any moment in history, has the equation between inhuman power and the human forces that challenge it ever stood differently? It is always: They are many, we are few. In fact, the human forces that stirred in the satellite revolt are conterminous with the Communist Empire. They stir, though you may not see or hear them, only in sporadic eruption and defeat, from the beaches of the China Sea to within air minutes of the Rhine River. They stir within the Communist Party itself.

For we further defeat meaning by our insistence on seeing Communism as a fixed, undifferentiated monolith. The monolith is made up of human units, each absolutely different from any other, at the point where each is an immeasurable mystery. It seems necessary to say it again and again: Communists are men and women; are subject hourly, therefore, to influence, reaction, change, growth. Few Communists, even in the Kremlin, can rest their eyes on another of their kind without wondering what exactly—what influence, reactions, reservations, "dangerous thoughts"—is at work in the mind behind the eyes that look back at him. For these stirrings—both in the viewer and the viewed—are not self-generating, but are reactions to a reality that encloses both.

We in the West have missed, too, from the first, it seems to me, another signal fact. The West has long buzzed around the satellite fringes of the Communist Empire, and must be presumed, in the ordinary course of things, to have had some effect. The satellite revolt was not sparked from the West. It was sparked by Communism itself. What touched off the revolt, like a lightning strike on an explosives chamber, was an energy discharged by the passage of Communism itself from one phase to another, marking changes which first found formal expression at the Twentieth Congress of the Soviet Communist Party. These changes have by no means run their course; they remain, therefore, in any rigorous sense, incalculable. All that can be said of them, with a qualified certainty, is that they manifest the pressure of great human forces, working within the cramped confines of Communist reality. Nevertheless, they work. Nikita Khrushchev at the uneasy pinnacle of power, Vyacheslav Molotov in Outer Mongolia, are alike evidence of the pressure of these forces. Molotov because he sought to repress them by main force. Khrushchev because he judged their energy more shrewdly, and seeing, at least with a politician's cunning, that things had gone too far for that, let the groundswell of those forces carry him to power, even if his purpose, on gaining power, was to clip, hobble, manipulate, and check them. Therefore, I say that these human forces are conterminous with Communism, though it was in the satellites (for reasons that we may bracket loosely as historical) that these forces stirred into open revolt.

I cannot bring myself to believe that this satellite revolution is not a permanent one, in the sense that, even if its energies are kept, henceforth, just short of exploding again, they will never again become inactive. Until events prove otherwise, I shall believe that they will continue active until— though in ways the probing mind cannot put a finger on, and over years that weary the heart at the thought of their length— they have transformed the dictatorship, not necessarily into something more likable in our terms, but into something different from what we have known. I am saying (always with the strong possibility of being in error) that sudden solutions seem to me unlikely. Rather, force will work on force—who knows under what frightful multiples of pressure? The human forces will work on the inhuman dictatorship which they are in passive revolt against, so that the end result is more likely to resemble a new fusion of elements, rather than an abrupt reversal or displacement of one by the other.

I am assuming, therefore, a process whose working out must, presumably, occupy the balance of the century. One taking place, moreover, in the absence of direct military action by East or West, in the absence of general catastrophe. I am assuming that there will be no world war, no apocalypse. (Obviously, if there is, all assumptions are meaningless since mankind will, in a matter of minutes, have undone the civilizing work of twenty thousand years.) Grant me, for a moment only, that assumption. Let us, for a moment, put out of mind (as my friend asked me to do) much that immediately weighs and presses on us, the apocalyptic anxiety now stirring among the human forces of the West, to which great governments are reacting, or soon must. For what also does the phrase mean: "To wage peace"?

Then—with apocalypse arbitrarily pushed aside—against my friend's questions I should like to set certain others. In the absence of any decisive action by the West, does not the race between science, streaking into space, and the agony of the human forces seeking to transform inhuman Communism, define the main lines of force for the coming decades? Is it not possible, too, to see in the events of the century's first half something like a vast, erratic, trial-and-error process, like any other in impersonal, unregulated Nature, in which there has been occurring in mankind as a whole, something like a molecular rearrangement, not only of reality but of man's ways of doing, thinking, and seeing that reality? Is this not a clue to the century's larger meaning, which the frightful details that we, as men, must chiefly suffer and sustain, distract us from or blind us to? Cannot we detect the further development of that meaning in that breathless counterpoint: the foreclosing energies of science and the human forces in revolt against what has pushed science to this extreme? In that process, does not the year 1957 suggest the beginning of culmination? Does it not crest, like a dividing ridge, perhaps the first of several, from which, looking off, we see (or think we see) the stress of history beginning to fall away in opposite directions? And later ages, looking back, may also set a finger on that ridge, and say of it: "Up to this point, one way. After it, something different in kind." Have we not, in fact, been standing for fifty years amidst the falling walls that mark the end of an age such as occurs once in a thousand or two thousand years? "End of an age" is a figure of speech. The meaning it attempts to catch includes a radical readjustment of reality (when that reality is the sum of all human relationships). It also includes a change which, in turn, amounts to a slight tilt in the general angle of man's vision, resulting in a new way on man's part of seeing the new reality and all those interrelationships. In short, not only is reality changing, but so is man, and therewith his way of weighing and assessing it all. Is that not what happens when ages end?

Heretofore, the end of an age has implied the beginning of another. What makes this one radically different, what causes in men a catch of dismay, is that this time man clearly has it in his power to end not only an age, but himself. And that, not in fancy, but in simplest nut-and-bolt reality. The layman's most gruesome fantasy can scarcely keep pace with the commonplaces of that reality. It is not the momentary weapons discrepancy between the West and Communism that need chiefly alarm us in the close of 1957. It is not even the giant rockets. It is what both are leading us toward. It is what lies beyond both. I asked to be permitted—for a moment only—an assumption: no apocalypse. Yet it is reality, too, and we must glance at it.

"Year's end, year's sweepings," an old woman, who could make any dry stem root and flower, and who also drank too much in secret, used to say in my boyhood. How large my assumption is, how precarious, is clear enough from the sweepings which 1957, in closing, dumped, like its unseasonably heavy snows, against our doors. All those sweepings heaped up piecemeal evidence on one point. The point is, of course, the sudden disclosure to millions in the West that it had dropped behind Communism in certain areas of scientific development, where, in a military way, a lag means a hazard. Sudden fear turned hazard into immediate peril. The shock was deepened by the seeping realization that responsible governments in the West had long surmised, and even rather narrowly known, about that widening discrepancy, and had neither acted with energy to close it nor clearly disclosed it to those it threatened. Instead it was disclosed by those sputniks, streaking into orbit. *They* first stirred, among the threatened millions, an anxiety, creeping and formless; hence, like all herd fear, pointlessly unsettling and toxic. In fact, this was a reaction, opposite and about equal to the vast inertia of our complacency about Communism, our past failure, amounting to a refusal, to take seriously its meaning, purposes, and, above all, its clenched will to achieve both.

In fact, the military hazard, while it must never be minimized, was offset not only by our lethal striking power, but by our overall technological superiority in contrast with the overall Communist productive inadequacy. This fact remained constant even if, in our general reluctance to grasp Communism as it really is and works, we had failed to grasp what the record clearly shows: that Communism has almost never indulged in sudden aggressive adventures, and has, in general, broken off quickly the few adventures to which it had incautiously committed itself. Behind that prudence lay the strictest practical considerations. The German General Staff used to require of the political masters of its state evidence of a 51-per-cent margin of favoring odds before indulging in military action. The political masters of the Communist dictatorship have themselves consistently required something much more like 90-per-cent favoring odds. Nor was there much reason to suppose, once the alert was blown and the will to act began to harden, that the West could not close the weapons gap, with the possibility, too, of those chance accelerations and break-throughs which cannot be counted on in timetables, though neither need they be counted out.

So the military hazard was passing. The greater one is what loomed beyond it. For example, there exists at this moment, as an official bureau of the Soviet government, a Department of Space Travel. In the last days of 1957, we witnessed a hassle over the organization by our Air Force of a Department of Astronautics. For example, we heard, within the last weeks, a top-ranking American military officer remark publicly, in passing, that control of the moon's surface was probably decisive for the defense of the West. For example, two space planes, one American and the other Soviet, are now on drawing boards, if, indeed, one or the other of them has not already advanced to experimental stages. These are mere random items.

In the last weeks of 1957, we watched and heard a general of the U.S. Air Force deliver an address, and listening, I found myself thinking:

> Wouldst thou know what man can say
> In a little? Reader, stay.

"This is not to imply," he said, "that we have deluded ourselves into believing that the types of ICBMs now being developed will be the ultimate weapon . . . It is well within reason that air/space ships will fight the next major conflict, and that control of space will determine victory."

Discount the timing and phrasing of this in any political terms you find relevant. The central portent of those words remains clearly stated. Hence, of course, President Eisenhower's proposal to neutralize space in his latest (as of this writing) reply to Premier Bulganin. The struggle for space is hurtling at us. We have no choice, no right, but to respond.

The reality that response encases is of the most blunt and mundane kind. The logic of that reality is a radical transformation of all life, as we have known it, and there is not one of us who has the right to object, or would wish to. It is simply becoming *necessary*. The process may be more gradual than, at the moment, seems likely. But it is geared to the acceleration of the new weapons and their velocities, and to the perspectives of space that open out beyond. Some may resist this or that encroachment, more or less justifiably, more or less tentatively. The momentum is against them since what is at stake is survival. At that price, none can resist. Henceforth, all are simply under necessity, which has largely deprived us of choices. Against freedom of choice history has set frightfulness of penalty. It is in the nature of roads that they go somewhere, and go nowhere else. If you are committed, by will or circumstances, to travel a road in one direction, and there is no turning off, you will get there and nowhere else.

There is the alternative: "To wage peace," and to achieve it. This means a general disarmament, East and West. I have no way of knowing, any more than the next man, whether a general disarmament is even possible. In the light of certain special knowledge and experience, I fear, perhaps more than the next man, that general disarmament holds perils for the West such as its leaders seem scarcely to have thought about. To me it seems that the Soviet Presidium can scarcely fail to feel with smiling unanimity, even a certain smugness:

"Peace hath its victories no less renowned than war." The alternatives are such narrow ledges, the drop beyond is so steep.

I could sum up simply by saying: We are entering the "naked year"—the naked years, more probably. The phrase is that of Boris Pilnyak, the gifted Russian writer who was destroyed in the Great Purge. You find "the naked year" too bleak and sensational a phrasing of what lies ahead? Be happy if you do not live to damn it as merely too literary. I find its prospect no more dismaying than I surmise the satellite millions find the rigors of their reality dismaying. Reality is not in itself dismaying. What dismays, what disheartens in the spin, is a reluctance to face reality exactly as it is—or as narrowly as mind can ever do. In that effort, it seems to me better to overrate than to underrate the harshness of its terms. For reality requires of men chiefly a strength to be equal to their necessity. Since that is the only true strength there is, only on such irreducible gravel can men truly base the foundation of their world, finding in its stripped terms the strength to live or die at need for what they hold true and good. History is merciless to men when ages end. Men survive the shocks, reform, regroup, persist, by clutching tight what they hold to be irreducibly good and true.

In fact, from the outset, I have been talking about human hope, though you may not have guessed it. I am asking upon what minimum terms hope can be had, fastened on, and clung to, as it must be, eight years past the mid-mark of this century. For hope is not something that can be entertained, taken gently by the hand or invited to lead us among Oriental rugs, mink coats, mink sofas, or *their* many miniatures and isotopes—not in an age like this one. In this age, hope is something that must be taken by the throat. That is to say, hope, to be durable and real, must begin with things exactly as they are, not as we suppose they were (even a few tranquillizing months ago), or as we wish they might be. History is moving, like our planes, with the speed of sound. The terms of hope are not to delude ourselves about this in order not to suffer in the shattering spins the fear that casts out hope. That is where hope sets out from now. The deadly enemy of hope, its smiling murderer—is illusion.

There are hundreds of millions of men, women, and children in the European East and in Asia who could tell you a good deal about this. They could tell you that hope begins on the farther side of a daily hopelessness, but that in that knowledge there is also strength. Therefore, they look out upon your smiling optimism—you must know this because it lies at the root of your inability to speak to them convincingly—with a measuring glance. They judge that hope for you (as it has been for them) can truly begin only when complacency has been eaten off as by an acid bath, consuming the temptation to illusion.

I had a friend and former comrade, a woman named Maria, now in her sixties, whom I last heard of as serving a twenty-year sentence in that same Arctic slave camp at Vorkuta which I mentioned earlier. The details of her life are such that, hearing them, I think you must ask: How could anyone go through this and still go on living? Her husband, when I last heard, was also serving a twenty-year term in a Siberian slave camp. Their daughter was serving a twenty-year term in another camp (charged with anti-Soviet student agitation, apparently in connection with that same True Work of Lenin Group that I mentioned). I remember well the night this child and future slave was born—a light rain was falling; the occasion was thought one for rejoicing. This slave had an older brother, born subnormal and kept in a State institution for such unfortunates. When, during World War II, the Germans neared Moscow, the Soviet secret police rounded up the inmates of such homes, and marched them out to do whatever a wall of mindless, terrified bodies could do to slow the German advance. The boy was never heard of again. His father was seriously wounded in the same battle.

Another friend brought me word of Maria in Vorkuta. She told him that, as a slave, for the first time she felt free, because there was nothing left that she needed any longer to fear since there was nothing left that life could do to her. That is why she goes on living. Finality had freed her even in slavery. This is the most radical extension of reality there is. Hope known on such terms is close to the daily reality of some 800 million living under Communism. Did you really suppose that 800 million souls could exist in terms of such reality, and that you could coexist with them in your own different terms and that all would continue to be well with you, if only Communism could be "contained"? Or that you might never have to re-define your hope in terms closer to theirs? Such reality in this age is, among other things, contagious and always on the march. In the 1930s, the busy inhabitants of London, Berlin, Hiroshima learned, in general without undue concern, about the bombing of Madrid, Guernica, Nanking. In the 1940s, the inhabitants of those first cities learned, in the italics of toppling walls, what it means to say, in the twentieth century, that reality is contagious and always on the march.

I mentioned the name of Boris Pilnyak. The name of Ilya Ehrenburg may be better known to Americans. Like Pilnyak, Ehrenburg, in the 1920s, seemed one of the hopes of Russian letters. By the 1930s, Ehrenburg had become so tireless and sodden a time-server of the dictatorship, had winked at, if not worse, the official murder of so many of his colleagues, that I, for one, could not bear to look at anything he had written and would turn from it with physical revulsion. If this seems excessive, it has a personal root. I suspected Ehrenburg, further, of condoning, if no worse, the Purge murder of a man who had befriended me, the Polish writer Bruno Jascienski (only those who have lived through those things can know the fierceness of the feelings they breed).

What right had I to judge Ehrenburg or the actions of any man in a concentration camp, including that great slave camp,

the Communist Empire, with whose diplomatic murderers
we chat and clink glasses? No right at all, I had to tell myself
at last. Which of us dare judge any other who has lived with
the business end of a revolver at the base of his brain? But
then something unforeseeable happened. The Communist
Party closed in, not long ago, on the Soviet writer Boris
Pasternak. And Ehrenburg, the time-server, at the end of
two abject decades, rose to defend him. This in itself seems
to me wonderful out of all proportion to the specific case. It
seems to mean once more: Communists are men; they change.
But that is not why I am laboring the incident. There is another reason. In defending Pasternak, Ehrenburg said this:
"If the whole world were to be covered with asphalt, one day
a crack would appear in the asphalt, and in that crack grass
would grow."

No one has said it so well. This is irreducible. On this, at
least, a man can stand in the end of the year 1957.

You may object that this is unreasonably bleak, that the
views I have set out above are unduly alarmist, and do not
even brush the American mood of the moment. I feel no
impulse to defend them or any wish to impose them on you.
I merely set them down for your consideration, lest a day
come when your children and grandchildren, and mine, with
the sea roaring clearly in their ears at last, have a right to
say, and with the bitterness that threatens to kill even the
hope of hope: "No one told us."

But I do not wish at all to leave just this sweeping of the
ends of other years. Life still forbids it. I wish to assert
something else radically opposite. Not long ago, somebody
found at the far end of the pond which lies just under my
windows, the footprints of a doe and a fawn. The beautiful,
shy creatures go there at night to drink. The teeming life of
this other creation is constantly around us out of sight. If, at

night, we sit completely still for a long time, we may catch
sounds or glimpses of it. Sometimes, it is the slightest displacement of a stem in the brush. Sometimes, it is the momentary, phosphorescent, red or green bead of an eye which is
looking back at us when it may see no questionable or dreadful shadows, darker than the rest. Sometimes, it is an animal
cry, chilling our nerves never more than at the moment when
it snaps off and silence falls in again. Days, weeks later, we
may come on some tufts of fur and little bones by a stone.
They tell us that Nature, from which we crave the illusion of
peace, is both beautiful and murderous. They warn us that
we can divide their aspects, accent one more than the other,
only at the price of unsettling the balance, of violating reality.
We do not know why and no one can tell us why. No one
knows why. No one has ever known why. There is only a
choice of guesses—in sum, the same old guesses, always the
same, under their diversity of form and emphasis, since man
began guessing. Only the "props" and the vicissitudes change
from age to age. The mystery remains exactly the same
mystery.

Put out of your mind so far as you can—at least in the way
that a judge instructs a jury to put out of its mind a scrap
of testimony that it has, nevertheless, plainly heard—what
weighs and presses on us. The political revolution which
reaches out for us. The scientific revolution. Put out of your
mind for a moment the thermonuclear fear, the rocketry and
the terrors that lie beyond. Under this appalling, dwarfing
mass that troubles us—troubles us all the more because most
of it we see the way an animal's eye sees *us* at night, as
shapeless patches of the darker dark—under this leaning
overhang lives man: people in our undifferentiated millions,
bounded by our household cares and happinesses, the fathers
and mothers of children, grandfathers and grandmothers of
grandchildren in whom we see the continuation of a pulse
that began with the Creation.

A note to his daughter Ellen, living in Wallingford, Connecticut, with her husband and children—a few weeks before his last heart attack.

Pipe Creek Farm
Westminster, Maryland
June   , 1961

Dear Little One:

I suppose I really should find out what the date is, but not knowing is, somehow, part of the fun of vacation.

Kinzer just popped off (as Sam Welles says) to take four pictures to an exhibit where she's showing. She will pick up Mrs. Summers, who is also hanging art. The show is in a little church over beyond Glyndon. I dislike such things, and rather meanly smitched out.

Imagine, being able to get up not caring what hour it is (actually it's earlier than usual); and then go down and study

Chinese and Italian. This morning, I went down at 8:30, could not tear myself away until 1:30. I'm a quiet child and play well by myself when let alone. I thought of the Italian as a brush-up, with the possibility in mind of an Italian journey. I find how much I've forgotten, or don't know. But the sentences are beginning to pick up quite a lot. For example, we are asked darkly: Where was the cook yesterday? We learn: She went to the post office and met the postman. Further: Last week, the postman brought a beautiful red rose (*una bella rosa rossa*) for the cook. The cook offered tea to the postman. Then: Is a handsome man, the postman, and the cook is not ugly (*non e brutta*—is a lovely word, *brutta*). You might think things were going nicely when, bang: Yesterday, I met Maria's brother and the postman in town; they were talking with that girl from the bookshop. (*That* girl—clearly, a bad look-out for the cook.) Chinese is much less exciting and confines itself to cow and sheep on mountain; though things took a questionable turn this morning when we learned: Man does not see small dog on mountain. (Somehow, one feels that is what has always been happening to the Chinese.) . . .

I wish I had a great bagful of joyous news to end up with. But I've spun out the little wisps I had. We haven't heard from John and Pat, and are inclined to let them get settled in, unjostled.

Oh, the *ochroleuca gigantea* Golden Nugget that I planted near the pump-house overflow, is ending its two years of convalescence with two big handsome gigantea buds. Love to everybody and how's Slugger?

Papa and g

r

a

m

p

o

About the Author

WHITTAKER CHAMBERS was born April 1, 1901, in Philadelphia and died July 9, 1961, in Westminster, Maryland. He went to Columbia from 1920 to 1924—his scholastic career was interrupted to make a trip to Europe, and never finished. He was a member of the Communist Party from 1925 to 1938. He joined *Time* magazine in 1939, first as a book reviewer, then as a writer and editor. He was an editor and writer on the staff of *National Review* from the latter part of 1957 to the middle of 1959. During much of this journalistic career, he continued to operate his farm in Westminster, maintaining a dairy herd, raising sheep, beef cattle and various crops.

Over the years, Whittaker Chambers did a number of translations, including *Bambi, Dunant—the Story of the Red Cross*, and a number of children's books. When he was on *Time* he wrote many of the cover stories, including profiles of Toynbee, Niebuhr and Pope Pius XII. As an editor and writer in the foreign news section, he displayed an extraordinary prescience and insight into the East-West conflict, based on his experience inside the C.P. and on his remarkable sense of history. He edited a *Fortune* series on the great philosophers (February 1942 through December 1943). He also contributed essays on the Middle Ages, the Venetian Republic, the Age of Exploration, the Enlightenment, and the Edwardians in *Life's Picture History of Western Civilization* in 1947. Likewise for *Life*, he was the author of "The Devil" (February 2, 1948), "Is Academic Freedom in Danger?" (June 22, 1953), and a report on the Soviet 20th Congress (April 30, 1956). His book *Witness* was published in 1952 by Random House, Inc.